Trade Unions and the State

Trade Unions and the State

THE CONSTRUCTION OF INDUSTRIAL RELATIONS INSTITUTIONS IN BRITAIN, 1890–2000

Chris Howell

PRINCETON UNIVERSITY

PRINCETON AND OXFORD

Library of Congress Cataloging-in-Publication Data

Howell, Chris, 1962–
Trade unions and the state : the construction of industrial relations
 institutions in Britain, 1890–2000 / Chris Howell.
p.   cm.
Includes bibliographical references and index.
ISBN 0-691-12106-0 (cloth : alk. paper)
1. Labor unions—Government policy—Great Britain—History—20th century.
2. Industrial relations—Government policy—Great Britain—History—
20th century. 3. Labor movement—great Britain—History—20th century. I. Title.
HD6664.H69 2005
331′.0941′0904—dc22   2004042069

British Library Cataloging-in-Publication Data is available.

This book has been composed in Goudy

Printed on acid-free paper. ∞

www.pupress.princeton.edu

Printed in the United States of America

10 9 8 7 6 5 4 3 2 1

For Susan, Jay, and Colin,
who keep me (relatively) sane

Contents

Acknowledgments   ix

CHAPTER ONE
Introduction: The Puzzle of British Industrial Relations   1

CHAPTER TWO
Constructing Industrial Relations Institutions   20

CHAPTER THREE
The Construction of the Collective Laissez-Faire System,
1890–1940   46

CHAPTER FOUR
Donovan, Dissension, and the Decentralization
of Industrial Relations, 1940–1979   86

CHAPTER FIVE
The Decollectivization of Industrial Relations, 1979–1997   131

CHAPTER SIX
The Third Way and Beyond: The Future of British
Industrial Relations   174

Notes   195

References   221

Index   237

Acknowledgments

THIS BOOK HAS BEEN a long time coming; I began it in 1995 when my (at that point, only) son was eighteen months old and I had finally started to get a good night's sleep again. Now I have a ten-year-old and a seven-year-old, and tracing the intellectual origins of this book, and acknowledging the debts incurred in its production, requires recovering memories long since repressed. Nothing prepared me, emerging from graduate school, for the way in which time becomes fractured, and sustained, coherent periods when one can work on a single project seem to disappear. The result is that this book, conceived when John Major was still firmly in power, was completed midway through the second term of Tony Blair's government.

Given the gestation period for this book, I have accumulated an enormous number of debts: intellectual, financial, and emotional. It is probably appropriate to begin with the money. The initial research for the book was done in 1995, when I had a German Marshall Fellowship, and the bulk of the writing took place from 1999 to 2000, when I had a research status appointment from Oberlin College. The book would never have seen the light of day without this support.

The research on the period of Conservative rule after 1979 relied heavily on the countless trade unionists—general secretaries, research officers, and others—who opened their files to me and explained the intricacies of bargaining, organizing, and legislative strategies. My thanks go especially to David Lea, Lief Mills, John Edmonds, Garfield Davies, Jon Robinson, Hilary Benn, and Pete Morris. My respect for the day-to-day work of union officials under the extremely difficult conditions of late-Thatcherite Britain grew with every interview. Jon Cruddas also provided an invaluable window into Labour Party–trade union relations.

The quality and sophistication of scholarship produced from within industrial relations departments and units at British universities is remarkable, and I am well aware of the arrogance of proposing a reinterpretation of British industrial relations from outside that intellectual environment. Nevertheless, I would never have been able to develop the arguments contained in this book, nor work through the implications of existing theoretical approaches, without the guidance of several British scholars. I owe the greatest thanks to John Kelly, who met with me several times and offered commentary on early versions of this project, and Lord Wedderburn, whose breadth of knowledge and intellectual generosity were remarkable. I also want to thank David Metcalf, Jeremy Waddington, Rebecca Givan, Rachel Bailey, and Simon Milner for direction and access to their unpublished scholarship. I doubt that any of these scholars will fully agree with the final product, and they are certainly not responsible for errors of fact or interpretation, but they nonetheless offered invaluable help. Dave Marsh played an important role in forcing me to clarify the argument of the book in his comments on a paper I presented to the European Consortium for Political Research in 1998 and then published in the *British Journal of Politics and International Relations*, under his editorship.

Aside from the rare solitary genius, intellectual networks are the lifeblood of progress in the social sciences. There is nothing like opening a file of accumulated Post-it notes and scraps of paper containing ideas for a project, only to discover that you have had the identical brilliant thought on three different occasions. A network of scholars willing to respond rapidly to queries, read drafts, and engage in debate over beer is a precondition for any kind of ambitious intellectual project. In this regard, I owe a special debt to David Coates and Colin Hay. Their prodigious scholarly output has influenced my own interpretation of British political economy more than they can know. Both are model social scientists, who have been unfailingly generous and supportive of this project but never willing to pull their intellectual punches in criticism (as far as I know); neither will be entirely happy with this book, but they should know that it is wrestling with their criticisms that has required the greatest expenditure of intellectual energy on my part.

In the course of the past eight years, countless people have read drafts of particular chapters of this book, commented on conference papers that explored some of the ideas in the book, or simply engaged in discussions that shaped the way in which I finally took the book. Special mention must go to Peter Hall and Kathy Thelen, who, for somewhat different reasons, have heavily influenced the argument contained in the second chapter; it is probably fair to say that almost every contribution to a theory of capitalist institutions in the past decade and a half has been shaped in some way by Peter's work, and that is certainly the case for me, even when I have been critical of this or that aspect of it. Peter's legendary generosity with feedback, and his openness to criticism, always make intellectual exchanges with him enjoyable and productive. Similarly, Kathy has overcome any qualms she may have had with my approach to institutional construction, and over the years has offered careful and copious commentary. George Ross and Andy Martin gave me the opportunity and the incentive to switch from research on French industrial relations to the British case, and both their own work and their commentary on mine has shaped my thinking on trade union strategy in important ways. I am also immensely grateful to Marc Blecher, Mark Blyth, Joel Krieger, Ursula Lawrence, Jonah Levy, Rianne Mahon, Jonas Pontusson, David Soskice, Peter Swenson, Mark Vail, and Dan Wincott, all of whom have read drafts, offered comments, or contributed to the way in which I have conceived of this project.

Finally, I owe an incalculable debt to my partner, Susan, and children, Jay and Colin. Throughout the research and writing of this book, my family has provided the perfect balance of support, distraction, and refuge. At one point I thought of dedicating a different book to each of them, but given how long it has taken to complete this book, it seems wiser to dedicate it to all three. Thank you.

CHAPTER ONE

Introduction:
The Puzzle of British Industrial Relations

> So though I'm a working man
> I can ruin the government's plan
> Though I'm not too hard
> The sight of my card
> Makes me some kind of superman.
>
> Oh you don't get me I'm part of the union
> You don't get me I'm part of the union
> You don't get me I'm part of the union
> Till the day I die, till the day I die.[1]

THIS BOOK BEGINS with a puzzle. Why did the British labor movement so quickly succumb to the radical reforming efforts of Conservative governments elected after 1979? This was a labor movement at the peak of its power and influence in 1979, when more than half of all British employees belonged to unions and more than four-fifths were covered by collective pay-setting mechanisms. Trade union power was widely acknowledged to be immune to state reform efforts because it was embedded in decentralized workplace institutions, rather than being dependent upon a favorable framework of labor law, and the British labor movement had only recently successfully turned back two major government efforts to limit its power. Such reform efforts were more likely to lead to the downfall of governments than to any decline in trade union strength. And yet, twenty years later, at the dawn of the twenty-first century, trade union density has almost halved; the extent of collective bargaining coverage and the numbers of strikes have collapsed to the lowest levels since the 1920s (or even earlier); where trade unionism exists, it is of a weaker, more marginal form, consulted more often than negotiated with; and various forms of individualized industrial relations have come to dominate the landscape of the British economy. It should be said that so unexpected and rapid was British trade union decline that it went largely unnoticed and unacknowledged among academics until the early 1990s, when evidence from workplace surveys confirmed the transformation of the British industrial relations system.

To put the question that first set the research agenda for this book in a somewhat different way, why was Thatcherism, which enjoyed much more mixed results in economic and social policy, so strikingly successful in the realm of industrial relations? In searching for an answer to this question, and exploring the puzzle of how a once powerful labor movement went into what may well be terminal decline, this book offers a reinterpretation of more than a century of British industrial relations developments, and constructs an argument about the centrality of state action in the establishment, mainte- nance, and reconstruction of industrial relations institutions. The importance of the British state's role has been its institution-building capacity rather than regulation or repression, and both the timing and the form of state action are intelligible in terms of shifts in the underlying patterns of British economic growth. I argue that, contrary to most scholarship, the state has played a central role in the construction of industrial relations institutions in Britain in the last hundred years or so, and that one can identify three distinct indus- trial relations systems, the first lasting from the early part of the twentieth century until the end of the 1950s, the second lasting a scant two decades before collapsing in the mid-1980s, and the third now firmly in place. For all the variations across industries, and idiosyncratic elements of industrial relations practice, each system formed a more or less coherent approach to the regulation of relations between business and labor, and each evolved in response to economic restructuring. Industrial relations institutions came under severe pressure as the basic structure of the economy changed, and the state, far from being abstentionist, played a crucial role in the construction of new institutions to manage, or regulate, class relations. How the state intervened, in turn, had important implications for the ideology, organiza- tion, and practice of British trade unions. It is the legacy of this crucial state role over more than a century, I argue, that explains why British trade union- ism was so vulnerable to Thatcherism.

The focus of this book is Britain, but the argument that it makes has much broader theoretical and empirical applicability. The next chapter intervenes in the theoretical debate concerning institution-building, arguing first that institutional theory needs to pay more attention to moments of crisis and disjuncture, second that economic patterning and class conflict are key triggers of institutional change, and third that states have particular capacities un- available to private actors, among them a privileged role in the narration of crises, and the ability to solve collective action problems. As such, the theory of institutional change offered in the next chapter anticipates both more dra- matic breaks in institutional development and greater synchronicity in institu- tional developments across the political economies of advanced capitalist soci- eties, along with a more central and distinctive role for states in institutional construction, than the main alternative theoretical approaches.

Furthermore, at an empirical level, I argue that Britain constitutes a critical case for any argument about the role of the state in institutional development. It has long anchored one end of the spectrum of state intervention in industrial relations. In contrast to accounts of industrial relations development in France or the United States, for example, which have tended to emphasize important roles for their respective states,[2] state abstentionism in industrial relations, and a concomitant emphasis on "voluntarism" on the part of private industrial actors, was the defining feature of accounts of British industrial relations until at least the end of the 1960s.[3] If it can be argued, as this book does, that the British state has in fact been a central actor in the construction, maintenance, and reconstruction of industrial relations institutions for over a hundred years, this suggests that, at least in the realm of industrial relations, accounts of institutional construction cannot afford to sideline the importance of state action anywhere.

INDUSTRIAL RELATIONS IN BRITISH POLITICS AND SOCIETY

In no other capitalist democracy has "the labour question" been as enduringly central to politics and political economy as in Britain. The British Labour Party, famously born out "of the bowels" of the trade union movement,[4] retained a tight institutional and organizational connection with the labor movement from the time of its creation until the middle of the 1990s, and even now the party constitution reserves an important role for unions; despite a persistent undercurrent of conflict, even Tony Blair's New Labour government has not yet attempted to sever the constitutional cord linking party and unions. The closeness of the party-union linkage has meant that party politics has been inextricably linked to industrial relations and the manner in which the labor movement is integrated into the British political economy. Every attempt to renegotiate the role of labor and the form of industrial relations has caused political tremors.

Concern over the labor question, though, goes well beyond party politics and the linkage between the Labour Party and the trade union movement. Well before the labor interest was represented in Parliament there were periodic bouts of middle-class panic in response to industrial conflict, and as British economic dominance gave way to the long drawn-out agony of economic decline, one of the most persistent themes has been trade union responsibility for economic failure. One can read explanations of British economic problems in the *Economist* magazine or the *Times* of London in the 1890s and the 1970s and find almost identical passages in both periods identifying restrictive work rules, resistance to technological innovation, and poor work habits as the source of those problems. Only the inclusion of delightful terms such as "ca'-canny" (the deliberate practice of "going slow" at work and limiting output on the part of workers) in the earlier period serves to date these accounts.

Political and public concern over economic decline and the labor movement's responsibility for that decline reached its apogee in the 1960s and

1970s in Britain. Industrial relations reform became a central part of the agenda of successive governments, and a plausible case can be made that industrial conflict and trade union resistance to those reform efforts brought down two governments: Edward Heath's 1970—74 Conservative government, following the stillbirth of the 1971 Industrial Relations Act and the mine workers' strike, which made Arthur Scargill a household name; and James Callaghan's Labour government, which collapsed in 1979 after an extended experiment with incomes policies resulted in a wave of strikes known collectively as the Winter of Discontent. These events had a profound political impact, launching Margaret Thatcher's leadership of the Conservative Party, contributing to that party's embrace of neoliberalism and radical industrial relations reform, and leading to the process of "modernizing" the Labour Party, which eventually led it to embrace "Third Way" policies and Tony Blair as its leader.

The argument here is not that the British labor movement necessarily bears responsibility for the charges that have been repeatedly brought against it; debate over the source of economic decline has been perhaps Britain's only consistent growth industry.[5] There is a strong case to be made that trade unions were as much the victims of decline as its cause, and that industrial militancy was more symptom of economic failure than cause. From the perspective of more than a century of debate, Britain's economic decline appears overdetermined. This is not, in any case, a debate that I wish to enter into in this book.

The point, rather, is the importance that public debates concerning industrial relations have played in British politics and society for more than a century. Regardless of the *reality* of trade union power, it became a central cultural trope, reappearing every time the level of industrial conflict became elevated or concern about economic decline heightened. Again, the two decades from the end of the 1950s until the end of the 1970s serve as the best indicator of the wider cultural impact of perceptions of industrial relations crisis. Two examples may illustrate the point. In 1959 Peter Sellers starred in the enormously popular film *I'm All Right Jack*, as a dour trade union shop steward, contemplating a small portrait of Lenin on his mantelpiece at home, and seeking to limit output and encourage militancy at work. Ian Carmichael played an employee whose efforts to work hard and ignore restrictive practices were constantly thwarted by the Sellers character. The film won several British film awards.[6] My first exposure to the cultural importance of British industrial relations came in 1973, when I was eleven and the Strawbs reached number two in the British pop charts with the song "Part of the Union." The song ended with the verse and refrain that begin this chapter, and it captured well the apparent power and influence of trade unions in Britain in the 1970s. Little wonder then that public debate over industrial relations reform has been so central to British politics. The story of the institutional development of industrial relations is an inseparable part of the wider trajectory of British politics and political economy in the twentieth century. An examination of the reform of industrial relations over this long period opens a remarkable window into the process by which political-economic institutions are first constructed, then maintained, and eventually transformed in capitalist societies.

THATCHERISM IN HISTORICAL PERSPECTIVE

Why was the rapid transformation of the British system of industrial relations in the period after 1979 so unexpected, posing substantial problems of explanation for scholars? After all, Britain's centralized Westminster system of politics places few political obstacles in the way of government reform efforts, and there is no question but that "taming the trade unions" was a core goal of Thatcherite Conservatism.[7] The reason this constitutes a puzzle lies in the manner in which the power of the labor movement had tended to be explained prior to the 1980s, and in particular, the role accorded the British state in the construction of industrial relations institutions.

Almost thirty years ago, John Goldthorpe launched a devastating critique of the dominant diagnoses of the crisis of British industrial relations and prescriptions for reform.[8] In the early 1970s two main versions of reformism, "liberal-pluralist" and "Tory reformism," emerged in response to the problems widely considered to be afflicting British industrial relations: a high strike rate, inflexible and restrictive labor practices, and uncontrolled labor costs. Liberal-pluralist reformism, which was intellectually dominant at that point, argued that these problems reflected a widespread "disorder" or "anomie" in the industrial relations system, and recommended efforts to institutionalize formal collective bargaining in the workplace and reassert both managerial and union authority through education and persuasion (see chapter 4 for an account of those efforts). Tory reformism, to which Goldthorpe devoted much less attention, on the grounds that it had been tried and found wanting, shared much of the liberal-pluralist diagnosis but identified trade union power as a prime culprit and prescribed legislation and sanctions to prevent the "abuse" of union power.

Goldthorpe, from the perspective of radical sociology, argued that reformers failed to recognize that the problems of British industrial relations were symptomatic of a fundamental shift in the balance of class power in the postwar period, in favor of labor, which had created something akin to an industrial relations stalemate. As a result, reformism both misdiagnosed the problem and promoted utopian solutions. Goldthorpe ended his critique thus: "Indeed, the further, more radical, conclusion may be suggested that at the present time British industrial relations are simply not in any far-reaching way reformable."[9] Goldthorpe was not alone. By the mid-1970s it was common, among academics, politicians, and political commentators, to argue that Britain was becoming "ungovernable," in large part because of the power of a deeply implanted labor movement that was autonomous of, and therefore immune to, state power.[10] As we will see later in this chapter, postwar industrial relations scholars constructed a highly sophisticated theoretical edifice to explain British industrial relations, one that rested on the notion of a largely abstentionist state and a decentralized workplace trade unionism, and that identified few sharp breaks in the institutional trajectory of industrial relations, and certainly no leading role for the state during periods of institutional transformation.

Yet a quarter century on, one can plausibly argue that British industrial relations have undergone massive reform, and in the process many of the problems of most concern to employers have disappeared. Most interestingly, and unexpectedly, the nature of this reform of industrial relations has not been of the liberal-pluralist variety but rather Tory reformism, in the form of the Thatcherite class project of using state power to restrict the actions of trade unions, limit collective bargaining, and free the hands of managers to organize the workplace as they wish. The state has not been as powerless as, and the labor movement has been more fragile than, anyone would have expected three decades ago. This requires a reinterpretation of British industrial relations.

It is worth stepping back a moment to explain in terms of intellectual autobiography why I have come to argue that understanding Thatcherism's impact on industrial relations requires a more thoroughgoing reconsideration of a century of British institutional development in this sphere. Prior to turning to the study of British industrial relations, I worked on France, which boasted a notoriously weak and excluded labor movement and an archetypal strong state whose central role in the regulation of industrial relations was well known.[11] I then became involved in a collaborative comparative project surveying the fate of trade unionism in Western Europe in the period after the second oil shock; within this project, my responsibility was Britain.[12] I had expected a striking contrast between Britain and France given the long-standing dominant interpretations of British industrial relations; in many ways the respective labor movement strength and state role in industrial relations in the two countries ought to have been mirror images of each other.

However, the experience of the 1980s and 1990s appeared to demonstrate similarity, not difference, as British trade unionism was far more vulnerable to the exercise of state power than anticipated. The question then was whether Thatcherism marked a break with the past—dominant interpretations of British industrial relations had been correct in the past but had simply been superseded by a determined reforming government—or whether state power has always played a central role in the institutional development of industrial relations, with the implication that the labor movement was always more dependent upon the actions of the state, its strength less autonomous of resources derived from institutions put in place by the state. This book makes the second argument. It argues that Thatcherism was, in fact, the *third* great project of state industrial relations reform in the period since the 1890s (when British governments first began actively trying to shape industrial relations institutions). In each case, the state responded to evidence of a failure of existing industrial relations to manage economic restructuring and industrial conflict with a purposeful, coherent project of institution-building, and in each case, the resulting system of industrial relations institutions shaped the resources, practices, and ideology of trade unions. This is not to say (as the next chapter will elaborate at some length) that trade unions, still less business, have been unimportant actors, or that their class strength has not constrained state reform efforts. On the contrary. The British state has nevertheless played a central role in determining the particular shape that industrial relations reform took on all three occasions.

The historical scope of this book thus serves *both* to contextualize the events of the 1980s and 1990s, by demonstrating that this was one more iteration of a long-term state role in the construction of industrial relations, *and* to explain why the British labor movement was more vulnerable to state-led institutional reconstruction than one might anticipate from the perspective of the 1970s. It is necessary to reinterpret the past in order to explain the present. In comparative perspective, this interpretation of the British case may in turn require that we rethink our classifications of national varieties of state intervention in the political economy, as the next chapter suggests.

Interpreting British Industrial Relations

This book offers a reinterpretation of the development of industrial relations institutions in Britain. This is clearly not a subject upon which little scholarship exists. Precisely because industrial conflict and debates over trade union power have been such contentious political and public issues, a staggering quantity of literature exists, and it is hard to identify any areas of research that have escaped academic scrutiny. The final section of this chapter will set out the main elements of the argument of the book and its contribution to that literature, and the next chapter will elaborate the theoretical framework employed. But it is first important to briefly discuss alternative interpretations of British industrial relations, particularly the interpretation that dominated debate until at least the end of the 1970s. Teasing out the assumptions contained in this theoretical approach is the starting point for any reinterpretation that is able to make sense of the impact of Thatcherism, and more recently Blairism, on British industrial relations.

From the 1950s through the 1970s British academic industrial relations were dominated by a pluralist theoretical paradigm (what Goldthorpe referred to as liberal-pluralist). The leading figures, including Otto Kahn-Freund,

Hugh Clegg, Allan Flanders, and Alan Fox, were influential both in the academy and in public policy. These academics were often found on public commissions and courts of inquiry, and their research efforts served as the raw material for the formulation of government policy. The best indication of the intellectual dominance of pluralism was indicated by the report of the Royal Commission on Trade Unions and Employer Associations, chaired by Lord Donovan and issued in 1968 (see chapter 4), which closely followed both the diagnoses and the prescriptions of pluralism, and which set the industrial relations policy agenda for the next decade.[13] Pluralism was always subject to criticism, particularly from its left, and as the 1970s wore on that criticism grew. However, while pluralism has fallen out of fashion in the last two decades, no overarching industrial relations theory has replaced it. Somewhat paradoxically, the influence of its main theoretical rival, Marxism, largely rose and fell in step with pluralism.[14] Of particular importance for this book is the role that pluralism and both alternative and subsequent interpretations of British industrial relations have attributed to the state.

It is also worth noting that the British tradition of industrial relations research has been dominated by empirical work.[15] Its primary focus has been the workplace, where hugely rich accounts of industrial relations practice have been made possible by a case study approach. Case studies have increasingly been supplemented by large-scale surveys, but even these have tended to center on the workplace rather than the sectoral level or the suprafirm institutions of union or business organization. The result is that the literature is "characterised by fact-finding and description rather than theoretical generalization."[16] Theory has been more an afterthought than a central focus of intellectual activity. This is of course itself a generalization, and industrial relations scholars have on occasion sought to step back from the detailed, finely grained studies of industrial relations in a given workplace or industry to seek some broader theorization of industrial relations developments.[17] Still, it remains true that while the theoretical architecture of pluralism is rarely invoked in discussions of contemporary industrial relations, no alternative paradigm has achieved anything like its widespread acceptance.

For pluralists, Britain was the classic example of the abstentionist state and the voluntarist industrial relations system. The best statement of this position was that of the foremost legal theorist of British industrial relations, Otto Kahn-Freund, who labeled the British system "collective *laissez faire*."[18] This implied "allowing free play to the collective forces of society, and to limit the intervention of the law to those marginal areas in which the disparity of these forces ... is so great as to prevent the successful operation of what is characteristically called 'negotiating machinery.' "[19] Kahn-Freund argued that a mature system of industrial relations, of which Britain was the best example, exhibited a sufficiently high degree of collective self-organization by business and labor that state intervention was unnecessary, and would serve only to impose conditions that unions and employer organizations could not and would not carry out. Kahn-Freund's view of the appropriate role of the state in industrial relations was clearly influenced by his experience in interwar Germany, where labor law was used to limit the autonomy of trade unions and ultimately incorporate them into the state,[20] but it also rested on the assumption that the relative power of business and labor organizations could be sufficiently leveled, in the absence of a significant and continuing role for the state, to permit self-regulation. The result from the perspective of the 1950s was, again in Kahn-Freund's words, that "there is, perhaps no major country in the world in which the law has played a less significant role in the shaping of these [industrial] relations than in Great Britain."[21]

Similarly, when Flanders attempted to set out the core principles on which the British industrial relations system was based in his evidence to the Donovan Commission, the first was the priority "accorded to collective bargaining over other methods of external job regulation."[22] This meant that legislation played a very limited part in the setting of wages and working conditions, tending to be reserved for areas of the economy where collective bargaining was too weak to operate, and that there was no legal regulation or legal support for collective bargaining. The second core principle was the priority accorded to "voluntary over compulsory procedural rules for collective bargaining."[23] This principle implied limited regulation of the relations between unions and employers, and hence an abstentionist and minimalist role for industrial relations legislation. The state and legislation, in other words, played a peripheral role in the British system of industrial relations, which was instead regulated by voluntary agreements between unions and employers. Thus, from the perspective of the 1960s, British industrial relations were characterized by a severely limited legislative framework, which relied on negative immunities rather than positive rights, and the processes of union recognition, bargaining, and industrial conflict were regulated by voluntary collective agreement rather than the state.[24] At this time British workers had no statutory right to strike, to union recognition, or to collectively bargain.

Thus the conventional account argued that British trade unions have traditionally relied on immunities instead of rights, that the state provided few individual protective rights at work, and that there was limited juridification of outcomes, with the single exception—a very big exception—of incomes policies, which were considered temporary despite being in operation in one form or another for the great bulk of the postwar period. Steinmetz has argued that disadvantaged groups have traditionally had two routes for making gains.[25] The first is to bring the state in on their side, while the second is to bypass labor law and the state through collective action. For the pluralists Britain was perhaps the purest example of that second route.

The implication of this account was that trade union strength, when it existed, was a result of the unions' own efforts and a direct result of market strength rather than state support of some kind. Parallel to, and influencing, the notion of an abstentionist state in British industrial relations was the doctrine known as voluntarism. It reflected, as Flanders put it in 1974, "the notion that unions have, as it were, lifted themselves into their present position of power and influence by their own unaided efforts in overcoming employer resistance and hostile social forces."[26] The basis of voluntarism, from the perspective of trade unions, was neatly summed up in Kahn-Freund's statement that "what the State has not given the State cannot take away."[27] Hyman's important recent account of varieties of European trade unionism firmly emphasizes both the voluntarism of British unions and, in comparative perspective, the historical continuity of British trade union traditions.[28] Their distinguishing feature, for Hyman, is their occupation of a terrain between market and class: between a focus on bargaining for improved terms and conditions within the labor market, and a model of class conflict in which trade unionism is a form of "anti-capitalist opposition."[29] And of great importance for trade union behavior is the fact that voluntarism, with its particular understanding of the sources of labor power, came to be internalized by the unions themselves.

The particular emphases of the pluralists were nicely captured by Clegg's classic and highly influential early accounts of British industrial relations, which began with chapters on work groups, shop stewards, and workplace bargaining and only then moved on to discuss employer associations and trade unions, ending with a discussion of the role of the state.[30] It made sense to begin with workplace bargaining and labor organization in the workplace because, as Clegg put it, "they are uniquely important in contemporary Britain compared with the past or with countries overseas."[31]

All pluralists agreed that the most important single fact in the development of British industrial relations in the postwar period was the growth of workplace bargaining, which threatened to displace the existing system of industry-level bargaining. The famous conclusion of the Donovan Report was that Britain now had two systems of industrial relations: industry-level bargaining had an elaborate set of formal mechanisms and procedures created by unions and employer associations, but the agreements that resulted were increasingly empty, setting minimum wages and grievance procedures but leaving the negotiation of real wages and working conditions to the firm, where collective bargaining was much less formalized and much more subject to conflict. The results were unofficial strikes and wage drift. Neither unions nor employer associations had much control over industrial relations at this level. Instead, power was in the hands of groups of workers and managers in the firm.

This account of a decentralized and voluntary system of industrial relations, unregulated by the state, overlay an essentially *market* view of the nature of workers' power. Wright has usefully distinguished between the associational and structural power of workers, with the former being a product of collective organization and the latter emerging out of the location of work-ers in the economy.[32] Pluralist accounts of British industrial relations empha-sized structural power, with power lying with the work groups inside the firm rather than with trade unions outside; the balance of power between workers and management rested on market factors: the level of employment, skill, and location in the firm.[33] Power was not, in other words, based on the collec-tive or organizational resources of workers, still less on political resources derived from the state. So it should come as no surprise that the primary explanation used by pluralists to explain the rise in the power of workers in the postwar period—and hence the problems of strikes, inflation, and so on—was tight labor markets. As Clegg put it in 1972: "The study of British indus-trial relations today is to a considerable extent the study of how a system of industrial relations fashioned at a time of unemployment or fluctuating employment, has reacted to a long period of full employment."[34] Workers became more powerful after 1945 because market conditions gave them greater bargaining power.

The pluralist view was not uncontested. Indeed in the course of the 1970s it came under increasing attack from Marxism and radical sociology. Gold-thorpe's 1974 critique cited earlier was only one of a range of responses primar-ily from the Left, and there was even an internal critique from Alan Fox, one of the original pluralist theorists.[35] Two parts of the pluralist account of British industrial relations came in for particular criticism: the nature of industrial conflict, and the appropriate response to it. Thus pluralism's critics argued that conflict was inherent in the capitalist wage relationship, that power was more weighted toward management in the workplace, and that, as Goldthorpe argued, worker power in the workplace, especially the growth in the power of shop stewards, was not so much a source of disorder as a genuine expression of class power.

Hence the response to pluralist prescriptions for reform was to ask in whose interests reform would be, and to question whether reform, either negotiated or imposed, would work. Goldthorpe argued that what the pluralists saw as general problems of British industrial relations—which, as a result, most groups in society might be expected to wish to ameliorate—were in fact only problems for management, and reflected a long-term and deep-seated growth in the workplace strength and hence bargaining power of workers inside the firm. Pluralist solutions were utopian because they failed to recognize that what industrial relations theorists saw as generalized anomie in fact served the interests of large numbers of workers. Similarly, Tory reformism, while more seemingly realistic in its willingness to impose reform, misidentified the culprit and hence focused its attention on trade unions, who were as powerless as management to control the power of labor in the workplace.

The important and surprising point, though, is that for all their differences over the nature of industrial conflict and what to do about it, pluralists and

their critics did not differ on the core assumption of the essentially autonomous firm-level and market-based nature of worker power in the firm. The
assumptions about the minimal role of the state in explaining labor power
were shared, and indeed enhanced, because pluralism's critics on the left were
even more likely to see the state as primarily coercive in its defense of capital's
interests. And if anything, the critics on the left went further in emphasizing
the workplace as the source of labor strength, in celebrating shop steward
power, and in distrusting the motives and role of trade union bureaucrats, a
perspective Zeitlin has termed "rank-and-filism."[36] Indeed, Clegg, in a theoretical conclusion to his 1979 book on industrial relations, perceptively noted
that "the difference between their [Marxist and pluralist] analyses of industrial
relations should not be exaggerated" and that there is "much common ground
in their answers" to the explanation of conflict and stability in industrial relations.[37] In the one area where Marxism ought to have had a clear superiority
over pluralism—its account of the economic determinants of class conflict—
the advantage was lost by positing a largely abstract and ahistorical capitalism,
which could no more account for broad shifts in labor strength than the labor
market analysis of the pluralists.

Much attention has been paid in this chapter to a historical snapshot of the
state of industrial relations theorizing in Britain. In retrospect, the dominant
pluralist interpretation of industrial relations was something of an accident of
timing. It emerged in the 1950s, a period of relative stability in the institutional
development of industrial relations. In most industrialized countries, the critical
construction phase of the postwar industrial relations system took place between 1930 and 1950, as a result of depression, war, and a postwar settlement
resting on new political and class compromises. Industrial relations institutions
in Britain did undergo some important development during this period, but the
basic contours of the system already existed, having been constructed between
1894 and 1921 (as chapter 3 details). Thus scholars, examining British industrial relations in the early 1950s, saw institutions that appeared to be operating
smoothly with little help or hindrance from the state; the theorization of an
abstentionist state was, in other words, an artifact of a particular time period,
one that was actually quite unusual in the limited degree of state intervention.
The 1950s were also a highly unusual period of apparently harmonious class
relations, as evidenced by popular reactions to the festival of Britain in 1951
and the coronation of Queen Elizabeth II in 1953.[38] At the time of the coronation, a pair of prominent sociologists could argue

> The assimilation of the working class into the moral consensus of British society,
> though certainly far from complete, has gone further in Great Britain than any-
> where else, and its transformation from one of the most unruly and violent into
> one of the most orderly and law-abiding is one of the great collective achievements
> of modern times.[39]

This was not a description of British class relations that would be recognized a decade later. Historically, it has been a rise in the level of industrial conflict, and public concern about the economic impact of such conflict, that has forced the British state to take a more active role in the regulation of industrial relations, and in the 1950s British governments had the luxury of being able to rely on existing industrial relations institutions to limit that conflict.

The pluralist interpretation of British industrial relations, with its emphasis on collective laissez-faire, voluntarism, and a relatively limited state, was therefore forged in a quite unusual period of British industrial relations history. Nevertheless, aspects of its interpretation were reinforced by events of the 1960s and 1970s (as we shall see in chapter 4), in particular the view that states had limited power to rein in trade union power, and that the strength of the labor movement derived from its autonomous power in the workplace. Initially, at least, the dramatic shifts in British industrial relations beginning in the 1960s were assimilated into the existing pluralist theoretical framework.

Of course the state abstentionist view has not survived unexamined to the present. Evidence from the 1960s onward of a steadily increasing tide of both individual and collective labor law forced some reconsideration of the role of the state, and the experience of the 1980s and 1990s accentuated that process, though the question of the *effectiveness* of state action in curtailing labor strength remained contentious.[40] The emergence of a burgeoning historical literature on the role of the state in encouraging union development in various industries has also chipped away at the abstentionist position.[41] It is no longer acceptable to construct industrial relations textbooks along the lines that Clegg and his collaborators first produced in 1954; government policy, labor law, and the public sector now all receive sizable attention.[42]

However, the traditional view of the abstentionist state, though superseded, has absorbed and refracted the more recent evidence of an expanded state role. State intervention still tends to be seen as incoherent, ad hoc, and narrowly political rather than systemic. This has had two implications. First, the focus has been on labor law, to the exclusion or marginalization of a much broader range of state actions that influence industrial relations. Indeed much of the discussion of the role of the state in recent years has come from academic lawyers.[43] Second, the very notion of state *intervention* implies a basic separation between the state and industrial relations, in which the latter could, and at one time presumably did, operate autonomously of the state. Thus the role of the state is seen not as an integral component of industrial relations so much as a regulator of conflicts that originate in the workplace. Legislation and other forms of state action are rarely seen as a central component of labor strength. Thus the increased role of the state in industrial relations has been recognized but not theorized.

It needs to be said that several scholars have argued that the constitutive role of the British state in the construction of industrial relations institutions needs to be more fully integrated into our understanding of the historical evolution of industrial relations. Most important have been Zeitlin and Tolliday's work on the role of the state in encouraging union growth and collective bargaining,[44] and Ewing's account of the interwar period.[45] Both not only offer an alternative historical reading of the role of the state but attempt to theorize it as well. Zeitlin and Tolliday emphasize a position of state autonomy and identify a range of state interests separate from those of business that lead states to foster trade unionism. Ewing is particularly valuable in expanding the notion of what constitutes state intervention and in emphasizing the institution-building role of the state. This book builds on that scholarship, both by extending the historical period to cover three great state projects of industrial relations reform, and by attempting to explain both the *logic* of state action (why states act in particular ways at particular times) and the consequences for institutional construction in the realm of industrial relations.

State regulation of industrial relations can take place in a wide variety of forms. The single most important reason why the abstentionist account of the role of the British state seemed plausible, at least until the 1960s, was that regulation was understood to mean legislative regulation through a comprehensive framework of labor law, and this Britain most certainly did not have. But in fact the British state has intervened constantly in industrial relations. There was scarcely an industrial conflict in the decade and a half before the First World War, or again in the 1960s, in which the state did not seek to bring about a settlement, often through detailed participation in the negotiations.[46] To be sure, intervention is not regulation, as Fulcher has reminded us,[47] and it could be argued that it has been precisely the absence of a better framework of labor law that has forced the state to intervene constantly in an ad hoc manner, cleaning up the mess of a failed industrial relations system. The remainder of this book argues that this would be to misunderstand the nature of state regulation in Britain, which achieved a high degree of coherence during each of the three periods of the past century.

THE ARGUMENT

This book examines a little over a century of industrial relations developments, from the late 1890s, when the British state first clearly articulated a public policy interest in the spread of collective institutions for the regulation of industrial relations, to the present. After 1979, Conservative governments formally ended that public policy presumption in favor of collective regulation, instead urging the decollectivization of industrial relations and the spread of individualized institutions for the regulation of social relations in the workplace. The Labour government elected in 1997 and reelected in 2001 has made few changes to this industrial relations framework, emphasizing that any further regulation of the labor market would take place primarily through individual labor law enforced through state agencies, not a revitalization of collective labor organization and collective regulation of industrial relations: the decollectivist system of industrial relations has been reinforced, even if alternative mechanisms of labor protection have been introduced.

In the course of the time period covered in this book three distinct industrial relations systems were constructed in Britain. Each new set of mechanisms to regulate industrial relations was a response to changes in the structure of the British economy and the increased industrial conflict that accompanied economic restructuring. But new industrial relations institutions did not emerge out of the interactions of business and labor in civil society alone. In each case, the British state played a crucial role in the early construction phase of new regulatory mechanisms. Once they were in place, the state could then partially withdraw from active regulation, leaving industrial actors to use the new institutions. The three systems of industrial relations that were put in place in the course of the last century were each coherent and intelligible responses to the economic challenges facing the British economy at the time of their construction: there was, in other words, a clear economic patterning that underlay institutional development, explaining the timing and form of reform efforts, which went well beyond short-term, reactive, and narrowly political explanations of the manner and trajectory of industrial relations. At the same time, however, the sets of institutions that were created were not the only ones that might have responded to economic restructuring, nor were they necessarily the best—the seemingly permanent crisis of British industrial relations speaks to the failure of industrial relations reform alone to manage capitalist crisis. There was, at particular junctures, an important measure of space for state actors to shape the design of institutions. Furthermore, as the next chapter elaborates, states have unique capacities, beyond those enjoyed by private industrial actors, when it comes to the construction and embedding of institutions.

The first system of industrial relations, which emerged in response to the long drawn-out decline of the old staple industries that had powered Britain's economic growth for much of the nineteenth century, was organized around industry bargaining between trade unions and employer associations. The institutions that made up this system of industrial relations served to limit competition, both between employers and workers, and between different employers in the same industry, creating a floor of terms and conditions of work and elaborating grievance procedures. Public commissions helped to privilege a particular interpretation of economic decline and industrial conflict, and created the political space for the spread of industry bargaining. This was not a set of industrial relations institutions that would have found widespread acceptance in the absence of an active role on the part of state actors, primarily because of collective action problems among employers. Board of Trade and Ministry of Labour officials repeatedly intervened in industrial disputes and used an assortment of mechanisms to urge the creation of collective bargaining institutions. Once in place, these institutions were remarkably successful in resisting pressure for their abrogation, even after labor movement strength and industrial conflict waned in the interwar period. An important advantage of this system of industrial relations for trade unions was that industry bargaining helped them gain recognition from employers and recruit new members where they might otherwise have found it difficult to force recognition.

This industry bargaining–based set of institutions began to collapse in the 1950s, when the center of gravity of the British economy shifted from the older staples to a set of industries that more closely approximated Fordist forms of growth. The absence of institutions for managing economic change and improving productivity *inside* firms generated higher levels of industrial conflict, much of it at the workplace level, unsanctioned and uncontrolled by trade unions. In this context, a second system of industrial relations began to develop, this one organized around the creation of collective workplace institutions to permit the negotiation of economic change. Within a relatively short period, about a decade and a half, workplace bargaining over not just terms and conditions but a broad range of aspects of work organization, a formalized role for lay union officials inside the firm, and an increasingly elaborate set of resources and mechanisms for decentralized collective bargaining became widespread in the economy. Again, public commissions played an important role in setting the terms of political debate concerning industrial relations reform, and state action (this time as much legislative as administrative) served to reduce the costs, particularly to trade unions, of decentralizing their activities, and to spread decentralized bargaining far beyond those firms and industries that initially experimented with these forms of industrial relations. Chapter 4 argues that this project of industrial relations reform was in fact significantly more successful than contemporaries acknowledged. Furthermore, the failure of alternative projects of industrial relations reform during this period, which had taken the form of offering a statutory route to union recognition in return for restrictions on industrial action, reinforced in trade unions the myth of bootstrap voluntarism, referred to by Flanders earlier, in which union strength was believed to be autonomous from state action and resources.

This second system of industrial relations rapidly came under pressure from the interaction of domestic and international economic factors, and from the particular manner in which employers responded to both those economic factors and the expansion in scale and scope of collective regulation inside the firm. The focus of the third system of industrial relations remained, like the second, centered on the firm, but it replaced collective regulation with individualized institutions that maximized the flexibility of employers in organizing work and managing their workforces. Collective regulation remained in parts of manufacturing, in older firms, and in the public sector, but even there it was less formal and increasingly circumscribed. In the 1980s, the British state once again played a central role in the articulation and spread of this new set of industrial relations institutions. Labor law and management of the public sector were the main tools of state policy. A slew of industrial relations legislation—six major acts of Parliament alone between 1980 and 1993— limited the capacity of trade unions to resist change and gave employers a free hand in restructuring their industrial relations, and action in the public sector served to demonstrate acceptable forms of industrial relations to private-sector employers. As noted above, and elaborated in some detail in chapter 6, the arrival of a New Labour government in 1997 after eighteen years of Conservative governments did not markedly alter this system of industrial relations, reinforcing its decollectivist tendencies while introducing some limited statutory reregulation of the labor market.

It was in this context that the chickens of voluntarism came home to roost for British trade unions. In both the first and second systems of industrial relations, important components of labor strength derived from institutions constructed or underwitten by the state: industry bargaining provided a mechanism for gaining recognition, while the costs of decentralized collective bargaining for unions were subsidized by the state and employers. Once the state and employers both withdrew from these institutions, trade unions found themselves much weaker than they, or most academic commentators, had anticipated. The result was a rapid and sustained decline in both trade union strength and collective regulation of industrial relations. One measure of this vulnerability has been the dramatic shift in trade union strategic orientation in the last fifteen years; in a partial recovery of strategies that briefly flowered at the end of the nineteenth century, and again in the early 1960s, trade unions have now turned their backs on voluntarism and endorsed a thoroughgoing juridification of British industrial relations, with the creation of a wide range of statutory rights at work. Unions, in other words, have finally acknowledged their dependence upon political resources and sought a political settlement that embeds a set of positive rights (in contrast to the negative immunities they enjoyed for most of the twentieth century) in labor law.

The narrative contained in this book brings state actors to the center of the stage. For that reason, it is easy to overstate the role of the state and the autonomy that it enjoyed. The next chapter will attempt to theorize more precisely the space available to states for institutional construction, and the relationship between state and class actors, but a brief disclaimer is necessary here. All states operate within a force field of class interests and constraints, and in capitalist democracies the "privileged position of business" is partially offset by the capacity of other social actors to mobilize political resources.[48] It makes little sense to isolate one actor, whether it be labor, business, or the state, as dominant when it is the relationships among them, and their shifting interests, alliances, and compromises, that shape the construction of industrial relations institutions. This book focuses on the role of the state, both in order to highlight some specific capacities and features of that role in the process of institution-building, and because the state's role has often been misunderstood in the British case. It is precisely the traditional undervaluing of state action in Britain that makes Britain a crucial comparative case for any discussion of the process of institution-building.

Nevertheless, business and labor were not mere bystanders, so understanding the "class drivers," to borrow Coates's marvelous term, is always going to be an important part of the story.[49] In this regard it is worth distinguishing between the purposeful role played by class actors in the process of institution-building, on the one hand, and the manner in which class formation served to shape the kinds of institutional responses that were available to the state, on the other. Each moment of institutional construction was preceded or accompanied by an increase in industrial conflict and an expansion of the organizational capacity of trade unions. The search for new industrial relations institutions was therefore in part a response to renewed labor strength and an effort to find a new manner in which to integrate the working class into capitalist society. In the British case, trade unions helped to trigger each new phase of institutional construction, but they played a less significant role in shaping the resulting institutions. Business interests played a much more important role, both because of the greater political influence of business throughout most of the last century and because firms were bound to have a privileged role in identifying the institutional implications of economic restructuring.

More important than directly shaping industrial relations policy, however, was the manner in which class formation in Britain constrained the kinds of institutions that could be constructed. There is a large literature on the way in which industrialization and empire shaped the organization and interests of business and labor, and created enduring class practices.[50] The dominance and international focus of financial capital, the small size and resistance to technological innovation of industrial firms, the fragmentation and craft outlook of the labor movement are all well known, and reference will be made to them in later chapters. Their importance for the purposes of this book is that they created a set of collective action problems that pushed the state to take a more active role in the construction of industrial relations institutions and, at the same time, made certain institutional responses to economic crisis all but impossible. British governments were thus simultaneously forced to act and constrained in the manner in which they could act.

The outline for the rest of this book is as follows. The next chapter steps back from the British case to examine theoretical approaches to the process by which industrial relations institutions are constructed, maintained over time, and then reconstructed. It argues that existing approaches do a much better job in explaining institutional continuity over time, and differences in sets of national institutions, than in explaining sharp breaks, moments of institutional discontinuity, and synchronous waves of institutional construction across countries. The rest of chapter 2 elaborates a theory of institutional construction that emphasizes two factors: first, a modified version of Regulation Theory in which changes in the growth regime trigger institutional crisis; and second, a set of capacities that are unique to the state in the process of institutional reconstruction, and which therefore make state action indispensable to the trajectory and shape of industrial relations institutions.

Chapters 3, 4 and 5 examine the three systems of industrial relations that have been created in Britain in the period since the 1890s. Chapter 3 covers the period from 1890 to 1940 (though it concentrates on the first half of that period), when the system of industry collective bargaining emerged. Chapter 4 examines the decline of the first system of industrial relations and then focuses on the various state reform projects undertaken between 1968 and 1979. It charts the growth of the second system of industrial relations, in which collective bargaining became decentralized to the firm level and expanded in scope to cover a wide range of workplace issues. Chapter 5 investigates the collapse of decentralized collective bargaining and its replacement by a decollectivist system of industrial relations. The logic and impact of Conservative reforms between 1979 and 1997 are examined in some detail. The structure of each of these three chapters is similar. They first outline the process of economic restructuring that triggered an upsurge in industrial unrest and the search for alternative institutional forms to regulate class relations, and examine the role of public commissions in shaping the discourse of reform. Each chapter then details the construction of new industrial relations institutions and the role of state actors (and conflicts among different state actors) in that process. The consequences of a particular sets of industrial relations institutions for the ideology, organization, and practice of trade unions forms the concluding section of each chapter. As noted above, the persistence of voluntarism on the part of British trade unions had the result that at potential turning points they largely rejected alternative industrial relations institutions. These chapters argue that institutions inherited from the past, and the reaction to them on the part of many trade unions, exacerbated the labor movement's vulnerability, a vulnerability that was exposed after 1979. The final chapter investigates the impact of the Labour government, in power since 1997, on the emerging decollectivist system of industrial relations. It concludes with a discussion of the trajectory of British industrial relations in comparative perspective.

CHAPTER TWO

Constructing Industrial Relations Institutions

INTRODUCTION

This chapter examines some theoretical and conceptual issues with regard to the institutional development of industrial relations, with particular emphasis on moments of institutional construction and transition—moments when, to paraphrase Gramsci, one set of institutions is dying while another is struggling to be born.[1] Industrial relations go to the heart of the ordering and regulation of class relations, and this chapter is concerned with those points at which industrial conflict cannot be contained within existing institutional structures and practices, and therefore employers, trade unions, and state actors seek alternative arrangements that promise to restore industrial peace, stable accumulation, and the legitimacy of capitalist social relations. In short, this chapter tries to explain why industrial relations institutions break down, and how new sets of institutions are constructed.

Jenson has suggested that social scientists deal with two types of political time: normal and epochal.[2] During the former, when political change is slow, incremental, and characterized by path dependence, explanatory frameworks that privilege continuity, stability, and order are appropriate. Most institutionalist accounts fall into this category, concerning themselves primarily with normal political time. Epochal political change is easier to envisage in theory than in practice, and there will always be a strong case for emphasizing recurring patterns and continuities with the past.[3] Nevertheless, it is the contention of this book that epochal political change—in this case, moments of rapid transformation in the institutions of industrial relations——is both more characteristic of capitalist political economies than most accounts acknowledge and requires somewhat different tools of analysis than those employed in explaining political change during normal time.

A quick glance across western Europe and North America in the past century suggests, as one might expect, both similarities and divergences in the trajectory of industrial relations institutions.[4] Collective bargaining institutions have tended to become more embedded and encompassing over time, at least up until the 1980s. Moreover, one can identify a "bunching" of reform efforts in several countries at broadly similar times. Governments and industrial actors (employers, their organizations, and trade unions) have often appeared to be attempting to solve similar sets of problems in these reform efforts, suggesting that country-specific explanations are insufficient. At the same time, one can identify quite distinct national trajectories and indications of path dependence in the way in which a set of industrial relations institutions, once constructed, close off certain alternatives and encourage others. Furthermore, the development of industrial relations is marked by periods of intense institutional restructuring followed by periods of relative institutional stability. The question, then, becomes how to explain the combination of continuity and discontinuity, convergence and divergence, in the development of industrial relations systems. And, it should be said, the existing literature is much better at explaining institutional continuity and divergence than discontinuity and convergence. In this respect it is representative of political science more generally.

It is worth resisting the temptation of promising to "bring something back in" to the conceptual and theoretical toolbox of political science. In the last two decades we have first brought the state back in, then employers, and more recently ideas (though labor still appears banished to the wilderness, awaiting rehabilitation), and there are obvious dangers in "bending the stick too far,"[5] of seeking parsimony or novelty at the expense of explanation. This account is interested rather in encouraging a shift in emphasis within comparative political economy by highlighting two features of institutional development. The first is the distinctive capacities of states, and the central role of states when it comes to the construction and "embedding" of industrial relations institutions. The argument here is not one of state autonomy, or the importance of the distinct interests of state actors, but rather that states have unique capacities both to narrate an authoritative interpretation of industrial relations crises (a discursive capacity) and to solve collective action problems for employers and unions (an institutional capacity). Employers, workers, and their collective organizations are rarely able to create stable mechanisms for regulating class conflict in the absence of action on the part of the state. States not only have distinctive resources for institutionalizing industrial relations practices; they also play a crucial role in the interpretation and narration of industrial crises, both of which contribute to the long-term legitimacy and stability of a given industrial relations "settlement."

The second shift in emphasis highlighted in this chapter is the importance of broad shifts in the pattern of economic growth in triggering periods of intense industrial relations reform. Patterns of economic restructuring help to explain both the discontinuities that characterize the development of industrial relations within individual countries and a certain synchronicity, or bunching, of industrial relations developments across countries at particular points. Economic change is too often relegated, within the study of political economy, to the status of a broad contextual factor, only rarely operating to shape and constrain.[6] But, at least with regard to industrial relations, new patterns of economic restructuring pose different sets of problems to states and industrial actors, shift the interests of those actors, and go hand in hand with heightened levels of industrial conflict, triggering a crisis of existing industrial relations institutions. Clearly, how actors interpret the pressures on industrial relations institutions caused by economic restructuring, and hence how they choose to respond, are by no means given. That is why the discursive and institutional capacities of states matter. But the timing and character of economic restructuring play an important role in explaining the trajectory of systems of industrial relations.

This chapter does not attempt a complete explanation of the evolution of industrial relations institutions. The existing literature identifies a range of factors—the structure and organization of employer associations and trade unions, the political complexion of particular governments, the impact of war—that are clearly important. But explanations incorporating these causal factors systematically underestimate the importance of state intervention and the impact of economic restructuring. The result is that alternative accounts fail to recognize, let alone explain, the coherence, and the pattern of stability and change over the *longue durée*, exhibited by the institutional development of industrial relations.

The Specificity of Industrial Relations Institutions

Given the focus on industrial relations institutions, the starting point for the theoretical discussion contained in this chapter is the burgeoning institutionalist literature. But this chapter seeks to better embed that literature within the Regulationist tradition of political economy (where I think it properly belongs), while simultaneously recovering the more political and institutional elements of the Regulation approach. It has been argued that because "institutional theories share an emphasis on finding order and stability . . . in general [they] run into trouble in accounting for political change."[7] The Regulation approach offers some promise in providing the basis for a more dynamic theory of institutional construction and reconstruction. The mutually beneficial relationship between Regulationist and institutionalist approaches lies in understanding, first, how economic change brings about change in institutions and, second, how institutions subsequently regulate and stabilize economic growth.

The institutions under examination here are industrial relations ones—systems of labor law, collective bargaining, collective organizations, strike practices, and so on—and the analysis reflects the specificity of those institutions. It is by no means obvious that theoretical approaches designed to explain the emergence and development of social programs, central banks, or training systems (some of the most frequently examined institutions within comparative political economy) should be the same as, or have the same emphases as, those seeking to explain the institutions of industrial relations.

The distinctiveness of industrial relations institutions is that they go to the very core of power and accumulation in the workplace, reflecting and regulating the inherent imbalance of power, and resulting conflictuality, between employers and their employees. This is not to say that training systems or social programs do not affect the profitability of firms or even the power resources of workers, but they do so in less direct ways than industrial relations institutions. Industrial relations regulate the wage relationship and hence the wage-effort bargain itself, directly influencing productivity, relative factor income, and accumulation. Thus it is to industrial relations institutions that employers and states turn first when seeking to (re)establish order in the workplace.

For industrial relations institutions, more than other kinds of institutions, the relevant social forces are class actors. Industrial relations institutions are socially constructed in the particular sense that they are a congealed form of class power: they reflect a particular moment of class power at the time of their construction. There is nothing necessarily fragile or contingent about class power. It is the changing economic interests of workers and employers that are likely to be decisive in understanding both the form and the direction of institutional change. What gives institutions in the sphere of industrial relations their stability over time is a rough stability in the balance of class power and the economic interests of workers and employers. That in turn rests upon a stable pattern of economic growth. It is when that form of growth breaks down, and consequently the interests and resources of class actors change, that one would expect the institutions that previously regulated industrial relations to mutate, whether that involves the creation of entirely new institutions or the investing of new functions and meanings in existing institutions.

It is important to incorporate the essential insight that institutions are socially constructed through political practice with a recognition that those institutions can nevertheless remain stable—frozen, as it were—over long periods of time and can come to shape political outcomes independently of the conscious action of social actors. In this sense the utility of the Marxist tradition of political economy, out of which Regulation Theory emerged, with its emphasis on the economic patterning of social relations, is that it points toward a process of institutional construction, deconstruction, and reconstruction that is not historically contingent, fluid, and open-ended but instead profoundly structured.

Industrial relations institutions thus display certain characteristics.[8] They are primarily defensive, created above all to suppress conflictuality, to restore order, legitimacy, and accumulation. It is that role which explains the importance of economic restructuring in disrupting expectations, and in changing the interests and power of industrial actors. But at the same time, industrial relations institutions, once created, can have unintended consequences. As

Zeitlin has reminded us, even institutions created by employers to restore order and limit encroachments on managerial control in the workplace can provide a measure of protection to unions and their members, offering unexpected opportunities for future gains.[9] Another way to think about the duality of industrial relations institutions is that they simultaneously reflect congealed class power and in turn constrain the way in which that power can be used. The institutionalization of class conflict does not eliminate it, but it does move it into different arenas where different forms of conflict and different actors can play a role. Just as Douglas Hay's classic account of eighteenth-century English law demonstrated how law and the legal system operated as a class instrument while constraining the rulers at the same time,[10] so industrial relations institutions regulate workers and class conflict and, at the same time, force employers to play by a set of rules that limit their capacity to manage social relations in the workplace just as they wish.

This discussion of the character of industrial relations institutions matters for the account that follows. Industrial relations institutions are always fragile, partial solutions to industrial conflict, reflecting shifting interests and power. The danger of a certain kind of institutionalist analysis is that it can be overly functionalist, downplaying conflict and power. For that reason, perhaps bending the stick too much, in this account I emphasize the role of industrial conflict, the moments of institutional crisis, construction, and reconstruction. But it is nonetheless true that industrial relations institutions survive in the long run only if they are able to respond to the needs and interests of employers, and to permit a particular pattern of economic growth. To echo Hyman, "There is far greater realism in a perspective which recognises that the terrain of industrial relations is above all conditioned by capital."[11]

NATIONAL MODELS OF CAPITALISM

The dominant approaches to the study of institutions, including industrial relations institutions, simultaneously emphasize the importance of distinct national traditions and institutional trajectories, and a high degree of continuity across time (often understood in terms of path dependence of some kind) in the physiognomy of national institutional configurations. While emphasizing variation across national cases, contemporary comparative political economy demonstrates a certain insensitivity to institutional variation across time. This insensitivity in part reflects a preference for political over economic explanation, though Pontusson has pointed out that explanations based on structural economic change are perfectly compatible with national distinctiveness.[12] In contrast, I argue that the institutional development of industrial relations is marked both by sharp discontinuities across time within countries and by a remarkable degree of synchronicity across countries.

Any theoretical examination of industrial relations must begin with Crouch's seminal account of European industrial relations developments, both because it is one of the few institutionalist accounts to focus on industrial relations and because it anticipates many of the theoretical innovations of more recent comparative political economy.[13] Crouch's account can be fairly easily assimilated into the "Varieties of Capitalism" approach, with its broad division between organized and liberal market forms of capitalism, and emphasis on divergent national trajectories from an early historical point of departure.

Industrial Relations and European State Traditions embeds an argument about ideal-typical forms of "rational social exchange" (different industrial relations institutions) into a historical argument about the sequencing of patterns of state-society relations. The argument in brief, shorn of Crouch's eye for detail and complexity, is that distinct state traditions for dealing with interest groups emerged out of state conflict with established religions in the eighteenth century and earlier, and out of state responses to the emergence of capitalist markets and business interests in the nineteenth century, such that those traditions were in place by around 1870. The emergence of labor as an organized class actor after 1870 was largely assimilated into that preexisting tradition, so that the trajectory of industrial relations was essentially set by the outbreak of World War I. Social Democracy only really appears as an explanation for the emergence of corporatism in countries that had already developed organized forms of state-society relationship; corporatism, in other words, was unavailable to countries with liberal market forms of interest group intermediation, regardless of the presence of Social Democracy.

Crouch uses a common theoretical framework to explain divergent and nationally distinct patterns of industrial relations development, and his account argues (in a manner consistent with the argument of this chapter) that states play an important role in the development of industrial relations systems, in part because contestation between employers and unions is seen as a potentially long-lasting equilibrium unless the state intervenes to expand the scale and scope of contacts and regulatory industrial relations institutions. This account replicates the dominant emphasis of institutional continuity within countries and diversity across countries. In particular the argument embodies a strong form of path dependence in which it is very difficult to explain or even recognize institutional discontinuity; broad patterns of economic restructuring play almost no part in the explanation after industrialization. The national industrial relations traditions are so broad as to wash out most industrial relations change within countries. It is interesting, in this respect, that Britain is acknowledged as an outlier by Crouch, the only "case of a powerful, long-established, but decentralized unionism" that never moved from industry-level to more encompassing forms of collective bargaining.[14]

In a similar vein, but not focused on industrial relations institutions, is the work of Dobbin on distinctive national traditions of policymaking, with its emphasis on industrial cultures and industrial policy paradigms.[15] Dobbin argues that countries develop distinct approaches to policymaking that both persist over time—again, path dependence is very strong—and shape how policy is made in new areas as novel problems or areas of policymaking emerge. The great strength of this approach, which will come to the fore in later sections of this chapter, is its discursive element: industrial cultures create collective understandings, which have the effect of explaining why certain issues come to be identified as problems requiring action, and delimiting the range of possible solutions. In general, Dobbin argues, states will tend to respond to new issues and problems in familiar ways and with familiar solutions.

The weakness of this approach is obviously knowing where these deep-seated national industrial cultures come from, why they persist over time, and why breaks or shifts occur. It is unclear how this approach explains both the similar developments that occur at particular historical points in several countries at the same time, and the sharp shifts in policymaking that occur in particular countries. Dobbin argues that the distinctiveness of the British model of policymaking is its emphasis on protecting firms from both the market and the state. Applied to industrial relations (as opposed to railway policy, which is Dobbin's focus), this might be shoehorned into the period of "collective laissez-faire" (with its emphasis on state abstention and collective regulation of industrial relations) in the middle of the twentieth century, but it cannot account for post-1960 developments in industrial relations. Nor, given the difference in industrial cultures, can this approach explain some important similarities in British and French industrial relations developments after 1968.[16]

In the last few years the approach known as "Varieties of Capitalism" (VoC) has emerged as the most fully developed form of institutionalist analysis within comparative political economy.[17] At the risk of imposing a coherence and set of shared assumptions on an approach that is still developing,[18] it is worth trying to tease out the core elements of the VoC literature because it speaks directly to the relationship between institutions in capitalist economies. The approach is distinctive in identifying interlocking institutions, at the national level, that reinforce and undergird particular patterns of strategic behavior on the part of economic actors. Institutions are important primarily for their ability to solve coordination problems for firms, and the interaction between sets of institutions creates incentives for certain forms of behavior. The linkages between institutions tend to inhibit change: it is not the effects of individual institutions so much as the interaction between a set of institutions that encourages a certain path dependence.

The importance of institutions within the VoC approach is less that they distribute power or sanction behavior and more that they facilitate deliberation and information flows among actors, permit "decentralized cooperation,"[19] and solve familiar collective action problems, such as the underprovision of training. Institutions are rarely able to perform these roles in isolation; rather, there are likely to be interactions and complementarities among institutions such that one set of institutions functions more effectively, or indeed may only function effectively, when accompanied by other institutions. These institutional complementarities imply that there is a tendency for institutions to reinforce one another, forming an interlocking ensemble of institutions spanning the spheres of industrial relations, the welfare state, finance, and so on, which makes the set of institutions resistant to change. Change in the sphere of industrial relations, for example, may be resisted because of its implications for corporate governance or the training regime.

Among capitalist economies, this approach identifies a fairly limited variety, two (or possibly three[20]) broad ideal-typical types of political economy: liberal market economies and coordinated market economies. The former rely primarily on unregulated labor and capital markets to solve coordination problems, while the latter rely more heavily on nonmarket forms of coordination (collective bargaining, long-term financial relationships between banks and firms, and so on).

In emphasizing the interaction effects among institutions, the VoC approach represents a significant step forward in institutional analysis. Comparative political economy has been treated over the past two decades or more to theoretical accounts that direct our attention to a whole range of political economic institutions: investment banks, peak-level and industrial collective bargaining institutions, central bank independence, employer coordination, training regimes, and so on. The VoC approach demonstrates that economic performance is the product not of isolated institutions but of the interaction between complementary institutions

The VoC approach identifies firms as the primary actors within capitalist economies, seeking to "bring firms back into the center of the analysis"[21] and suggesting less prominent, less strategic roles for both state actors and organized labor. The primary role of states within the VoC framework is to induce "economic actors to cooperate more effectively with each other" through the construction of institutions that encourage "better forms of coordination among private-sector actors."[22] This is a particularly valuable insight because it emphasizes (again, in a manner consistent with the argument of this chapter) the capacities of states, and their role in institutional construction, rather than the autonomy of states from major interests in society, something that has always been a somewhat dubious claim for capitalist democracies. States clearly matter because their rule-making and coercive powers serve to reinforce coordination. But while states have certain capacities, the VoC approach does not imbue them with independent interests or autonomy. Thus states do not impose policies but rather induce private actors to act in their own interests by better coordinating their activities.

Several of the contributors to Hall and Soskice's *Varieties of Capitalism* volume point to the tendency within the VoC approach to "underplay the importance of the *political* dimensions of political economies"[23] and emphasize the need to take politics and policymaking more seriously.[24] Thelen, in particular, has commented on the underdeveloped role of politics and power in the construction and maintenance of institutions, and on the need for the VoC approach to pay more attention to the political settlements underpinning a stable ensemble of institutions.[25] The VoC theoretical framework offers an extremely thin notion of politics and state action, in which governments act largely at the behest of employers, and the state's function is essentially that of encouraging coordination among economic actors. States do not appear to have interests distinguishable from those of employers, nor do they have the capacity to act independently, still less against, employer interests, and managing the political economy is a fundamentally cooperative venture, involving facilitating information flows and the coordination of activities.

Labor, moreover, is a minor actor in the VoC approach; trade unions often appear to exist only in order to solve collective action problems for employers, having little independent existence or history. The limited role attributed to labor is both a reaction to its current weakened state, at the dawn of the twenty-first century, and the product of a reinterpretation of the relative roles of unions and employers in the process of institutional construction in earlier periods. Yet what this approach renders invisible is that class contestation over the central institutions of capitalist political economies has been a persistent feature of the postwar period, expressed both in synchronous strike waves, particularly right after World War II and again between 1967 and 1979, and in major debates within most advanced capitalist societies over the direction of economic and social development, in which the labor movement played a central part: *autogestion* in France; the extension of codetermination in Germany; wage-earner funds in Sweden; industrial democracy and the alternative economic strategy in Britain; industrial policy in the United States. The danger of the VoC perspective—with its emphasis on the coordination problems of capitalist economies rather than on conflict or the exercise of power—is that it flattens that history, explaining the failure of those more radical political-economic projects as overdetermined, a restoration of equilibrium rather than a result of political conflict and the exercise of power in a contingent historical process.

It is not clear what is gained by redefining the ubiquitous conflict between employers and workers as a coordination problem, and what is lost is the sense that power is being exercised by actors with different interests and unequal resources and capacities. In working within the framework of a smoothly functioning, self-adjusting political economy, the VoC approach finds it difficult to describe, still less explain, the moments of crisis and conflict that are a central part of comparative political economy. A web of class relationships, compromises, and struggles (both between and within classes) structure the kinds of political settlements that are possible and the range of viable institutional arrangements. In a sense, this is an obvious point. But unless the obvious is stated, it becomes more plausible to ascribe to institutions what are in fact the attributes of social relationships, and to slowly replace the "powering" function of institutions with that of coordination.[26]

Thus, while the VoC approach provides a highly sophisticated theory of institutional interaction, it shares with the other approaches discussed in this section an emphasis on continuity over time and distinct national traditions. Interlocking institutions reinforce particular patterns of behavior, making radical changes of direction less likely. Furthermore, the VoC approach explicitly rejects a general convergence of capitalist economies toward a single type. Rather, there may be some convergence within each type or family of capitalist political economy—Britain converging on the United States, Sweden on Germany—but distinct varieties of capitalism remain.[27]

Discontinuous and Synchronous Institutional Development

The historical development of industrial relations institutions across the capitalist world suggests the need to modify the dominant emphases within comparative political economy so as to recognize both that periods of rapid institutional construction (in which discontinuity is more evident than continuity) coincide with periods in which the process of economic restructuring accelerates and changes in form and, furthermore, that these periods are often synchronous across capitalist countries. There are uneven waves of industrial relations institutional development that are suggestive of an underlying economic patterning, explaining both national discontinuity and cross-national synchronous developments. Silver has recently provided evidence of just such an economic patterning in her examination of the impact of product cycles and capital mobility on key industries in the period from 1870 to the present.[28] While her interest is primarily in explaining historical and geographic patterns of labor unrest, the argument is compatible with that made here about the timing of projects of institutional reconstruction. The trigger appears to be new patterns of economic growth, which in turn generate industrial conflict. From this, efforts follow to reconstruct industrial relations in order to restore industrial order.

Cronin's study of strikes in Britain identifies a wave pattern in which strike waves "represent a transition between distinctly different patterns of [economic] activity"[29] and are manifestations of "new attitudes and novel strategies produced by the impact of 'long waves' of economic growth upon the working class."[30] Thus strike waves are a response to the impact of qualitatively different patterns and processes of economic growth on the expectations, opportunities, and forms of collective organization of workers. Cronin notes strike waves in Britain during 1889–92, immediately before and after World War I, and during 1968–72, arguing that temporal variation in the form of strike waves is more significant than sectoral variation. In the course of such strike waves, the most strike-prone industries are "the large, strategically important industries most thoroughly entangled in the ups and downs, pressures and tensions, of the market. They feel most quickly and intensely the economic and technological changes that accompany each distinct phase of economic evolution."[31] They are "specially sensitive to the new situations caused by the qualitative transformations of the economy."[32] During these periods economic restructuring disrupts existing patterns of behavior and generates resistance in the form of industrial conflict.

Arguing that "waves of intense structural reform characterize trade union development,"[33] Waddington has identified a similar wavelike pattern, following the same chronology, in the evolution of trade union mergers in Britain. Merger waves map onto the common dating of Kondratieff cycles, with mergers accelerating during the two transitions from upswings to downswings (1910–20 and 1968–74), while also being characterized by qualitatively different kinds of merger in the two transitions.[34] Mirroring Cronin's study, a new pattern of economic growth triggers industrial conflict, to which employers, unions, and the state respond with the construction of new industrial relations institutions. Trade unions respond to these developments with mergers, which facilitate new forms of collective bargaining: national multiemployer bargaining in the first period and decentralized workplace bargaining in the second. It is worth noting, for the argument made later in this chapter, that in both periods the merger wave was facilitated by state action to make mergers easier.

Cross-national historical industrial relations data have limitations,[35] but it is clear that, not only does a pattern of discontinuous wavelike periods of intense institutional reconstruction mark industrial relations development beyond Britain, but that these waves are to some extent synchronous.[36] In other words, there are international cycles of strikes, union development, and changes in the structure of collective bargaining. These cycles are not random but coincide with the transition points between upswings and downswings in Kondratieff cycles. As Kelly summarizes the argument: "There is, in my view, enough empirical evidence to show that the Kondratieff economic turning points are associated with major upheavals in industrial relations, and these can be discerned through patterns of union membership and density, strike activity, union mergers, collective bargaining and a variety of other institutional changes."[37]

Of course, correlation is not causation, and the reason why long waves are controversial within the study of comparative political economy is that the causal mechanism that explains transitions between upswings and downswings, and back again, is unclear. Nor is it obvious why there is some regularity, with roughly twenty-five-year upswings and roughly twenty-five-year downswings, to the waves. Explanations range from shifts in innovation and investment, to generational effects.[38] The authors emphasizing the mapping of industrial relations developments onto Kondratieff cycles tend to rely on worker mobilization as the primary motor of change. As the next section will demonstrate, my preference is for a more Regulationist mapping of industrial relations institutional development because the causal mechanisms are clearer. But the point remains that we can identify periods in which the process of economic restructuring accelerates and existing patterns of growth are disrupted, triggering higher levels of industrial conflict, which we can characterize as strike waves, which in turn set off a search for new sets of industrial relations institutions to manage and regulate the conflict and its underlying causes. This suggests both that industrial relations institutional development is discontinuous—marked by periods of rapid restructuring followed by longer periods of relative institutional stability and only incremental change—and that capitalist economies often experience these periods of rapid institutional restructuring at roughly the same time. Broadly similar economic growth regimes pose similar sets of regulatory problems, though the solutions to those problems will often differ from country to country.

REVISING REGULATION

It follows from the preceding sections that a comparative political economy capable of offering an adequate account of the institutional development of industrial relations is one that recognizes three factors. The first is the importance of broad structural constraints on political action, in particular on projects of industrial relations reform, of which the most important emanate from changing patterns and processes of economic growth. This is not a call for a determinist structuralism, but simply an echo of Katznelson's recognition that actors "are embedded agents operating within relational structural fields that distinguish the possible from the impossible and the likely from the less likely."[39] Second, institutions need to be taken seriously as necessary mechanisms for managing class relations. Employers and workers rarely confront each other nakedly in the workplace and the labor market: a panoply of industrial relations institutions, both cooperative and coercive, structure that relationship. Third, sharp ruptures, in which sets of institutions are rapidly replaced or transformed in function, are every bit as important a feature of institutional development as continuity and path dependence. The historical evolution of industrial relations systems is marked by periods of institutional flux and discontinuity that follow a discernible and coherent pattern. A modified form of Regulationist analysis offers some promise of providing the basic elements of an explanation of this kind.[40]

It is important to recognize that there is no single Regulation Theory; there are multiple schools of Regulationist analysis, and there has been a certain dissipation of the original shape of Regulation Theory.[41] This is all to the good, and reflects both the shifting interests of scholars working within the Regulationist framework and the need of those scholars to confront serious theoretical and empirical problems encountered as the theory matured. Much Regulation Theory is now in fact barely distinguishable from the VoC approach, emphasizing distinct national variants of capitalism and focusing attention on the institutional determinants of different national forms of economic management.[42] Nonetheless, for all the diversity within the family of Regulation theories, there are several shared assumptions that have obvious advantages for a project of the kind attempted in this book.

First, Regulationist accounts understand capitalist growth to be a profoundly contradictory, unstable, and crisis-ridden process that will not occur naturally. Left to their own devices, subject only to regulation by invisible market hands, capitalist economies will exhibit a range of crisis tendencies and generate high levels of social conflict. Change within capitalist economies is therefore the product not only of exogenous shocks but more often of a steady accumulation of internal contradictions. It is for this reason that capitalism requires institutions to regulate or stabilize growth, one of which is clearly the industrial relations system, which manages the relationship between capital and labor. The Regulation approach is, above all, *an institutional account of capitalism*, which recognizes that the very "improbability of capitalist reproduction" ensures its "socially embedded, socially regularized nature."[43]

Second, Regulation Theory goes beyond identifying crisis tendencies to offer a historicization of capitalist development centering on the different growth dynamics (or "regimes of accumulation") of different phases of capitalism. While economic restructuring, instability, and crisis are permanent features of capitalist economies, distinct patterns of growth lasting longer than a business cycle or two can be identified. This suggests that, while core features of capitalist growth remain, the forms of linkage between production and consumption, the role of financial capital, the microeconomic and macroeconomic functions performed by wages, and so on undergo change. This form of periodization emphasizes "the strategic possibilities any given period gives for different actors, different identities, different interests, different coalition possibilities, different horizons of action, different strategies, different tactics."[44] As such, it anticipates that each growth regime will be accompanied by its own distinct regulatory institutions and political settlements.

Third, Regulationists suggest that the shift from one growth regime to another is likely to create pressure for a change in the regulatory institutions, and/or that the evolution of those institutions may themselves come to threaten accumulation. Thus, within this theoretical framework, one would anticipate that periods of relative institutional stability will alternate with periods of more rapid institutional transformation. Of course,

> since transitions between periods never involve a total rupture, path-dependent 'conservation-dissolution' effects can occur. Change can transform and re-functionalise earlier social relations, institutions, or discourses, conserving them in a new pattern; or, alternatively, can dissolve them into elements that are selectively articulated into new relations, institutions, or discourses.[45]

Nevertheless, the Regulationist approach is consistent with Jenson's distinction between periods of normal and epochal political change. Moments of institutional transformation and fluidity will both follow and be accompanied by heightened levels of social conflict, and the breakdown of existing class compromises and political settlements. These compromises and settlements then need to be reconstructed under quite different conditions, when class interests and resources have changed. Thus, while the Regulation approach shares much with that of VoC, it differs in two critical respects: its explicit linkage between a form of economic growth and a set of regulatory institutions; and its expectation that institutions can only ever offer partial, limited, and temporary solutions to the instability of capitalist growth, with the result that institutional development is likely to be marked by periods of rapid change.

Clearly, the Regulation approach also has a number of unresolved problems. It has always had a tendency toward being too grandiose, promising a broad theory of historical development appropriate for all capitalist societies. And, despite the fact that Regulation Theory first emerged in the mid-1970s as an explicit critique of structuralist Marxism, it too easily slides into functionalism and structuralism, in which shifts in growth regimes automatically generate parallel and matching shifts in the regulatory institutions to restore stable accumulation.

For the purposes of this chapter, two more small-scale theoretical problems are of particular interest. The first relates to the periodization of regimes of accumulation (and the question of how one operationalizes such regimes). The main growth regimes on offer—extensive and intensive, Fordist and post-Fordist—are pretty crude, operating best as ideal types rather than concrete descriptions of actually existing economic regimes. The labels that Regulationists give growth regimes are shorthand for a "bundle" of characteristics, and one can ask whether all the elements of a given regime change at the same time and, if not, which ones trigger pressure for changes in the regulatory mechanisms. How, in short, does one identify a period in which one growth regime gives way to another?

The second problem is equally fundamental. It concerns the role of politics and ideas in the transformation of regulatory mechanisms and institutions. What are the political and ideational conditions of existence for accumulation, and how much political and ideological "space" is there for the resolution of crises, both of accumulation and of the regulatory mechanisms?[46] This in turn raises the question of the degree to which alternative resolutions, and hence multiple sets of regulatory institutions, are possible. Above all, it is important to recognize that, with the important exception of Jessop, Regulation theorists have undertheorized the state, and its role in managing crisis and constructing or transforming regulatory institutions.[47] In this regard, Regulation Theory and the VoC approach share an underdeveloped role for politics and state actors.

How might the Regulation approach be modified to resolve these problems? The prominence within early versions of Regulation Theory given to the growth regime itself was misplaced. Indeed I am not convinced that Regulation Theory works at this macro level; it is better conceptualized as a theory of regulation rather than a theory of capitalist growth. Conventional Regulationist periodization suggests an overly *stage-ist* interpretation of capitalist growth patterns. Different patterns of economic growth do not need, and indeed are unlikely, to neatly succeed each other. Rather, we can expect them to persist and coexist. It is striking, for example, that when Swenson offers three employer labor market strategies, two of them, cartelism and segmentalism, closely approximate extensive (pre-Fordist) and Fordist forms of labor regulation, respectively.[48] Yet for Swenson, these are not stages but rather strategies appropriate to firms in particular markets. Thus, one might label a period in which core industries are dominated by a large number of small producers competing on the basis of labor costs as a period of extensive, pre-Fordist growth, but that should not obscure the coexistence of multiple industrial structures.

It is useful to think of each growth regime as composed of a bundle of elements. Fordism, for example, is usually understood to describe a regime of demand-led growth in which there are mechanisms linking productivity advances to increases in purchasing power.[49] Within this growth regime, technology and forms of work organization permit the mass production of broadly identical goods, and productivity gains come through economies of scale. Competition takes place among a small number of large firms with entry limited by the capital-intensive nature of production, and wages are not the main source of competition. Managerial control over the work process is expected to be high, and labor-management relations are of the low-trust variety. Skill requirements for labor in mass production industries are relatively low, and labor supply is quite rigid.

We can label this bundle "Fordism" as a kind of shorthand, but that may obscure more than it illuminates. There are dangers involved in reproducing the tight interdependence among elements that is characteristic of the VoC approach. Some, but not all, of these elements are likely to be present at any given time and place. Jessop has suggested that we think of broad growth regimes as families, composed of several (possibly national) variants, differing in many ways and sharing only a basic underlying growth dynamic. For Fordism, that is a form of link between wages and productivity and the spread of mass consumption, while for post-Fordism it is the emphasis on supply-side flexibility.[50]

There is also no particular reason to anticipate that all the elements of the bundle will come under pressure at the same time, or that a unique set of regulatory institutions will be associated with each regime of accumulation. One might expect, instead, a certain phasing of changes in the regulatory mechanisms. The various transformations in the growth dynamic in Britain over the past century brought in their wake a series of phases of intense industrial restructuring that occurred on a somewhat different timetable from, for example, changes in the financial system. In the British case, pressure for change in the industrial relations system came primarily from changes in industrial structure (which changed the competitive pressures acting on firms) and the organization of work inside firms (which encouraged a restructuring of relations between employers and workers), rather than other aspects of the growth regime.

As the next chapter will illustrate, the decline of old staple industries in Britain was experienced as a crisis, and transmitted to the industrial relations system as such, well before newer Fordist industries established sufficient weight in the economy to encourage the creation of industrial relations institutions that would respond to their specific needs. In fact, I will argue that the longevity of the first system of industrial relations system, with its emphasis on industry-level collective bargaining, lay in its ability to act as a transitional form that regulated the decline of pre-Fordist industries while not interfering in the development of Fordist industries.[51] Similarly, the second system of industrial relations, in which decentralized collective bargaining replaced industry and national bargaining, was transitional, regulating the shift from Fordism to post-Fordism in Britain; it was also one of several possible sets of industrial relations institutions that might have achieved this task, and it was never fully implemented, being overtaken by the Thatcherite vision of a decollectivized and juridified system of industrial relations.

A crisis of a particular pattern of economic growth does not cause a new set of regulatory mechanisms to come into being; still less can any new regulatory institutions be guaranteed to ensure stable, orderly economic growth. But the transition from one pattern of economic growth to another will create a set of problems that are not easily resolvable using existing institutions, and that crisis will encourage the search for new regulatory mechanisms. During periods of structural crisis, the search for new institutions is "experimental, trial-and-error, and chaotic . . . more successful experiments are selected in an ex post manner; and, through their co-evolution, are re-institutionalized and retained as the basis for a new repertoire of governance mechanisms."[52] Nothing could be further from automatic reproduction. Even during periods of stable economic growth, regulatory institutions are fragile, provisional, and contested, and will undergo evolution in response to political and industrial conflict. It is nevertheless during periods of crisis that the most fluidity and possibility exist in the process of institutional selection and construction.

Thus politics and class conflict play a central role in the construction of new sets of institutions, with industrial conflict in the form of strike waves playing a particularly important role in triggering the search for new industrial relations institutions. There are multiple possible regulatory forms—though they are neither infinite nor arbitrary—and the remainder of this chapter will examine the process in which the failure of an established pattern of economic growth leads to the widespread perception that a crisis exists, and then to the construction of one among several systems of industrial relations institutions. It is at this point that the undertheorization of the state within the Regulation approach is most significant. Neither "the economy" nor class actors (employers and unions) will spontaneously produce the industrial relations institutions needed for new patterns of economic growth. The state is a site of both experimentation and implementation; it is best positioned to select successful regulatory experiments, institutionalize them, and extend them throughout the economy.[53] That process is both one of concrete institution-building and a discursive one, in which crisis is narrated and new institutions and practices are discursively constituted and naturalized.[54]

INDUSTRIAL CONFLICT AS TRIGGER

As economies restructure, they create pressures for new industrial relations institutions that are better able to regulate the relationship between business and labor under new economic circumstances. States then play a central role in the construction of new industrial relations systems when it becomes clear that existing regulatory mechanisms have failed. Stated in this way, the argument has a deeply functionalist ring to it. How are broad economic pressures transmitted to the industrial relations system? What actually triggers state action? Why one form of action rather than another? The point here is that the state plays a central role in mediating between economic change and new regulatory forms. State intervention to construct new industrial relations institutions may fail and produce prolonged economic crisis—indeed, this is a plausible interpretation of postwar British political economy. And any resulting system of industrial relations will always be partial, provisional, and contingent. Nevertheless, economic change does create pressures to which any state will be forced to respond.

The signal that a set of industrial relations institutions is failing to manage economic restructuring is likely to be an increase in the level of industrial conflict because industrial disputes are the most direct indication of the failure to institutionalize and channel class conflict. Class conflict is never going to be eliminated, but a system of industrial relations is a form of class compromise, embodying a particular balance of class power and a consequent set of distributional outcomes.[55] Increased industrial conflict accompanied every period in which economic restructuring accelerated in Britain. Strikes functioned crudely as canaries in a coal mine, indicating the failure of industrial relations institutions and drawing public attention to the need for institutional reconstruction.

It is not only an increase in the *level* of industrial conflict that matters in triggering a state response but also the *form* that industrial conflict takes. Different types of strike waves are likely to lead to different interpretations of the causes and appropriate responses to an industrial relations crisis. In Britain, industrial conflict took quite different forms, depending in part on the form of economic growth and in part on levels of union organization and state policy: national strikes in the energy and transport sectors in the 1910s; unofficial strikes in manufacturing in the 1960s; public-sector strikes in the 1970s. The particular form that each strike wave took generated distinct political projects of reform. High levels of unofficial strikes in the automobile industry in the 1960s, for example, played an important role in privileging an interpretation of industrial relations crisis that focused on the underdevelopment of workplace industrial relations institutions. Every major project of British state reform of industrial relations followed from an upward spike in the strike rate. Industrial conflict triggered the process of constructing a new set of regulatory mechanisms in industrial relations. But heightened levels of conflict did not determine the manner in which the state responded. Explaining the role played by states in institutional reconstruction is the topic of the next section.

THE STATE AND INSTITUTIONAL CONSTRUCTION

State actors play a central role in the construction of industrial relations institutions by virtue of a set of unique public capacities, of which I emphasize the following: enforcing and systematizing institutional change; narrating an authoritative interpretation of industrial relations crisis; solving the collective action problems of employers and unions; and anticipating and crafting alliances among private industrial actors, though it is important not to forget the state's overt coercive power.[56] The role of the state is most significant in the movement from crisis to the construction of a new set of institutions designed to manage crisis. Thus a state role is most likely to be visible in the construction phase of institution-building and may be less necessary or less visible for the maintenance of existing institutions. That was certainly the case in Britain in the middle of the twentieth century, when apparent state abstention masked the central role state actors had played in constructing the industry-level bargaining system of industrial relations earlier in the century.

To repeat an earlier point, the role of the state is not necessarily a product of state autonomy or a set of distinct political or bureaucratic interests, though those might exist. On this, the VoC approach is correct in emphasizing the extent to which state action results from attempts to solve coordination/conflict problems for industrial actors. The British state has never been in the position to impose industrial relations institutions on business and labor, nor has it had any particular wish to do so. It has responded to social conflict and economic failure, and it has attempted to mobilize support for the reform of industrial relations. The construction of a narrative to explain conflict and failure, and the emergence of a prescription for change, never came from the state alone. And, it is worth pointing out, the long-term stability of each system was possible only when there was a broad political consensus between the dominant political parties. It makes no sense to call this state autonomy. There has always been a certain implausibility to the claim of state autonomy in capitalist democracies, but particularly in the sphere of industrial relations, which is the very core of wage regulation and the accumulation process in capitalist economies. The importance of the state is that it has certain capacities, and can perform certain functions that industrial actors alone cannot. Above all, it alone can create a *system* in place of a set of scattered experiments.

States intervene in the restructuring of industrial relations institutions because they cannot afford not to. The industrial relations system is the collective form, and regulatory mechanism, of the basic unit of the capitalist mode of production: the wage relationship. That relationship is inherently conflictual, as Marx and Polanyi each pointed out a long time ago (though for somewhat different reasons). The social, economic, and political consequences of industrial relations failure—in the form of strikes, unemployment, inflation, political crisis—make it implausible that any state can adopt a noninterventionist stance for long.[57] But states also intervene because business and labor may be unable to construct institutions themselves, even though they may want them and see them as beneficial. States can institutionalize practices, generalize them beyond a few leading sectors of the economy, and, above all, solve collective action problems by limiting defection, for both business and labor organizations. States may act against the wishes of industrial actors, for their own reasons. But more often, states will act because other actors cannot (the others may be timid, divided, concerned with short-term interests, have sunk costs in existing institutions and be generally unwilling to challenge existing industrial relations institutions) and because states can perform functions and have capacities unavailable to interest groups.

In an important contribution, Swenson has emphasized the role of state actors in *anticipating* potential alliances between segments of business and labor interests.[58] This is not precisely state autonomy: state actors are not imposing policy on employers, nor are they even seeking to persuade employers of the necessity of certain action. Rather state actors are anticipating that the benefits of a policy will lead to acquiescence, and they are crafting policy in such a way as to increase the chances of its eventual acceptance by business interests. This is a capacity that only state actors possess, and it ensures a central role for the state in institution-building. Wright, following Rogers and Streeck, has suggested that "positive class compromises" are possible when labor is able to solve problems capitalists cannot solve on their own—corporatist wage restraint being the most obvious.[59] This occurs, according to Wright, when a labor movement develops the associational power to prevent defection on the part of either its own members or employers. Recalling Crouch's argument, the state can make these positive class compromises possible by expanding the scope and density of exchanges between employers and unions. States can act as guarantors of agreements, prevent defection through legislation, boost the associative power of labor, and provide side payments (for example, in the area of social policy) to encourage agreement.

That said, it is easy to overemphasize the degree of mutual interest, and the lack of conflict, between business and labor in discussions of positive sum compromises and cross-class alliances.[60] Industrial relations institutions, because they seek to regulate conflict in the workplace, under conditions characterized by a fundamental asymmetry of power, always have a limited and temporary character, and are ultimately dependent on the relative power of different classes. Alliances are less likely than fragile compromises.[61]

Narrating Crisis

The most thorny theoretical problem for the argument being made in this chapter is how economic crisis gets translated into a particular form of state action, because crisis "is never a purely objective phenomenon that automatically produces a particular response."[62] It is worth distinguishing between economic failure, which has an objective character, and economic crisis, which is a more subjective condition.[63] Economic failure creates the conditions under which competing interests struggle to define and interpret the failure. The construction of a condition of political crisis requiring a state response involves the successful interpretation of failure, and it has an important discursive component.

In the process of institution-building, the capacity to define the nature of a problem, and hence limit the range of permissible solutions to that problem, is of particular importance. Lehmbruch has directed out attention to the emergence of "hegemonic discourses" that underpin successful and long-standing sets of national institutions:

> *Policy discourse* refers to sets of basic beliefs and assumptions about the normative values, objectives, and regularities underlying the formation of public policy and

serving to define the meaning of collective action and to establish the collective identity of the social actors who share this specific discourse.[64]

The point is that "when crises arise, the societal repertoire of possible responses is limited to those that are cognitively conceivable, normatively legitimate, and instrumentally feasible inside the dominant discourse."[65] This is similar to Dobbin's claim that industrial cultures create collective understandings of problems and narrow the set of policy responses.[66]

Actors—state and nonstate alike—interpret the world in various ways, and their ideas are cognitive shortcuts, which mediate between actors and the structures that constrain their ability to act.[67] Thus a structural constraint is mediated discursively—as, to use an example from Hay, when ideas about globalization lead state actors to scale back economic and social agendas in anticipation of the likely constraints, whether those constraints exist or not.[68] Blyth has also argued that "ideas are weapons," and that conflict over ideas plays a central role in institutional construction, reducing uncertainty in periods of crisis, permitting certain kinds of collective action, and providing blueprints for new institutional construction.[69]

Of course, there are limits to discursive construction, in that ideas need some resonance with experience—"some understandings are likely to prove more credible given past experience than others"[70] —but nonetheless the capacity to impose an authoritative interpretation of a problem is crucial to the choice of institutional solutions to that problem. Hall's work on policy paradigms suggests that possession of a coherent policy paradigm is a precondition for the ability of states to resist outside pressure and ensure some degree of independent action on the part of the state.[71]

State actors have some advantages in both the narration of crisis and the construction of a "hegemonic discourse" permitting institutional reform. The work of Fuchs on the emergence of protective labor legislation in Britain and France emphasizes the capacity of state actors (factory inspectors in her account) to "infuse with value" (borrowing Selznick's evocative phrase) political-economic institutions that in turn enabled "institutions to mobilize the kind of commitment that is necessary for institutional adaptation and weathering crises."[72] In Britain, a central role in narrating industrial relations crisis has been played by state commissions, set up as impartial bodies representing business, labor, and usually academia, which, through investigation and hearings, take on the role of narrating crisis. Thus the 1894 Royal Commission on Labour, the 1917 Whitley Committee, and the 1968 Royal Commission on Trade Unions and Employers' Associations all provided both an interpretation of crisis and the cover of impartiality, which legitimized a much greater degree of state intervention in the construction of industrial relations institutions while also selecting certain forms of intervention as more appropriate than others. Furthermore, supposedly impartial commissions and public inquiries helped to build a degree of political consensus, so that state policies were not rapidly and easily reversed.

To be clear, the state commissions that investigated Britain's industrial relations problems, and the reports they produced, were not impartial; they provided a "class telling" of British industrial relations and, without exception, emphasized industrial order over other goals.[73] Nevertheless, the composition of these commissions, and the extensive research undertaken on their behalf, made theirs the privileged interpretation of crisis, the one to which even those who disagreed had to respond. State commissions, as quasi-public bodies, simultaneously possessed the imprimatur of the state while maintaining at least the appearance of autonomy from it. Thus a political space was cleared for the state to act in the construction of industrial relations institutions, and those institutions enjoyed a certain initial legitimacy derived from the recommendations of state commissions. To be sure, state commissions have not been alone in the narration of crisis; other state actors (the British Treasury, for example) and nonstate actors have proposed alternative narratives. Indeed the state commissions themselves were often created in response to pressure from outside the state. Once again, strikes usually played a central role in helping to create a sense of crisis and urgency. Indeed, as later chapters will demonstrate, particular tropes about the causes and costs of industrial disorder have reappeared on a regular basis in Britain.

Thus a certain sequence has repeated itself in Britain over the past century: an acceleration in the process of economic restructuring put pressure on the existing institutions of industrial relations, which in turn led to heightened levels of industrial conflict, which created a political crisis, usually fueled by "public" concern that something be done, which encouraged the state to set up a commission to investigate the causes of industrial conflict, which finally provided the political space for state action to attempt the reconstruction of industrial relations institutions.

FORMS OF STATE REGULATION

The important comparative question is, therefore, not whether states seek to regulate industrial relations through the construction of institutions, since that is a necessary task for all states, but rather what form state regulation takes. It is here that different countries solve common problems in different ways. Industrialized countries have tended to go through broadly similar phases of economic restructuring as economies first became national and then global, and as mass production industries first arose and then went into crisis. But they constructed different industrial relations systems to manage the conflict that arose from economic change. Multiple regulatory forms are compatible with a given growth regime, in that different industrial relations institutions can act as functional equivalents.[74] For example, industry-level collective bargaining can take labor costs out of competition where employers and unions are strong enough to create such institutions. But state "extension" procedures, which extend by legislation agreements made in one area (firm, region, industry) to other areas, can have the equivalent effect, and are more likely where employers and unions are too weak to create industry-level bargaining institutions, as, for example, in France.

This highlights something that has been underdeveloped thus far. The context within which state actors engage in the construction of industrial relations institutions is structured not only by broad patterns of economic growth but also by the organization and historical development of social classes. Attention must be paid to the class context, which limits and selects from the set of possible regulatory institutions. As Coates has put it:

> Whether then states expand their role—to orchestrate capital-labour relations, or to tilt the balance of power between sections of the dominant capitalist class—varies over time and between national capitalisms: but it does not vary randomly. Rather, the degree and scale of state action vary with the balance and character of class forces surrounding it.[75]

Thus, in the example above, industry-level bargaining was simply not an available industrial relations institution in France, because of the organization of employers and labor interests. There is, in short, a class context as well as an economic context, and these are not abstract ideal-typical classes but rather specific historically constructed classes. It should be unremarkable that particular employers and trade unions may respond to similar periods of intense economic restructuring, and evidence of the failure of existing industrial relations institutions to contain industrial conflict, in different ways. Britain's labor movement, the product of early industrialization and a strong craft tradition, and British business, marked by a sharp divide between industrial and financial interests, the latter with strong imperial and international pretensions, responded to industrial relations crisis in quite specific ways; indeed it is the particular physiognomy of class in Britain that explains why industrial relations reform has been so difficult, and so fraught with conflict.

Thus the state is constrained, on the one hand by the failure of existing institutions of industrial relations and the resulting intensification of industrial conflict, and on the other by the strength, organization, and influence of industrial actors, all of which limit the possible set of new industrial relations institutions. But the state does have a degree of autonomy in the way in which crisis is narrated and in the particular solution, embodied in a project of industrial relations reform, that emerges out of crisis.

A wide range of elements comprise an industrial relations system, and a state can focus on any of them as the basis for a reform project. First, the state can regulate the basic rights of employers, workers, and their organizations, though, overwhelmingly, it has been trade unions that have been subject to regulation. These include rights of association, rights to engage in strikes and lockouts, rights to bargain, rights of recognition, and rights to consultation, information, and participation. Which rights the state provides, the balance of individual and collective rights, how they are provided, and what limits are placed on action all help to structure the relative power of industrial actors. Second, the state can regulate collective bargaining, influencing its level, coverage, and scope, and what provisions exist for conciliation, mediation, and arbitration. Third, the state can directly regulate the outcomes of the relationship between business and labor, through minimum-wage legislation, cost-of-living adjustments, work time reductions, and so on. Incomes policies, whether statutory or underwritten by the state, also come under this heading. Finally, the state, can regulate industrial relations by influencing the context, and the relative power of the actors, through macroeconomic and social policy. Full employment and extensive and generous welfare programs, as Esping-Andersen has demonstrated,[76] may create a measure of decommodification that is likely to bolster the bargaining power of workers and their unions.

The public sector is a special case of state regulation because the state is the employer and therefore able to directly recognize unions, limit strikes, organize bargaining, introduce "human resource management" policies, and so on. Regulation of public-sector industrial relations is tremendously important, not just because of the size of the public-sector, but also because the state can use the public sector as an example of "best practice," encouraging the adoption of similar policies in the private sector and tying contracts and other benefits to the generalization of public-sector industrial relations. This has been of particular importance in the British case, where the clearest, purest forms of the industrial relations institutions favored by the state have often been constructed first in the public sector.

Path Dependence and the Structuring of Class Relations

This chapter has been concerned primarily with periods of institutional reconstruction, when institutions undergo quite rapid metamorphosis. However, once created and bedded down, institutions have structuring effects that are important in explaining both periods of relative institutional stability and future periods of institutional reconstruction. The comparative advantage of institutional analysis lies in explaining the effects of institutions on the behavior of actors: how institutions limit and select strategies, shape interests, provide resources, and influence the relative power of actors.[77] Industrial relations institutions structure the environment facing employers and trade unions, and as such they encourage certain kinds of practice. Once in place, institutions become a part of the landscape of the workplace and the wider economy; they are difficult to dislodge and continue to influence the conduct of industrial relations well after the conditions of their original construction have passed. Institutions—labor law would be a good example—provide resources for industrial actors and encourage certain kinds of industrial practices rather than others. The notion of path dependence[78] (when a particular course of action becomes extremely difficult to reverse, and creates incentives for industrial actors to seek solutions that modify existing institutions in incremental ways rather than create entirely new institutions), is of tremendous importance for understanding how industrial actors respond to industrial relations reform projects.

Industrial relations institutions also have discursive effects because industrial relations systems embody "a system of meaning" that acts as a form of social regulation, influencing notions of justice and the expectations of industrial actors.[79] In the British case, the early decision of trade unions (in the first decade of the twentieth century) to seek *immunities* from civil and criminal law for collective action rather than explicit trade union *rights*, became, by the second half of the century, discursively constructed as providing "trade union privileges," which were more readily vulnerable to political attack.

Thus the form of institutional regulation matters because different forms have different effects. Recall Zeitlin's argument that the long-term implications of a particular set of industrial relations institutions are subject to unintended consequences and not necessarily predictable. For example, in the absence of a legal right of union recognition, British unions depended on industry-level bargaining and arbitration machinery to get recognition indirectly. This worked relatively well until the end of the 1970s, but it had the effect that unions for the most part failed to develop strong recruitment capacities, and were dismissive of proposals to legislate on recognition. Thus the organization, the practice, even the ideology of British unions were heavily influenced by that particular set of industrial relations institutions. This in turn encouraged the vulnerability of British unions to the Thatcherite project of industrial relations reform.

That said, one can identify periods when meaningful alternatives are possible, when existing industrial relations institutions are perceived to be failing in some way but before new institutions are established. Pierson has noted that over time the scope for change and the array of possible alternatives has a tendency to narrow.[80] As the remaining chapters of this book will indicate, there were several moments at which intense debate took place within the British trade union movement over the direction in which to push industrial relations institutions. These debates naturally took place when public policy indicated a reconsideration of the existing system of industrial relations.

This chapter has argued that understanding the trajectory of industrial relations institutions within the advanced capitalist world requires paying attention, not only to the emergence of distinct national systems of institutions, but also to a degree of convergence across countries in the timing and form of efforts to reform industrial relations; furthermore, it requires explaining not only the periods of institutional stability but also the periods of rupture, when new sets of industrial relations institutions emerge.

Incorporating recent insights from institutional analysis into the Regulation approach to political economy—recovering, as it were, the essential institutional core of Regulationist accounts of capitalist development—offers theoretical promise in this task. Within this approach this chapter has emphasized two factors: the unique discursive and institution-building capacities of states, and the distinct economic patterning that undergirds the timing and form of state projects of industrial relations reform.

The remainder of this book describes the construction of three distinct industrial relations systems in Britain. Each new set of mechanisms to regulate industrial relations was a response to changes in the structure of the British economy and the increased industrial conflict that accompanied economic restructuring. But industrial relations institutions did not emerge out of the interactions of business and labor in civil society alone; in each case, the British state played a crucial role in the construction phase of new regulatory mechanisms. It is to the origins, characteristics, and consequences of these three systems of industrial relations that we now turn.

CHAPTER THREE

The Construction of the Collective Laissez-Faire System, 1890–1940

Introduction

Between 1890 and 1921 the first national system of industrial relations was created in Britain. It was refined, extended to new parts of the economy, and provided with greater legislative buttressing in the ensuing thirty to forty years, but its essential elements were in place within three years of the end of the First World War. This industrial relations system was a coherent and intelligible response to the process of economic decline and accompanying economic restructuring, which accelerated in the last two decades of the nineteenth century and the early part of the twentieth century, and the waves of strikes that were both cause and effect of economic change. This chapter examines why this particular manner of regulating relations between labor and capital emerged in Britain at this time, and the role that the state played in shaping industrial relations institutions.

The 1890s are a good place to begin an examination of state activism in the sphere of industrial relations. The state had acted before, both to put down strikes and to establish the legal position of unions, creating a basic right to organize and act collectively, primarily in the 1871 Trade Union Act and 1875 Conspiracy and Protection of Property Act. But the state played a minimal role in regulating industrial relations, and it had acted primarily to maintain order and safeguard property relations, rather than as a conscious agent of economic intervention. The 1890s saw the start of sustained state interest in the construction of industrial relations institutions. For the first time, in 1893, the British government intervened in a strike, in the coal industry, to seek and promote a settlement between unions and employers, and the 1894 royal commission on Labour created the presumption in government policy that collective bargaining between unions and employers was a public good. Much of the development of this first set of industrial relations institutions followed from arguments made in the report of the royal commission, which articulated an early version of the doctrine of collective laissez-faire.[1]

This industrial relations system had five principal elements. First, there was the presumption within public policy that trade unions play a positive role in "organizing" the labor side and providing an interlocutor with which to bargain. Second, another presumption held that industry-level bargaining should be the dominant form of regulation of industrial relations, so that all (or at least the main) employers in an industry would bargain as a group with the relevant unions. Third, the main content of these industry-level bargains had two elements: disputes procedures to regulate and reduce conflict, and industry-wide minimum standards (wages and hours) and/or sliding scales and cost-of-living adjustments designed to reduce wage conflict. Fourth, a particular kind of state role emerged, one characterized by limited direct regulation; instead of legislating wages, conditions, and bargaining structures the state acted to provide arbitration and conciliation services, to intervene in strikes to bring about a settlement, and to pass auxiliary legislation to underpin and encourage industry bargaining. Fifth, there was the attempt to insulate collective organization and action on the part of trade unions from judicial oversight. This system became more formal as time went on, and from 1945 onward the state adopted a new macroeconomic stance that encouraged a certain decommodification of the labor market, and changed the balance of power of unions and employers, but the core institutions of the first industrial relations system were unchanged by post–Second World War governments, both Labour and Conservative, until the 1960s.

This set of industrial relations institutions had two main goals, sometimes explicitly articulated and sometimes not. The first goal was to minimize overt class conflict, that between employers and workers, so as to permit economic restructuring. This was of particular importance in a range of industries where, because of growing economic interdependence, disruption would have broad national economic consequences. The second goal was to stabilize market competition, that between different employers in the same industry, in a set of primarily older, declining, staple industries characterized by a relatively large number of employers, low capital requirements for entry, and competition largely based on wage costs or other forms of labor exploitation. This first industrial relations system used trade unions and collective bargaining to reduce or manage both forms of conflict, but did so leaving managerial authority inside the firm largely unaffected; bargaining was centered at the industry level, not the firm, where employers were free to organize the labor process as they wished.

The form and timing of the construction of this industrial relations system reflected the pattern of restructuring, and a set of attendant problems, facing the British economy during this period. These problems are outlined in the next section. But economic pressures were not unmediated. The curious combination of strength and weakness exhibited by the class organizations of labor and capital created a set of what were effectively collective action problems. Craft unions, a weak peak organization of labor, loose industry-level employer associations, and the absence of a peak employers' organization created decentralized, poorly coordinated class organizations, subject to internal competition.

There were certainly occasions when particular employers, employers' associations, groups of workers, and trade unions opposed the construction of an industry-level bargaining system, or elements of it, but it was also the case that there was a role for the British state to act where employer associations and trade unions wanted to but could not. At the same time, the structure and capacity of the state shaped how, and with what effect, the state itself was able to act. The state was not monolithic, and quite distinct industrial relations projects resided within the judiciary and different government departments. The interplay between state actors therefore helped to shape the outcome. Furthermore, royal commissions, as quasi-state actors, played a central role in shaping public discourse on reform. Finally, the effect of this first set of industrial relations institutions itself on the ideology, organization, and practice of both employers and unions had important consequences for how industrial relations were reconstructed in the next period of intense industrial relations reform, the 1960s and 1970s.

The plan for this chapter is as follows. The next three sections examine the challenges posed by economic restructuring in the early decades of the twentieth century and the reasons why industry bargaining offered one possible solution to those challenges. The fourth section documents the rising tide of industrial conflict and the parallel growth in concern on the part of the state and elite opinion about the inadequacy of existing industrial relations institutions and the widespread perception that these institutions were in need of reform. The bulk of the remainder of the chapter explores the different forms of state response, including a period of judicial activism between 1893 and 1901, the 1894 royal commission on Labour, the role of the Board of Trade in the decade and a half before the First World War, the impact of the Whitley Report at the end of that war, and the scaling back of state intervention in the 1920s. The sections on the reports of the 1894 royal commission and the Whitley Committee emphasize their role in shaping public discourse and channeling perceptions of disquiet or crisis into concrete projects of industrial relations reform. Two final sections contain a summary of the impact of state intervention, first on collective bargaining institutions and then on trade union structures, practices, and ideologies. As the next chapter argues, these in turn played an important role in shaping union reactions to later reform efforts.

It is worth emphasizing that this chapter is not attempting to provide a comprehensive account of the evolution of British industrial relations during a period covering more than sixty years, nor is it even an exhaustive treatment of the role of the state in this area. Such a task would scarcely be possible were this chapter ten times its current length, such is the mass of historical material. Nor is it even something to which this chapter aspires. Instead it constructs a framework linking economic restructuring, class organization, and state intervention to the construction of a particular set of industrial relations institutions. It offers what are, in effect, snapshots that concentrate attention on key periods and processes of institutional construction that illuminate the main argument of the chapter. The account of necessity zooms in on some parts of the story and zooms out on others. While that permits me to highlight the central parts of my argument, it has the effect of throwing into shadow those periods and processes which already form part of the conventional account of the early evolution of British industrial relations.

ECONOMIC DECLINE AND THE RESTRUCTURING OF CLASS RELATIONS

The period covered by this chapter was marked by two significant sets of economic developments. First, from the late 1880s until the First World War, the long decline of the staple industries that had spearheaded Britain's industrial revolution from the late eighteenth century through the nineteenth century first became visible and a subject of public debate. This decline was accentuated by intensified competition from challengers to British economic supremacy during the Great Depression from 1873 to 1896.[2] Then, between the two world wars, as the decline of those older industries continued and indeed accelerated, a set of newer industries, oriented more toward domestic consumers and reliant upon new technologies and forms of factory organization, emerged somewhat hesitantly and in a manner heavily influenced by existing forms of labor management. Even during this period, though, the older staple industries remained sufficiently important for the British economy as a whole that their characteristic forms of industrial relations and class organization continued to be the model for rest of the economy.

Economic restructuring is a constant feature of capitalist economies, but this period both posed a new set of challenges for the British economy and heightened existing ones. Perceptions of these challenges, and of potential solutions to them, held by employers, trade unions, and different branches of the state came to be reflected in their projects of industrial relations reform. The regulation of the social relations between capital and labor was itself a major component of the process whereby economic restructuring was itself managed. The precise fit between the problems posed by economic restructuring and the solutions offered remains to be seen, and one would expect those solutions to be refracted through the class and other interests of the participants, the legacies of past practice, and the simple capacity of industrial actors and the state to construct certain kinds of industrial relations institutions.

In fact, the central elements of the first industrial relations system, described in the previous section, were predictable and plausible responses to the particular form that economic restructuring took in Britain in the first half of the twentieth century. These elements were designed to reduce conflict both between workers and employers and among employers. The resulting solution was not the only one possible, and we shall see how alternatives fell by the wayside. But the match between the pattern of economic growth and the industrial relations system, which ultimately helped to regulate economic growth, was not coincidental. This first industrial relations system reflected the crisis and decline of pre-Fordist competitive capitalism, a kind of capitalism based largely on extensive growth, in which the institutions of industrial relations served to limit and manage the competition and social conflict that accompanied this kind of growth.

The manner in which the British economy was restructured during this period, and the consistent theme of decline and crisis, is well known and rehearsed in practically every account.[3] Debates among economic and social historians have rarely challenged the central elements of this story. Rather debate has been over the causes of decline: the relative blame that should be attached to trade unions, poor management, the flow of financial capital, the role of empire, exchange rate and trade policy, and so on.[4] This is not terrain I want to enter, but a more recent scholarship that has emphasized the particular structure of labor and product markets, and the incentives those markets created for firms, is of particular relevance to the argument made in this chapter.[5] As Gospel has argued, throughout this period British firms faced an abundant supply of labor, especially craft labor, which had the effect of discouraging the development of internal training regimes, the replacement of labor with capital, internal labor markets, and the payment of "efficiency wages." Persistent high unemployment between the world wars only exacerbated this situation. At the same time product markets were relatively small, heterogenous, and fragmented. Firms had to produce a wider range of goods for diverse markets, making standardization, and its attendant forms of technology and work organization, inappropriate. This situation was only reinforced in the 1930s after the introduction of tariffs redirected British exports toward smaller, less sophisticated imperial markets. The relatively small size of British firms, and the fact that many of them produced for markets characterized by intense levels of competition, further inhibited capital investment on the part of firms. The adoption of technologies and practices that were widely diffused in the United States and Germany at this time was therefore discouraged in Britain by the markets faced by British firms.

At the risk of some degree of simplification, one can identify two groups of industries in Britain during this period, each sharing a set of important characteristics and distinct one from another.[6] The old staple industries—textiles (especially cotton), coal, iron and steel, shipbuilding, some parts of engineering—tended to be characterized by a large number of small firms, intense competition, heavy export dependence, and low profitability. In some of these industries low capital requirements also made for relatively easy entry. Growth was "extensive," involving the addition of new units of labor, capital, and raw materials rather than the more efficient use of these inputs. (Coal was a particularly good example of this industrial structure. Between 1904 and 1914 the industry saw a 45 percent increase in its workforce but increased output by only about 10 percent. Technological innovation was very slow, in part because competition and the large number of small producers made investment difficult. As late as 1940, only about 60 percent of coal was cut by machines in Britain, compared with close to 100 percent in the United States and Germany.[7] In 1919 there were still 1,452 mining companies owning 3,300 mines.) These old staple industries were also facing increased international competition from more efficient producers, or loss of export markets because of tariffs. Added to these woes were the overexpansion of iron and steel and shipbuilding during the First World War and the growth of alternatives to coal in electricity generation. The net result was a highly competitive and brutal form of capitalism in which undercutting, particularly wage competition, was endemic, thereby creating high levels of industrial conflict as competition among firms affected wages and conditions, and led to resistance from workers and unions.

A second group of newer industries—motor vehicles, electrical engineering, chemicals, and glassmaking—was characterized by a quite different industrial structure. Each industry tended to be dominated by a small number of relatively large firms, often organized in cartel form. These industries produced consumer goods primarily for the home market and were often sheltered from foreign competition by transportation costs or other factors. But even the firms in these industries were limited by the labor and product markets that they faced. The British automobile industry, for example, did not adopt the central elements of American Fordism.[8] Smaller, less egalitarian markets, and a preference on the part of (more affluent) consumers for quality and continuous design changes, made highly capital-intensive mass production unprofitable. In fact, Henry Ford's attempt to export the features of his U.S. operation was a disaster. The most successful automobile producer in Britain between the world wars was William Morris, who did not even introduce a moving assembly line until 1933 and relied heavily on high-skill handwork. For all the differences between the newer and older industrial structures, British product and labor markets encouraged both kinds of industries to uses strategies that Gospel has labeled as "externalization" of work and employment relations: relying on the external rather than internal labor market to set wage levels; hiring and firing in response to product demand rather than offering job security; work intensification rather than investment in new technology; and rudimentary managerial hierarchies rather than the more bureaucratic management and personnel institutions that were developing in larger German and American firms.[9]

For the purposes of this chapter, three features of British economic development are important in the period between the last decade of the nineteenth century and the Second World War. First, the industrial structures of the older staple industries and the newer, more consumer-oriented industries diverged in a number of important ways. The problems of wage competition and of limited capacity for collective action on the part of employers within the staple industries were much more severe than in the newer industries. Second, the size and importance to the entire economy of the staple industries, coupled with their agonizingly slow decline, ensured that the problems faced by this sector of the economy, and the industrial relations solutions adopted there, would come to shape state policy, and the industrial relations system as a whole, well into the interwar period. The first system of industrial relations was, in essence, born of the prolonged crisis and decline of Britain's old staple industries. Third, because of the distinctive product and labor markets that they faced, even the newly emerging industries were often characterized by the managerial structures, employment relations, forms of work organization, and technologies of the older industries. That is to say, much of the familiar landscape of Fordist mass production was entirely absent from British industry during this period: standardization, line assembly, and mass production were limited; piecework actually became significantly more prevalent during the first half of the twentieth century; scientific management, including the home-grown Bedaux System, did not appear until the late 1920s and even then its influence was limited;[10] and what productivity improvements did appear were more the result of work intensification than technological innovation.

This account of the restructuring of the British economy in the late nineteenth and early twentieth centuries implies a high degree of continuity, as staple industries remained an important sector of the economy and restructuring took place without radical shifts in technology or the manner of production. Why, then, when so much recent scholarship has downplayed the degree of technological change, indicated the weak and late implantation of mass production and scientific management, and demonstrated the diversity of individual industrial experience, was this, nonetheless, a turning point for the development of industrial relations institutions? The two decades leading up to the First World War did not so much see a transformation of this industrial structure as a transformation of relations between workers and employers, as the latter sought to manage decline and competition. The intensification of national and international competition was crucial less because of any changes in technology and industrial structure it induced than because of the dramatic changes in the social relations of production it produced. It was not economic change itself that generated social conflict, but rather changes in the relations among workers, and between workers and employers.[11]

Price has argued that Britain exhibited a remarkable continuity in the social relations of production over the long period between 1750 and the 1880s, even during the periods of intense economic growth that characterized the industrialization process. This long period saw the spread of capitalist market relations to ever larger parts of the labor force, but it saw only limited restructuring of the labor process. In fact, for the most part employers and managers responded to economic change by *evacuating* from direct supervision of large parts of the labor process, choosing to rely on the expertise of labor rather than to claim particular technical expertise for themselves. Thus the paradoxical result came about that labor was simultaneously more dependent (in the sphere of market relations) on capital by virtue of being proletarianized yet was more autonomous (in the sphere of production) by virtue of remaining in control of the labor process. For that reason, unions during this period sought to control the labor supply, in order to reduce dependency in the labor market, rather than to control the labor process, over which workers still had a fair degree of control.

This changed between 1880 and 1914, when the intensification of competitive pressure on British industry led employers to try to gain control of the labor process in order to reduce labor costs and increase productivity. As noted above, there were important constraints on the ability of employers to increase productivity; industrial structure and fragmented markets made it difficult, and risky, to make the investment necessary for new technology and to make gains from new forms of work organization, even in the absence of worker resistance. Given the market incentives they faced, it was not even economically rational for many firms to follow the innovations of their American and Germany counterparts.

But regardless of the ability of managers to extract productivity increases, this period saw a much greater intrusion of managerial authority as managers resorted to traditional methods to either reduce labor costs or increase output, or both: sweating, the replacement of skilled by less-skilled workers, piecework and bonuses, and so on. This managerial initiative was experienced by workers in somewhat different ways—often as more disruptive and threatening for skilled than semiskilled workers[12]—but the result was heightened subordination and insecurity, which led, especially as the economy pulled out of depression in the 1880s, to industrial conflict, most spectacularly in the strike wave of 1889–91.

By the middle of the 1920s this battle had been largely won by employers. They and their managers had gained control over the labor process in part because of the form taken by the first industrial relations system, which freed them to organize the workplace largely as they pleased. The next decade saw almost complete managerial freedom to restructure the labor process, and it was during this later period that the British economy underwent more rapid modernization, with the growth of new industries, the rationalization of industry through mergers, and the spread of new production techniques. But as Price puts it: "In Britain the key break in class relations had occurred with the rupturing of the mid-Victorian compromise in the late nineteenth century which had been largely accomplished without the necessity for a distinctively 'managerial' ideology."[13]

The British economy also became more interdependent at the turn of the century with the rise of industries that were crucial for the success of the national economy. Thus strikes in the energy industry (especially coal) and transportation (rail, docks, shipping) would have a very rapid and serious impact on the rest of the economy, and would be hard for any government, however laissez-faire in theory, to ignore in practice. As Lloyd George, then president of the Board of Trade, put it in 1908, "There is no trade in which, if you get a dispute, you will not find a whole link to other industries involved, which suffer in consequence."[14] Even the *Economist* urged government action in 1907, saying that "railway strikes and railway lock-outs cannot be permitted. They are contrary to public policy."[15] Furthermore, as unions became stronger, the absence of industrial relations institutions able to overcome employer resistance to granting recognition, and able to channel disputes into bargaining and to manage conflict through arbitration and other procedures, led to growing numbers of strikes. And all these problems would become much more serious during wartime, when full economic mobilization was necessary.

The Benefits of Industry-Level Bargaining for Employers

The period covered in this chapter was one of transition from pre-Fordist competitive capitalism, when the industries that had powered Britain's industrial success in the nineteenth century were in decline, to a newer, mass production Fordist economy. The transition was very slow, and, as the next chapter demonstrates, Britain only ever developed a flawed Fordism. But the transition created a set of economic problems that were expressed in the form of strikes: strikes in response to wage cutting, strikes over the shifting "frontier of control" in the firm, strikes in crucial industries, strikes for recognition.

Time series data on strikes from the 1890s to the 1990s show particular peaks in the 1890s, in 1910–14, and in 1919–21; indeed, if the measure of percentage of union members involved in strikes is used, levels in the 1890s, the 1910s, and the 1920s have never been surpassed, even during the industrial conflict of the 1970s.[16] During this early period, strikes in the coal industry dominated strike statistics, comprising more than 30 percent of all days lost. It was these strikes which forced the British state to take a role in constructing new industrial relations institutions, ones able to better manage the economic transition.

The industrial relations institutions that became widespread during the period covered by this chapter offered partial solutions to the problems outlined above, primarily in their potential to stabilize market competition by taking wages and hours out of competition, and by channeling industrial conflict into disputes procedures and collective bargaining. Bowman has drawn our attention toward the ways in which business seeks to stabilize the market by reducing competition among individual firms.[17] Competition is, after all, often fatal to a firm. The problem for business is how to reduce competition while preventing defection and maintaining freedom of maneuver. Cartels maximize freedom from outside control, but they have almost no sanctioning power to prevent defection. State regulation can prevent defection but at the price of state control of prices, profits, and so on. In the first system of industrial relations in Britain, trade unions and industry-level bargaining were the most common solution to this particular collective action problem. Trade unions policed their own members through procedure agreements and a centralization of internal control, and policed business through minimum wages and standards to limit destructive competition between firms. From the perspective of business, unions provided some external sanction against defection while exercising only limited control over work organization and the labor process within the firm, and agreements with unions were, ultimately, easier to terminate than state regulation.

The last chapter made reference to Dobbin's work on national industrial culture, with its argument that political culture both shapes the perception of what constitutes a policymaking problem and delimits the range of legitimate solutions.[18] Dobbin argues that British industrial culture emphasizes shielding firms from both market competition and political interference. Thus British policymakers have permitted, and in many cases encouraged, collusion and forms of cartelization to stabilize market competition.[19] When forced to choose, policy (in marked contrast to the situation in the United States) "protected firms rather than market competition."[20] In this respect, the institutions of the first system of industrial relations meshed well with both the industrial culture of Britain, which protected firms from markets, and the choice of instruments to that end; reliance on industry-level bargaining limited the need for direct political regulation of industrial organization and market competition (in contrast this time to France).

Thus multiemployer industry bargaining had a set of advantages for employers.[21] It conceded recognition to unions in return for forcing unions to work within disputes procedures that limited the ability to strike and shifted regulation of conflict away from its source to the national level. It concentrated bargaining at the national level, where employers' associations were strongest, again, away from areas of local labor strength. It took wages out of competition. Finally, all these agreements encouraged managerial prerogative, both by explicit management rights clauses and by ensuring that bargaining was external to the firm, leaving employers free to organize the workplace as they wished.

Clearly, many employers had no interest in this form of regulation, and even many that did were too ideologically opposed to unions to accept it. Industry-level collective bargaining was a second-best solution for most employers, who would have preferred not to have to deal with unions at all. Pressure from competitors and from labor, whether organized or not, forced employers to join employer industry associations and contemplate participating in collective bargaining.[22] That is why it was often necessary for the state to encourage participation in industry bargaining and even to legislate the creation of bargaining institutions. But the important point is that this particular set of industrial relations institutions was less threatening to employers than alternatives, which, for example, might have embedded union representation and rights inside the workplace. Industry-level bargaining left managerial prerogatives largely alone, and permitted employers to limit union activity and influence inside the firm. Nothing in this system of industrial relations prevented different arrangements within the firm, and some businesses—particularly in newer consumer-oriented industries—chose to create workplace institutions as well. In a sense industry bargaining can be seen as a transitional form, which provided a partial solution to the situation faced by firms in older, declining industries while not acting as an obstacle to larger, more capital-intensive firms. It was not until the 1950s that the weight of the economy shifted toward these newer firms and alternative industrial relations arrangements began to be contemplated. What is clear is that industrial relations institutions were used in part to manage economic decline.

The Emergence of Industry Bargaining

Prior to the 1890s huge swaths of industry were without bargaining of any kind, and where bargaining did exist it was primarily of the district variety.[23] Only cotton weaving had a form of industry bargaining. Milner estimates that the coverage of collective bargaining was only about 7 percent in 1895.[24] The bargaining institutions that did appear, usually on a geographic basis, in the second half of the nineteenth century were designed *both* to manage industrial conflict and to regulate market competition during the Great Depression, from the early 1870s until the mid-1890s; in industries and districts where trade unions were too strong to dislodge, employers sought to negotiate institutions that reduced wage competition between employers, permitted wages to respond rapidly to price changes, and reduced worker resistance to falling wages. Sliding scales, in which a fall in prices of a certain magnitude triggered wage reductions, were widely used,[25] though this attempt to reduce industrial conflict by relying on automatic mechanisms could actually exacerbate wage competition.[26] Also widespread were boards of conciliation and arbitration, sometimes termed "alliances," which regulated competition among employers, often functioning as cartels to restrict output and keep prices and wages up. Phelps Brown describes the Birmingham Alliance, in which unions acted as enforcers of minimum terms and conditions, striking against recalcitrant employers and receiving the promise that only their members would be employed and that higher prices would be translated into higher wages.[27]

However, institutions such as these were always fragile and collapsed on a regular basis as economic conditions changed. Trade unions accepted them only in periods when their bargaining power was limited; pressure from their members led to the abrogation of sliding scales in a number of industries in the 1890s as labor market conditions improved. Without either legal underpinnings or a stronger institutional presence, the alliances were weak mechanisms for preventing defection.

From the 1890s to the outbreak of the First World War a different set of institutions emerged, but with the same dual function of limiting industrial conflict and regulating competition among employers. These institutions tended to combine industry-wide procedure agreements with district level wage and hour setting, usually incorporating a minimum wage. Procedure agreements outlined the stages of bargaining, often requiring conciliation or arbitration before a strike or a lockout could take place. A government report on collective bargaining in 1910 (written by George Askwith, who appears in an important role later in this chapter) counted 1,696 agreements covering 2.4 million people (about a quarter of the labor force) and contained a wealth of information about the main elements of collective agreements. It made clear that wider, district or industry, agreements protect "against the danger of being under-bid by firms obtaining their labour upon easier terms."[28] The agreements with the broadest coverage tended to be procedure agreements with more or less elaborate conciliation and/or arbitration schemes, all stages of which had to be exhausted before a work stoppage was possible; the building trades, coal mining, iron and steel, engineering, cotton spinning and weaving, and railways all signed procedure agreements, sometimes incorporating wage provisions as well, between 1893 and 1909.[29]

It is important to recognize that these agreements were signed largely at the behest of employers. Even after strikes or lockouts in which employers clearly defeated a trade union, they sought not to eradicate the union but to get an agreement that forced the union to police its own members. For example, Burgess has shown, for the engineering industry, that the agreement that employers and the Amalgamated Society of Engineers signed after the 1897–98 lockout gave complete freedom to employers to organize the workplace as they wished but also created an elaborate conciliation scheme that deliberately strengthened the union's national leadership over district committees so as to limit strikes.[30] Employers used trade unions to police their members, as "the universal feature of these developments [was] to secure a greater disciplinary power over the men by denying the legitimacy of unilateral action and undermining the autonomy of the local units of union organization."[31]

The price business paid for limited state regulation of the economy during this period was the collective laissez-faire industrial relations system. Fragmented ownership, brutal market competition, and long-term industrial decline were managed by a set of industrial relations institutions in which trade unions and collective agreements substituted for direct state regulation of competition. These industrial relations institutions permitted increased managerial control over the labor process inside the firm while seeking to limit explosions of worker militancy and set a floor under wage competition.

Perhaps this sounds a little too neat, and it is. Two important qualifiers are necessary. First, there is the danger of inferring the function and effect of institutions from the purpose of their construction. These industrial relations institutions were constructed at a point when unions were relatively weak, and while employers could not dislodge them, the form that the institutions took reflected the interests of employers more than unions. Trade unions, through procedure agreements and wage minimums, helped to regulate the labor market and manage conflict while leaving employers free to organize production. As Hyman has pointed out, it was not until this period that, within unions, "the notion of 'rank and file' came to be counterposed to that of 'officials.' " [32] Nevertheless, once established, these institutions created opportunities for trade unions to stabilize their membership and to make gains on behalf of those members. Zeitlin has argued that industry-wide agreements, in the long run, actually encouraged the diffusion of job control in the workplace, toward workers and unions, by reinforcing the existing division of labor and discouraging individual firms from developing specialized personnel functions.[33] Industrial relations institutions, indeed institutions of all kinds, have a plastic character that allows them to perform multiple functions depending on the context. During wartime, or when labor markets tightened, institutions designed to protect employers could provide trade unions with important advantages.

The second qualifier is more central to the argument of this chapter. However rational or functional for business interests this system of industrial relations was, it was not likely to appear, or at least to become entrenched, without the state acting as midwife. A combination of employer recalcitrance, union radicalism, the fragility of industry agreements and their vulnerability to changing economic circumstances, and a state interest in preventing damage to the national economy or the war effort through industrial conflict led the British state to take a leading role in the construction of this system. All these factors were important, but the weakness of the class organizations of capital and labor stands out because it speaks to the collective actions problem faced by those seeking to construct this first system of industrial relations.

In his classic comparison of Swedish and British industrial conflict, Ingham pointed to the way in which the industrial structure that results from particular patterns of industrial development influences the form, especially the degree of centralization, of employer and labor organizations.[34] Ingham argued that low levels of industrial concentration, a complex technical and organizational structure resulting from a relatively old, layered industrial system, and high levels of product specialization and differentiation resulting from early industrialization had the effect, in Britain, of making employer solidarity extremely difficult. Fragmented ownership, typically with large numbers of small producers, made collective organization on the employers side difficult. It is no surprise that a single authoritative employers' organization did not emerge in Britain until 1965, after a decade of rapid mergers. The same industrial structure produced a labor movement of enormous complexity, combining powerful craft unions, a handful of strong general unions, relatively few industrial unions, and a weak trade union confederation, the Trades Union Congress (TUC).

The issue here is not the strength or weakness of class organizations, per se, but their capacity for conducting industry-level bargaining. Neither employers nor trade unions were organizationally well suited to overcoming the collective action problem of multiple employers engaged in often brutal competition with one another, and multiple unions either competing with one another for members or representing different groups of workers within the same industry. Furthermore, as markets and industries became national, trade union strength within an industry was likely to remain geographically uneven, making the organization of the labor side difficult. In this context a role for the state emerged, not imposing a set of industrial relations institutions, but creating conditions under which employers and trade unions could overcome their own lack of organization.

The Reemergence of "The Labour Problem"

A set of economic problems and a few scattered and fragile experiments with forms of collective regulation of class relations were not enough to construct a national system of industrial relations. In part because of the collective action problem outlined above, and in part because of resistance to collective regulation by elements of the employer and labor classes, some action on the part of the state was necessary. But it was also unclear just what direction state intervention should take, and to what end. The central elements of what became the first system of industrial relations were not obvious. This section charts the process by which the British state first became committed to a particular approach to manage industrial relations, and then acted to implement it. That process involved both the definition of what constituted "the labour problem" and intrastate conflict over conflicting solutions.

Regulation of class relations was not virgin territory for the British state. Between 1871 and 1875 legislation had created a legal environment designed to permit collective action on the part of labor, and to put employers and workers on an equal legal footing.[35] In 1871 the Trade Union Act was passed, offering protection to unions from prosecution for restraint of trade. It was accompanied in the same year by the Criminal Law Amendment Act, however, which undid much of the effect of the first act by proscribing a wide range of tactics used by unions to pressure employers in the course of industrial conflict, including most forms of picketing. In response to trade union pressure, the Conspiracy and Protection of Property Act was passed in 1875, which gave immunity to unions from prosecution for the crime of simple conspiracy as long as a strike was in furtherance of a trade dispute. It also explicitly legalized peaceful picketing. Finally, also in 1875, the Employers and Workmen Act ended the criminal liability of workers for breach of contract. Both in substance and in the symbolism of language, the law of master and servant was replaced by legislation that put employers and workers on a more equal footing.

However, as the focus on what constituted criminal activities suggests, the public debates during this period had taken place within a discourse of law and order, and equality before the law.[36] During the long "mid-Victorian compromise," the framework of labor law was constructed to incorporate respectable workingmen, those represented by responsible craft unions, and to extend the principles of Gladsonian liberalism to labor organizations. This was an industrial parallel to the process of franchise extension. It was a reward for the forgoing of militancy in the industrial sphere and radicalism in the political sphere. It was a process and a discourse in which the economic implications of social conflict were rarely debated.

This changed at the end of the 1880s, with the militancy of the New Unionism. The scale and the nature of strike action, with the involvement of previously unorganized groups of workers, created a moral panic within elite opinion, accompanied by a demand that something be done. Content analysis of leading periodicals and *Times* editorials for the period from 1880 to 1893 demonstrates this rising concern.[37] But what was relatively new, and is of importance here, is that the discourse shifted from concern simply with the issue of law and order, and protection of property, to the economic implications of industrial conflict. The strike wave associated with the New Unionism coincided with growing doubts about the international competitiveness of the British economy. Typical was the opinion of the *Economist*:

> We have rivals to contend with who, if they do not possess superior energy, have nevertheless the most modern English machinery and the advantage of location and high tariffs with which to fight us. A prolonged fight between masters and men, even though it may have good reasons to back it, gives a handle to all these competitors.[38]

This theme continued to be prominent well after the level of strikes declined. Between November 1901 and January 1902 the *Times* ran an influential series of articles on the practice of "ca'canny" within British industry, understood to mean the deliberate strategy of limiting output of work.[39]

The first system of industrial relations was constructed *after* employers had crushed the radical potential of the 1889 strike wave, and had imposed restrictive settlements on workers and their trade unions in the course of the 1890s. It was precisely after the immediate threat had disappeared that employers, the state, and moderate union leaders sought to construct mechanisms that would both prevent future industrial conflict on that scale and manage the process of economic restructuring, which had become much more salient. The strike wave was the trigger, but how it would be interpreted, and what industrial relations mechanisms would form the response, remained to be worked out.

There was in fact no single state response. There were actually three, a judicial, a legislative, and a bureaucratic, though the latter two worked in parallel, reinforcing each other. These different responses reflected the fact that the "ruling elite itself was seriously divided as to the best strategy to adopt in containing labour unrest,"[40] and it was this division that created space for the initiatives of the Board of Trade that are discussed below. Much of the commentary on the state response has focused on the judiciary and its attempt to restrict the scope for strike action and picketing through a series of legal decisions in the 1890s, culminating in the famous *Taff Vale* decision in 1901. But far more important, in the long run, was the impact of legislative and bureaucratic intervention. Together, they created a new set of assumptions about the benefits of trade union organization and collective regulation of class conflict, and they permitted institution-building in the sphere of industrial relations.

THE JUDICIAL ONSLAUGHT

Beginning with *Temperton v. Russell* (1893) and culminating in *Taff Vale Railway Company v. Amalgamated Society of Railway Servants* (1901) and *Quinn v. Leathem* (1901), the British judiciary tore a series of giant holes in the protection which the 1875 Conspiracy and Protection of Property Act, and 1875 Employers and Workmen Act, had supposedly afforded trade unions and workers.[41] While that legislation provided protection from criminal liability, the courts developed a set of new doctrines of civil liability covering interference with trade, conspiracy to injure, picketing, and inducement to breach of contract. Their net effect was that "effective trade unionism premised largely on collective action, was rendered virtually impossible."[42]

It is impossible to interpret this judicial onslaught as other than a deliberate response to the rise in industrial conflict, on the part of one branch of the British state. The 1890s saw "the convergence of judge-made law and the vigorous assertion of hostility towards unions that was displayed in the literary and journalistic organs of opinion."[43] The legislation protective of unions and strike action had been in place since 1875, but the courts were largely silent for the next decade and a half as the mid-Victorian compromise held. Klarman's exhaustive study of the new judicial activism of the 1890s concludes that these decisions cannot be explained with regard to precedent or legislative intent. Quite different standards were applied to labor markets and product markets, and indeed different standards were applied within the labor market, to employers and to unions. Rather, ideological and class bias on the part of judges is the best explanation of the case law that emerged during this period. Ideological bias manifested itself in the preference given to individualism over collectivism, and while class bias is more difficult to identify, the courts do appear to have been influenced by the drumbeat of concern about declining economic competitiveness as they sought to curtail trade union action.[44]

This cycle of judicial intervention came to an end in 1906 with the passage of the Trade Disputes Act by the new Liberal government, which provided blanket immunity to trade unions for action taken in furtherance of a trade dispute, an immunity that remained essentially unchallenged until the next wave of moral panic concerning strikes in the 1960s. The 1906 act effectively prevented the use of labor injunctions, the most potent weapon in the hands of employers seeking to prevent strikes, for sixty years until the House of Lords decided to review the use of labor injunctions in *Stratford v. Lindley* in 1965.[45] British labor law has been characterized, as Lord Scarman put it, by "a shifting pattern of Parliamentary assertion and judicial response—a legal point counterpoint which has been more productive of excitement than of harmony. The judges have been . . . reluctant to abandon common law and equitable principles unless unambiguously told to do so by statute."[46] It was this that the Trade Disputes Act achieved, and which permitted the construction of the collective laissez-faire system.

The Trade Disputes Act had been preceded by the report of the Royal Commission on Trade Disputes and Trade Combinations, set up in response to *Taff Vale*.[47] Trade unions refused to give evidence before this royal commission, and it produced a narrow and legalistic defense of the judicial decisions of the preceding decade. It did, however, recommend that legislation create a set of positive rights for trade unions, declaring them legal associations and declaring strikes legal.[48] These recommendations were overwhelmed by the demand of trade unions for judicial immunity, and their influence over the new Liberal government.

This episode of judicial activism is important less for its direct impact on industrial relations, which was relatively limited and brief, than on the ideology and practice of the British labor movement, which in turn had a long-term effect on the evolution of the industrial relations system. In the second half of the 1890s, some elements of the labor movement had come to look favorably on an alternative model of industrial relations, influenced by New Zealand's Industrial Conciliation and Arbitration Act, passed in 1894.[49] This introduced a conciliation process followed, if conciliation failed, by compulsory arbitration. It promised a route to gaining employer recognition through legislation and labor courts in return for severe restrictions on the right to strike. Its primary appeal was to relatively weak unions that were unlikely to be able to force recognition through strike action, and its greatest champion in Britain was Ben Tillett, secretary of the London Dockers union. But Tillett's campaign to gain trade union support was undercut by hostile judicial decisions, and his resolutions in favor of the New Zealand legislation at the TUC annual conferences in 1899 and 1900 were heavily defeated, with opponents making it clear that they "could not trust the judges of this country to give a fair and impartial verdict on any question as to the conditions of labour which might be remitted to them."[50]

For the largest, most influential unions, the degree of hostility manifested in this phase of judicial activism was interpreted to mean that no framework of labor law, even one embodying positive rights for unions, could offer protection from judges except blanket immunity from the scope of judge-made law. As Klarman puts it:

> Ironically, the unions chose to pursue absolute tort immunity principally because the judges had proved themselves so unrelentingly hostile to union interests that only legislation placing the unions beyond the judicial grasp would afford adequate protection.[51]

It was this that the unions and their representatives pressed on the 1906 Liberal government. Its achievement in the Trade Disputes Act effectively closed off one alternative industrial relations future, until at least the 1960s. It meant that there was only limited, minority support within the labor movement for a range of legislation, positive rights instead of negative immunities, that might have afforded rights and protections to unions. It made the ideology of "voluntarism" virtually hegemonic within the labor movement, and it gave birth to the notion of "trade union privileges," that unions were somehow above the law, something that made them ideologically and politically vulnerable half a century later.

From 1906, with some minor exceptions, the British judiciary was quiet, reflecting both the waning of labor militancy and the formula of immunity. But this was at best a negative solution, which said nothing about how the relations between labor and capital would be regulated, beyond that employers could not rely on the protection of the courts. Parallel to the phase of judicial activism, and extending well beyond it, was a quite different approach to the regulation of class relations, one that emphasized joint, collective regulation through industry-level bargaining. The institutional elements of this system of industrial relations were constructed in three stages. The first two stages corresponded to the two main elements of this system: the identification of bargaining with unions as a public policy good, which took place relatively quickly, with the 1890s and the first decade of the twentieth century being the critical period; and the construction of industry bargaining, which took much longer and was done industry by industry, with 1911–21 being the key period of construction. Both stages can usefully be viewed through the public inquiries set up by the state. The third stage, lasting from 1922 to the outbreak of the Second World War, was a period in which there was first some retrenchment of the industrial relations system and then, in the 1930s, a good deal of legislative buttressing of industry bargaining.

THE 1894 ROYAL COMMISSION ON LABOUR

The Royal Commission on Labour, which reported in 1894, was created in response to the dramatic upsurge in strikes mentioned earlier. It took as its aim the investigation of the causes of industrial conflict, of how strikes could be prevented or best settled, and of what, if any, role legislation could play in reducing conflict. The commission took extensive evidence from employers, trade unionists, and experts, and for the purpose of gathering evidence divided itself into three committees, one examining heavy industry (mining, iron and steel, engineering and shipbuilding), one transport and agriculture (including shipping, the docks, and railways), and one light industry (textiles and clothing) and construction. The very exhaustiveness of the commission's inquiries gave its eventual recommendations greater legitimacy. The commission issued majority and minority reports, corresponding to the employer side and the labor side. The majority report was, unsurprisingly, more influential. But it is important that the minority report did not disagree with the industrial relations prescriptions of the majority report. Rather it argued that only state control—socialism—would remove the causes of strikes.

The report made two central arguments. First, and most novel, it argued that "organisation," of both employers and workers, reduced conflict:

> On the whole, and notwithstanding occasional conflicts on a very large scale, the increased strength of organisations may tend toward the maintenance of harmonious relations between employers and employed . . . peaceable relations are, upon the whole, the result of strong and firmly established trade unionism.[52]

The report recognized the potential collective action problem, arguing that class organizations needed to be sufficiently encompassing to permit multiemployer bargaining:

> It is usually admitted on both sides that strong organisations have been proved by experience to be almost a condition precedent to the success of voluntary methods or institutions of conciliation and arbitration, *so far as these institutions extend beyond the limits of a single establishment to a whole trade or district.*[53]

It also remarked that some witnesses "allege that the action of strong trade unions is beneficial even to employers by preventing them from destroying each other through unlimited competition."[54] The commission argued that strong, encompassing class organizations were less likely to enter into conflict, because the "leaders of associations on either side are likely to have broader views than individuals and local men."[55] The view that trade union leaders are, by virtue of their position, inherently more moderate than rank-and-file members became a hallmark of both the first and second systems of industrial relations in Britain, challenged only in the Thatcherite period, when the reverse assumption became dominant. Similarly, the report explicitly argued that strong trade unions act as enforcers of industrial peace, seeking alternative means of resolving disputes and preventing local strikes.

Second, the royal commission made a strong plea for voluntarism and a limited role for legislation, arguing that only solutions acceptable to both industrial actors would be durable, and concluding that "many of the evils to which our attention has been called are such as cannot be remedied by any legislation."[56] The role of the state was to encourage business and labor to bargain with each other. The majority report recommended minimal legislation (to make conciliation available), though a significant minority within the majority added a call for compulsory arbitration. Neither did the labor side argue for greater juridification of industrial relations, calling only for a broader role for the Board of Trade in collecting data and disseminating it to the public.

To a remarkable extent, the report of the 1894 royal commission articulated the essence of collective laissez-faire, and this became the cornerstone of public policy for the next eighty-five years. The importance of the report was not only its policy prescriptions, which were few, but also its public articulation of the assumptions underlying those policy prescriptions. The arguments that direct legislative regulation of class relations would engender resistance and enfeeble collective organization, and that strong trade unions recognized by employers would serve to limit and channel industrial conflict into bargaining procedures, proved enormously influential. They served to shape public discourse, to offer an official imprimatur and justification for public policy. By the end of the first decade of the twentieth century, these assumptions were repeatedly being publicly evoked by leading political figures. Winston Churchill, then president of the Board of Trade, insisted that trade unions provided the "necessary guardrails and bulwarks" of capitalism,[57] and Prime Minister Campbell-Bannerman justified his government's support for blanket immunity for trade unions in the 1906 Trade Disputes Act with this paean to unions:

> the great mass of opinion in the country recognise fully now the beneficent nature of trade union organisations, and recognise also the great services that those organisations have done in the prevention of conflict and the promotion of harmony between labour and capital.[58]

THE BOARD OF TRADE

The next twenty years saw a new role for the state. The Board of Trade was the main agent of state action, taking on the role of apostle for the collective regulation of industrial relations. The shift in responsibility for managing industrial conflict to the Board of Trade was an important stage in the evolution of the state's role. It is worth emphasizing that what changed was not primarily the provision of new tools, or capacities for state action, but rather the willingness of state actors to intervene in industrial relations conflicts. In fact, the 1867 Conciliation Act and 1872 Arbitration (Masters and Workmen) Act had permitted the Home Office to encourage voluntary forms of conciliation and arbitration, but Home Office officials never made any use of the legislation, refusing to intervene even when requested by employers and unions. The Home Office saw its role as more or less exclusively the maintenance of law and order. After the 1894 royal commission report, another piece of legislation designed to encourage conciliation was passed, the 1896 Conciliation (Trade Disputes) Act. This legislation gave no more powers of compulsion than earlier legislation; it simply permitted government officials to inquire into the cause of disputes and to mediate or conciliate if both parties wanted such action. There was one crucial difference, however: responsibility for conciliation went not to the Home Office but to the Board of Trade. In part this marked the rising importance attached to the economic causes and consequences of industrial conflict, but it was also part of what Davidson has termed the "refinement of the machinery of civil intelligence."[59] In response to growing concern with industrial conflict, a Labour Statistical Bureau was created within the Board of Trade in 1886, which was then placed in a newly created Labour Department (still within the Board of Trade) in 1893.

The 1896 Conciliation Act was the thin reed used for the highly interventionist role played by the Board of Trade in the decade and a half until the outbreak of the First World War. It intervened in practically every industrial dispute of note, and in each case it recommended the creation of procedure agreements and bargaining institutions, as Phelps Brown put it, guiding "the parties towards 'permanent machinery.' "[60] The memoirs of George Askwith, the principal conciliator at the Board of Trade, offer an invaluable glimpse into its work.[61] Two points of particular importance come across from Askwith's memoirs. First, he makes clear that, in case after case, the source of industrial conflict was increased competition leading to undercutting of established wages and conditions, *and* that the same industrial structure of multiple competing small employers made resolution of conflict impossible without the intervention of the state. Thus a dispute in the Northamptonshire army boot industry saw "a mass of unorganised employers, each competing against the other,"[62] and in the Nottinghamshire lace industry "severe and undercutting competition had arisen from France, Scotland and elsewhere; and outside the city walls large factories had been erected at Long Eaton to escape the city rates of pay."[63] Similarly, persistent conflict on the docks resulted both from the "pools of casual labour" and from the lack of "cohesion among employers, and no section of employers who dared come forward and give a lead."[64] Compensating for the lack of organization was also relevant for the trade union side; Askwith noted that when he convened a meeting of the boilermakers union in 1909 in London to resolve a dispute, it may have been the first time most of the delegates had met each other, with the result that the meeting helped "weld the society together."[65] The problem identified by Askwith was not that the industrial actors resisted a negotiated settlement, or state intervention, but rather that they were unable to reach a settlement themselves because of weak organizational capacity.

Second, a central principle of government action that emerges from Askwith's memoirs is the emphasis on not simply settling conflicts (firefighting, as it were) but on the repeated efforts to construct industrial relations institutions to prevent future conflict. In all cases this involved trade union recognition and agreement on dispute procedures, ideally with regular bargaining between employers and unions. Askwith was explicit in this respect:

> I had determined that whenever possible, in the cases coming to my lot, I would try to end the lock-out or strike, but in all cases where an opening occurred in the course of settling the strike, I would go farther and endeavour to suggest and establish means by agreement between the parties in a firm or an industry for the prevention of future strikes and better relations between employers and employed.[66]

During this period the Board of Trade stretched its statutory powers under the Conciliation Act to intervene, often in highly innovative ways, to settle industrial conflict in such a way as to encourage collective regulation in the future. Despite the emphasis of the 1896 act on conciliation, and its anticipation that arbitration would be used only as a last resort, almost three-quarters of settlements under the act prior to the First World War involved arbitration, and a further innovation, not anticipated in the 1896 legislation, was the use made of ballots of workers to demonstrate strength of feeling. The Board of Trade also used the publication of its inquiries into disputes to discredit those who were opposed to the collective regulation, either employers who refused to recognize unions, or unions considered syndicalist.[67] What was critical about state intervention was the manner in which the British state used industrial conflict to shape a new industrial relations system, to "universalize a system which employers and unions had long been evolving for themselves."[68]

Halévy described Askwith as a "secret dictator" constructing "piece by piece throughout the United Kingdom a vast written code governing the relations between employers and employed, which if not strictly speaking law, nevertheless possessed a very binding force."[69] This account speaks to the influence of the Board of Trade, but neither Askwith nor the other conciliators were dictators, secret or otherwise. Their ability to act depended entirely on support from employers and unions.

On those occasions when an industrial dispute, because of growing economic interdependence, was likely to be especially damaging to the national economy, a greater element of compulsion was likely. The half decade before the First World War saw both more strikes and more potentially damaging strikes as coal, docks, and railroads experienced industrial conflict. This was the period of the Triple Alliance between the rail, mining, and transport (dockers') unions. As a result, state intervention became both more frequent and more laced with legislative compulsion. During the railroad strike of 1907, the threat of legislation setting up compulsory arbitration led the employers to agree to create boards of conciliation that effectively provided for an industry-wide agreement. Similarly, the mining strike of 1912 led to legislation that created joint boards in each district with the power to set wage minimums. But legislation followed only when divisions among employers made it impossible for them to reach agreement without the threat of compulsion to prevent defection.

Measuring the impact of this type of state intervention is inevitably difficult because we cannot know what industrial relations institutions would have emerged in the absence of a state role. The number of boards of conciliation and arbitration increased 500 percent between 1894 and 1913,[70] and new institutions of collective regulation were constructed in several major industries, including mining, textiles, and the railways. Between 1906 and 1914 the Board of Trade intervened in over 85 percent of major industrial disputes, resolving 75 percent of them. At least 17 percent of joint boards of conciliation and arbitration operating in 1914 originated as a by-product of settlements brokered by the Board of Trade, and these affected 27 percent of the organized labor force.[71] The foremost historian of the Board of Trade offers this cautious evaluation:

> it would appear that the shift in the labour policy of many organised employers after 1900 from confrontation to collaboration with the unions in the process of collective bargaining was, if not initially inspired, at least reinforced by the efforts of the Board of Trade's Labour Department.[72]

This evaluation fits with the argument of this chapter, that the primary role of state intervention was not to impose solutions and institutions on the industrial actors but to solve collective action problems, and to use the settlement of strikes to encourage the construction of industrial relations institutions.

The prewar period saw industrial relations legislation as well as more informal state intervention, which formed important components of the new industrial relations system. The 1906 Trade Disputes Act has already been mentioned, along with legislation affecting the mining industry. The 1909 Trade Boards

Act permitted the state to set up bargaining bodies, comprised of business and union representatives along with government officials, in low-wage industries where the industrial actors were not sufficiently organized. These bodies could then set minimum wages and conditions, which had the force of law in each industry where a trade board existed. The goal was explicitly to reduce wage competition and the resultant industrial conflict. As Winston Churchill, president of the board of trade in 1909, argued: "the good employers are undercut by the bad, and the bad are undercut by the worst."[73] Here, in microcosm, the new industrial relations system is visible. Where business and labor were sufficiently strong, the state tried to persuade them to create stable bargaining arrangements. Where they were not, the state did not directly regulate industry; rather, it set up bargaining institutions in embryo and allowed employers and unions to set wages, in the hope that they would develop into autonomous collective bargaining arrangements. Here, legislation ultimately enforced wage rates but was mediated by a form of collective bargaining institution.

Thus whereas in 1889 cotton weaving was the only industry to have a national collective bargaining agreement, by the outbreak of the First World War national agreements existed in engineering, shipbuilding, cotton spinning, construction, printing, iron and steel, and footwear.[74] Most of the coal industry operated under a single agreement, and collective bargaining was well established in many other industries; a Labour Department study estimated that 2.4 million workers were covered by industry-wide or district agreements in 1910, and that number excluded local-government workers and those covered only by firm-level agreements.[75] The outlines of the first industrial relations system were now in place, at least for the older staple industries, the ones most subject to a fragmented industrial structure and heightened competition. Collective bargaining was the result of growing organization on the part of trade unions and employers, and was a response to the industrial restructuring engendered by economic decline. But industry-level bargaining agreements would not have been as widespread in the absence of state action; in the manner of their intervention, government officials turned industrial conflict into industrial relations institutions.

WAR AND WHITLEY

The second stage in the development of this system of industrial relations took place during and immediately after the First World War, when industry bargaining became the preferred industrial relations institution. In the period immediately before the war, state intervention had focused on recognizing trade unions and creating conciliation machinery, but during and after the war the focus became regular collective bargaining, covering a range of bargaining issues.

This section will treat the impact of the First World War on industrial relations only briefly, even though national industry-wide collective bargaining took an enormous leap forward during the war as a result of state intervention. State intervention, in contrast to the prewar period, was direct and usually embodied in legislation. In part the limited attention paid to the wartime period in this chapter is because the story is well known and documented; every account of the development of British industrial relations, emphasizes the role of the two world wars. It is also because while the First World War "was important in terms of consolidating and extending this system of industrial relations,"[76] it did not change the trajectory of institutional development; war simply provided an opportunity for the state to extend elements of the prewar system of industrial relations more widely, and wartime developments largely maintained the existing industrial relations trajectory, keeping its essential components (emphasis on strong employer and union organizations, collective laissez-faire, industry bargaining) rather than shifting to a different, perhaps more statist, form of regulation. Indeed the experience of war made it clear that British governments were not seeking an alternative, more juridical industrial relations system, having been stymied previously in that goal by union and employer opposition. Rather, collective laissez-faire was precisely the goal. For the British state, wartime provided an opportunity to encourage the collective regulation of industrial relations and also to use public debate about postwar reconstruction to further shape discourse in that direction, which was what the Whitley Committee did.

The effect of wartime mobilization was to impose compulsory arbitration and a prohibition on strikes and lockouts on vast swaths of British industry. In "controlled establishments" profits were limited, and all work rules, customs, and practices that restricted production were suspended. The Munitions Act, passed in 1915 and subsequently amended to extend its reach, effectively imposed union recognition and industry bargaining in many areas for the duration of the war. The war extended national pay bargaining to the chemicals industry, road transport, wool, the railways, coal mining, and the public sector itself, for a total of at least four and a half million workers. If the million people in agriculture covered by statutory pay regulation are included, over a third of the employed labor force was covered by national pay bargaining by the end of 1917.[77]

War also encouraged the centralization of union and employer organizations,[78] largely because national wage bargaining shifted power to national officials, and because trade union officials became responsible for preventing their own members from damaging production through unofficial work stoppages and restrictive practices. This produced tension between local and national levels within unions where local officials had traditionally been responsible for bargaining, such as in the rail and engineering industries. The 1917 Trade Union (Amalgamation) Act, by easing the voting requirements for union mergers, also had the effect of encouraging mergers among unions and thereby contributing to larger, often more centralized, unions.[79]

As the war drew to an end and it was clear that more direct state regulation of industrial relations would be unacceptable to either business or unions (nor was there any expressed desire to maintain it within the wartime government), plans for the reconstruction of industrial relations were needed. The Whitley Committee was set up as part of this reconstruction process in late 1916. Its composition included employers and union leaders (though with no direct representation for the TUC) and a number of experts, described by one commentator as "mainly labour sympathisers."[80] The absence of both the TUC and employers' associations, despite the growing prominence of these organizations during the war, was an indication that any recommendations would likely emphasize industry- or district-level collective bargaining, familiar features of the first system of industrial relations, rather than peak-level corporatist bargaining. The preparation for postwar industrial relations reconstruction was precipitated by the anticipation of a resurgence of strikes once the wartime controls were lifted; indeed the recommendations of the Whitley Committee were forwarded to the Commission on Industrial Unrest, which was created in early 1917.

The Whitley Committee articulated the same principles of organization and voluntarism used by the 1894 royal commission. Its goal was to recommend mechanisms that would permit "continuous cooperation between employers and employed in each industry with a minimum of government interference."[81] Once again, strong class organizations were crucial: "an essential condition of securing a permanent improvement in the relations between employers and employed is that there should be adequate organisation on the part of both employers and workpeople."[82] What was novel was that the Whitley Committee now advocated a particular form of bargaining institution, the Joint Industrial Council (JIC), as the core of a new industrial relations system. Joint industrial councils were to be permanent industry-level bargaining arrangements, intended to encourage continuous cooperation rather than cooperation only in emergencies, and they were to be created in every industry where there was not existing industry-level bargaining machinery. The report issued by the committee recommended three levels of bargaining machinery—workplace, district, and industry—but the emphasis of the report, and the energy of government efforts after its approval, were directed almost exclusively at industry-level bargaining because of employer resistance to workplace bargaining. Industry bargaining responded to the very real collective action problem facing employers, while workplace bargaining challenged managerial prerogative. Where employers saw benefit to bargaining within their own firms, they were free to create bargaining machinery; a role for state action, and hence the focus of the Whitley Report, appeared where achieving multi-employer bargaining voluntarily was difficult.

The report argued strongly that state action was no substitute for voluntary collective bargaining between employers and unions, but it did see an important role for the state in encouraging the creation of joint industrial councils in industries where something similar did not already exist. The report urged the government to approach employers' organizations and unions to propose the formation of joint industrial councils, to chair meetings bringing the two sides together, and to circulate "information from industry to industry so that all should have the benefit of the experience of all."[83] As with the 1894 royal commission, state intervention was to be informal and administrative, to help overcome divisions within the employer or union side, or mistrust between the two sides, and to spread what would today be called "best practice." The distinctiveness of the British state's intervention in industrial relations remained.

However, two pieces of legislation did follow the Whitley Report, and they closely followed its logic. The 1918 Trade Boards Act amended the original 1909 act of the same name to widen the conditions under which trade boards could be created. The 1918 act empowered the newly created Ministry of Labour to set up trade boards not just in low-wage industries but also where employers or unions were too poorly organized to create bargaining institutions on their own. This extension of the role of trade boards followed from a recommendation of the Whitley Report, which envisaged that ultimately there be "two classes of industries in the country—industries with Industrial Councils and industries with Trade Boards."[84] Thus the goal was that all industries would be covered by one or the other; the power to create trade boards could also be used by government officials to persuade employers and unions to set up JICs instead. Again, the labor market was to not to be directly regulated by the state, but neither was it to be left regulated only by market forces. Rather, regulation would take place as a result of either collective bargaining or institutions that mimicked collective bargaining, with the hope that they would develop into entirely voluntary collective bargaining institutions.

The second piece of legislation was the 1919 Industrial Courts Act, which empowered the Ministry of Labour also to create industrial courts in order to look into important industrial conflicts. The role of public opinion in influencing such disputes (and courts tended to be created to avert a national strike, in notorious "trouble spots," and where a strike was likely to be highly disruptive to the public) was the justification used for the Industrial Courts Act. The vast majority of the seventy-five courts set up between 1919 and 1965 were composed of three people, one representing employers, one labor, and a neutral chair. Both pieces of legislation demonstrated a preference for indirect state intervention and for the creation of institutions to mimic regulation by employers and trade unions.

Following the acceptance of the Whitley Report by the cabinet, favorable comment in the press, and a survey of employers and union organizations, the Board of Trade set up meetings in a range of industries where bargaining machinery did not exist, and encouraged industrial actors to first attend and then create institutions along the model of the Joint Industrial Council. It is clear that state encouragement in various ways played a central role in the creation of many of the joint industrial councils.[85] The railways and docks got joint industrial councils following the recommendations of a government inquiry and the intervention of the prime minister. Many of the industries that accepted joint industrial councils readily were ones that had been first organized during the war as a result of state action. And Charles estimates that a further eleven industries required state persuasion to set up their joint industrial councils. It is important to be clear that state action was necessary not so much to overcome an ideological objection to bargaining but because the industries were too poorly organized to set up bargaining institutions on their own. The problem was thus one of collective action. Ministry of Labour officials recognized that they could not compel collective bargaining, and they did not try. But the momentum for the creation of joint industrial councils was encouraged by government action, either threatening to impose trade boards in poorly organized industries or promising that the resulting councils would be "the sole authoritative voice of an industry" in well-organized industries.[86]

The period between 1918 and 1921, after which no new joint industrial councils were created, saw an extensive and ambitious experiment in the state-sponsored construction of industrial relations. Whitleyism "constituted a public and official recognition of trade unionism and collective bargaining as the basis of industrial relations," and collective bargaining "was authoritatively pronounced normal and necessary, and was extended, potentially if not actually, over the whole field of wage-employment."[87] Evaluating this experiment is not easy. Seventy-four joint industrial councils were created, covering about two million workers,[88] and by 1921 there were sixty-three trade boards, covering about three million people, mostly women.[89] By no means did all the joint industrial councils survive, and among those that did, there was a wide range in the frequency and scope of bargaining. But it is clear that the state was able to direct bargaining toward a particular kind of industrial relations institution: industry bargaining. The decade of the 1920s was not a propitious time for the development and spread of collective bargaining, as we will see below. But the institutional form of the Joint Industrial Council survived, and when collective bargaining was again considered in the 1930s, it took the familiar shape of the joint industrial council. When employers and trade unions came to construct collective bargaining machinery, they picked institutional forms they were familiar with. It is also worth noting that, after the Second World War, joint industrial councils were created in every one of the newly nationalized industries; hence the expansion of the public sector through the extensive nationalization program also served to spread the Whitley model of industry bargaining.[90]

DECLINE AND CONSOLIDATION

The first half of the 1920s proved to be the high-water mark for the spread of industry-level collective regulation of industrial relations (whether by collective bargaining or trade boards) until the Second World War. Gospel has estimated that by 1920 there were 2,500 multiemployer agreements, covering half the working population,[91] and Milner's time series data suggest that 57—60 percent of those in employment were covered by either national collective agreements or statutory wage machinery in 1925.[92] No new joint industrial councils or trade boards were created until the 1930s. Trade union density peaked at 45.2 percent in 1920 before collapsing to 22.9 percent in 1933,[93] the coverage of collective bargaining and statutory wage machinery also halved by 1930,[94] and highly publicized experiments in peak-level concertation, such as the National Industrial Conference, failed to take hold.

Nevertheless, the core elements of the first system of industrial relations remained in place, and after a relatively brief period of decline in the 1920s the impact of the Depression revived efforts to stabilize markets using industrial relations institutions to limit market competition. What is remarkable, given that union density halved in such a short period, is not that the tide of industry-level bargaining ebbed in the 1920s but that the industrial relations institutions created over the previous three decades were not washed away altogether. The defeat of organized labor in the 1926 General Strike provided ample opportunity for employers and the state, had they wished, to construct an alternative form of regulation.[95] However, after 1926 "no major group of employers withdrew recognition at national or district level" outside of the coal industry.[96] That we can identify an essential continuity from the prewar and First World War period through the interwar period testifies to the useful social and economic function that the first system of industrial relations performed. The system of industrial relations survived this period primarily because enough employers believed that it benefited them. In Clegg's words: "by 1939, therefore, it must be assumed that organized employers in Britain had secured a system of collective bargaining which suited them."[97]

The period immediately following the First World War did see the failure of an attempt to create a permanent peak-level forum for the negotiated resolution of industrial problems, the National Industrial Conference (NIC).[98] In 1919 six hundred trade unionists and three hundred employers met and selected representatives for a provisional joint committee that, it was hoped, would examine and offer recommendations in the areas of industrial relations procedures, a minimum wage, maximum hours, and unemployment. Yet after several meetings and no progress, the joint committee resigned in 1921. At the end of the 1920s another attempt to use peak-level bargaining to solve industrial problems, the Mond-Turner talks, also failed.

The reasons for the failure of these experiments have been exhaustively examined by scholars.[99] The fragmentation and disunity of the main employer and labor organizations, and their inability to overcome the divergent interests of their members, overwhelmed the NIC, not least because the threat of industrial unrest that had propelled the creation of the conference in 1919 had subsided by 1921. The Mond-Turner talks suffered from the unrepresentativeness of the industries participating on the employer side. Mond and his fellow progressive employers came from larger firms, in more modern industries, less concerned about the conditions of brutal market competition in declining industries. Fulcher has also examined this period in order to explain the failure of attempts to create central regulation, in contrast to Sweden, and he has argued that employers had no need to create such regulation, because the state took on the role of controlling unions, and unions were not strong enough to require a coordinated employer response.[100] It is certainly the case that the British state was more prepared in the 1920s to intervene to prevent strikes, though its repressive role was relatively muted, even after the defeat of the General Strike in 1926.

The organizational weakness of employers and labor, the structure of British industry, and the role of the state help to explain why one possible industrial relations trajectory, central regulation through the construction of corporatist institutions, did not occur. Given the nature of class organization in Britain, corporatism was probably structurally unavailable. However, not only is there no natural progression from industry-level to peak-level bargaining, but as Lowe has argued, the development of one could undermine the other.[101] The short-lived NIC, with its discussion of a minimum wage and hours of work, threatened the autonomy of joint industrial councils. The Whitley Committee, in its composition, was explicitly noncorporatist; it followed the path of industry bargaining laid out in the prewar period. The institution of joint industrial councils held out the promise of managing industry-specific problems of market competition and industrial conflict, which were quite different from the problems that corporatist institutions had the potential to solve. Industry bargaining and corporatist peak-level bargaining were two alternative trajectories for British industrial relations, not different way stations on the same continuum.

THE TREASURY VERSUS THE MINISTRY OF LABOUR

The indirect administrative role played by the Board of Trade was central to the spread of collective industrial relations regulation in the decade or so prior to the First World War, particularly after the 1906 Trade Disputes Act limited the industrial relations influence of the judiciary. In 1916, as a concession to the Labour Party for support of the wartime governing coalition, the Ministry of Labour was created, and the industrial relations functions of the Board of Trade were transferred to it. Yet, paradoxically, this achievement of a long-term goal on the part of organized labor soon coincided with a decline in the influence of the new ministry over the development of industrial relations policy.

This decline can be attributed to a number of factors, including the leading personnel of the Ministry of Labour; to a certain extent it lacked "archetypal Edwardian pro-consuls" like George Askwith, willing to engage in such a single-minded crusade to create procedures to manage industrial conflict.[102] But the main source of the Ministry of Labour's impotence was less changed personnel or changed practice than changed context. The core principles on which ministry officials operated were strikingly similar to those of the old Labour Department of the Board of Trade. The ministry emphasized "industrial self-government," meaning that employers and unions should collectively regulate conditions in their industries with as little interference from the state as possible, with strict impartiality between capital and labor, and, where state intervention did take place, its central goal was to create industrial relations procedures to manage conflict. These were barely changed from the guiding principles of the 1894 royal commission.

After 1921, however, a new rival for influence over industrial relations policy arose to challenge the Ministry of Labour: the Treasury. As the threat of industrial unrest declined, and with it the urgency of a strategy of containment, the view of the Treasury, which was more influenced by laissez-faire than collective laissez-faire, prevailed over the Ministry of Labour. The British Treasury, as the most potent locus of the interests of financial capital within the state, had a quite different set of priorities from those of government departments that saw themselves as catering to British industry. The precedence accorded the interests of the City of London are a persistent theme of Britain's long, painful economic decline. The Treasury's influence within the state increased after 1919, when the head of the Treasury was made head of the civil service, and all recommendations for increased expenditure had to be submitted to the Treasury before going to the cabinet.

From 1921 onward the Treasury waged an unrelenting war on the industrial relations functions of the Ministry of Labour. It attacked the very goals of strengthening trade unions and using trade boards to create a minimum wage, on the orthodox economic grounds that both destroy jobs by interfering in the labor market, even arguing that having industrial relations officials created rather than reduced industrial unrest! At the Treasury's urging the Cave Committee on reform of the trade boards recommended in 1921 that the 1918 amendment to the Trade Boards Act (expanding the conditions under which trade boards could be set up) be repealed. The government chose not to legislate such a change, but it endorsed the spirit of the Cave Report, and after that point the creation of new trade boards slowed to a trickle. The ministry was sufficiently intimidated by Treasury pressure that even prior to the Cave Report the ministry had, for the first time, refused to accept the minimum wage proposed by the Grocery Trade Board. In 1922 the Geddes Committee challenged the very principle of state intervention in industrial relations, and the existence of the Ministry of Labour, but the cabinet rejected such a radical proposal. The Treasury achieved a similar end, though, through the use of its budgetary powers to restrict the industrial relations functions of the ministry, including a refusal to accept the appointment of local conciliation officers. Economies forced on the Ministry of Labour reduced the staff in its Industrial Relations Department from 229 in 1919 to 28 in 1924, and led to the disbanding of the Labour Intelligence and Joint Industrial Council divisions.[103]

As a result, the Ministry of Labour was able to have an influence only at the margins of public policy, though that influence was discernible. The ministry's consistent arguments in favor of collective laissez-faire, and against legislative compulsion, served to limit challenges to the main outlines of the first system of industrial relations. This was particularly important following the General Strike, when some employers and members of the Conservative Party wanted to use the defeat of the labor movement as an opportunity to repeal the 1875 Conspiracy Act and the 1906 Trade Disputes Act and introduce compulsory strike ballots and arbitration. The 1927 Trade Disputes and Trade Unions Act was far less punitive, primarily preventing public-sector unions from affiliating to the TUC and threatening the Labour Party's source of funding from unions by insisting that union members contract into rather than out of paying the political levy.

This essentially negative role—limiting challenges to the existing institutions of industrial relations, but not extending them—changed again with the onset of the Depression, which accentuated competitive pressures, encouraging smaller firms to resort to wage undercutting. The British state became more active in seeking to stabilize markets and, once again, looked to industrial relations institutions to limit competition. As the Ministry of Labour reported on its activities in 1934:

> It has been the deliberate policy of the Department to take every opportunity of stimulating the establishment of joint voluntary machinery or of strengthening that already in existence. It cannot be doubted that the operation of lower conditions than those observed by no less successful and efficient employers creates a problem which is bound to become more prominent unless there is an increase in voluntary co-operation and in recognition of agreed standards.[104]

To a certain extent, the threat of strikes resulting from wage competition provided the impetus for state intervention, but unions were simply too weak to impose bargaining, and, for the most part, it was employers who sought external protection from competition. During the 1930s the Ministry of Labour played the familiar role of broker, encouraging employers and unions to reach agreement and to create permanent bargaining machinery. But the state's role was also more direct, and legislation played a bigger part in the construction of industrial relations institutions.

The 1934 Cotton Manufacturing Industry (Temporary Provisions) Act and the 1938 Road Haulage Wages Act illustrate this form of state action, in that they made wage levels set by joint union and employer boards legally enforceable across their respective industries. The cotton industry suffered particularly badly in the Depression, and wage cutting led to two large strikes in 1932. Initially the Ministry of Labour appointed a conciliator who helped both sides to reach the "Midland Agreement," which set out a new conciliation process and a set of market stabilizing measures. When this agreement collapsed, because it was being ignored by smaller firms and nonfederated firms, the unions and the employers' association that represented the larger manufacturers supported the 1934 legislation, giving the force of law to the Midland Agreement.[105] Similar high levels of competition characterized the road haulage industry. Once again the Ministry of Labour was instrumental in creating a National Joint Conciliation Board for the industry, and once again it was insufficient to set industry-wide wages and conditions. The 1938 Road Haulage Wages Act set up a national wages board and ten district wages boards, comprised of employers, unionists, and some independents. Once the boards recommended wage rates, the Minister of Labour could make them legally enforceable.

The two, by now familiar, points to note are, first, that industrial relations institutions took on the broader function of not only regulating class conflict but also regulating market competition, and, second, that the practice of the British state was to construct embryonic institutions for collective regulation, even when one or both parties were too weakly organized to do so themselves, and to provide them with legal buttressing if necessary. The state was seeking to encourage collective laissez-faire, when the opportunity arose, not simply to regulate competition. The result was that, as Clegg has argued, "the 1930s must be one of the most productive periods of state intervention in industrial relations."[106]

Collective bargaining was extended in the 1930s, in part as a result of state action, and in part from the spread of bargaining into new areas independent of state action. Furthermore, even where collective bargaining already existed, there is evidence that more employers were willing to join employer federations to use the benefits of dispute procedures and industry-wide terms of employment.[107] The Ministry of Labour refused to act unless both unions and employers supported its actions, and its willingness to intervene followed from a renewed interest in collective bargaining on the part of employers:

> Most extensions of collective bargaining came where unions were relatively weak.
> They lacked the strength to force the employers to the bargaining table; and in most

instances the employers did not have to be forced. They wanted to come, if they could have the assurance that their competitors would not be able to undercut them by evading the agreement.[108]

It was this assurance that the British state was willing to provide in the 1930s.

THE STATE AND INSTITUTIONAL CONSTRUCTION

The period covered by this chapter saw the construction of Britain's first national industrial relations system, one centered on industry-level bargaining between trade unions and employer organizations. At the beginning of the period, only the cotton-weaving industry had a collective bargaining procedure, and collective wage-setting covered fewer than one in ten of the labor force. Milner's time series data on the coverage of collective pay-setting institutions charts the changes over the next fifty years.[109] His estimates for those covered by national collective agreements *and* statutory wage machinery (primarily trade boards) show a rise in coverage to 15–16 percent in 1910, 50–57 percent by 1918 (with 17–20 percent accounted for by statutory machinery), and 57–60 percent by 1925 (with 22–25 percent accounted for by statutory machinery). Coverage then declines to 29–30 percent in 1930 (with only 10 percent a result of statutory machinery) before recovering to 38–40 percent in 1935 (9–11 percent accounted for by statutory machinery) and 49–52 percent in 1940 (with 12–15 percent the result of statutory machinery).

Two points are worth making about these figures. First, if one excludes the First World War and its immediate aftermath, the overall rate of coverage shows a relatively steady upward progression rather than wild fluctuation. While the war clearly had an important impact on the development of British industrial relations, it is hard to see its impact as determinative. Second, the importance of statutory wage regulation in the form of trade boards was most important early in the interwar period, when as many as 20 percent of employees benefited from minimum-wage legislation. As trade union density declined, direct state wage regulation came, for a brief period, to substitute for collective bargaining, creating an alternative, statutory floor under wage levels. Thus the role of the state was important in spreading the coverage of industry-level collective wage-setting, both through the encouragement of voluntary bargaining institutions and through the spread of statutory wage-setting machinery. By the Second World War, the central elements of what became known as collective laissez-faire were in place, faithfully following the path laid out by the 1894 Royal Commission on Labour.

This first system of industrial relations enjoyed a high degree of political consensus, permitting the long-term stability of these bargaining institutions. It is remarkable that the core elements of state policy on industrial relations remained the same for a period of close to seventy years, until the 1960s, encompassing Liberal, Conservative, and Labour governments, two World Wars, and two depressions. This degree of consensus is explained by the nature of the economic problems that the country faced, the role that industrial relations institutions played in solving those problems, and by the success of public inquiries, such as the 1894 royal commission and the Whitley Committee, in mobilizing public opinion and creating political space for the construction of this set of industrial relations.

Despite the fact that plenty of studies have demonstrated, for this or that industry, that the British state played an important part in creating the conditions for collective bargaining to take place, state intervention in British industrial relations still tends to be seen as the exception, or at least as ad hoc, incoherent, and reactive. In fact, what industry-by-industry studies miss is that state intervention was the rule, not the exception, it was coherent, and it was consistent: state action encouraged the construction of a particular set of industrial relations institutions whenever the opportunity arose.

State intervention in Britain during this first construction phase took a distinctive form, one that sets it apart in comparative perspective. The British state appeared at best a silent partner in this system of industrial relations, organized as it was around a limited role for labor law in the regulation of social relations, with the provision of immunities to override common law and permit voluntary collective bargaining, no statutory obligation to bargain, no statutory right to union recognition, no compulsory arbitration, and only limited regulation of the internal affairs of trade unions. There was very little direct legislative intervention, and very little action that directly aided the spread of trade unions. Instead, the most important action of the state was to encourage the creation of bargaining institutions, either indirectly through persuasion and mediation during disputes, or directly in industries marked by high levels of conflict, in the public sector, and through trade boards. The British state helped to construct a bargaining structure rather than a comprehensive legislative framework of industrial relations. There was also direct intervention by the state on an industry-by-industry basis as part of efforts to reorganize declining industries. State action to restructure a declining industry was always accompanied by reform of industrial relations to ensure that union recognition and collective bargaining existed. Mining, rail transport, cotton, and iron and steel were only the largest industries to see this kind of construction of industrial relations institutions, the price paid by employers to be saved from destructive competition. All in all, the main influence of the state was through its intervention in industrial disputes, with the goal of creating permanent bargaining institutions, and through its creating a climate of opinion in which collective bargaining with trade unions was presumed to be in the national interest.

The British state was not monolithic with regard to industrial relations policy. The pre–First World War Board of Trade and later the Ministry of Labour were in competition with the Treasury for control of labor policy, with the former having the upper hand at key points in the first two decades of the century before losing out to the Treasury in the 1920s. Broadly, the influence of the Board of Trade and the Ministry of Labour waxed and waned with the strike rate; they were most able to play a role when industrial conflict was high, at which times it could credibly be argued that state intervention was needed to reduce conflict. Similarly, the judiciary was consistently hostile in its decisions to undermine the legal basis of union strike activity, and was influential until the 1906 Trade Disputes Act banished judges from a role in the regulation of class conflict.

State intervention had an economic function. It responded to the particular economic context of the long decline of Britain's old staple industries (encouraged by growing international competition) and of accelerating national economic interdependence, such that industrial conflict in one industry could rapidly affect production in other industries. Thus collective bargaining was rarely simply a concession to the growing strength of organized labor. Instead it enlisted the support of organized labor in an effort to regulate markets. State intervention was required to overcome the resistance of some employers to collective bargaining and to fashion the institutions of collective regulation. The first system of industrial relations contained a "positive sum class compromise" for trade unions and employers.[110] From the perspective of employers, industry bargaining enlisted the support of unions in limiting industrial conflict through procedure agreements, and it established minimum industry-wide rates of pay, wage predictability, and a reduction in wage competition while choking off local wage variations. At the same time, managerial prerogative in the workplace was reasserted and embedded in collective agreements. Nothing in the system of industry bargaining precluded individual firms from developing particular workplace industrial relations institutions if they chose. The first system of industrial relations offered, in short, both managerial control in the workplace and market control over wages in the labor market.[111] Trade unions gained recognition through industry associations, which helped them to both recruit and maintain members, and some leveling up of conditions in localities where they were weak. Industry agreements were probably also less vulnerable to abrogation in bad economic times than individual firm-by-firm agreements, and, as Zeitlin has argued, industry-level industrial relations institutions formed a beachhead from which unions could advance in better economic times.[112]

Although the manner in which the British state intervened was distinctive and important, this cannot plausibly be termed state autonomy. Bargaining could not be imposed on business and labor, and when legislation was used it was only after both had signaled that they wanted it. Even during wartime, when the capacity of the state to impose industrial relations was relatively great, the British state used the opportunity to extend and encourage the form of industrial relations that had been developing for the previous two decades rather than to impose a different one. The state acted primarily when levels of social conflict were so high that it had to intervene, and when it could encourage industrial relations practices that solved some collective action problem for business and labor. It acted to reduce conflict and to regulate competition, and it acted on the presumption that regular industry-level collective bargaining was the way to achieve those ends. Because of the fluctuating economic conditions in each industry, bargaining was unstable. Sometimes, as in the 1930s, the state was drawn into more direct regulation of the industry, and industry bargaining institutions went through cycles, becoming active and then moribund, as the need for bargaining varied.

ALTERNATIVES AND CONSEQUENCES

During this period there were two points at which alternative sets of industrial relations institutions were considered. First, between 1895 and 1906, some employers, trade unionists representing weaker unions, and members of public commissions raised the issue of compulsory arbitration, based on the experience of New Zealand, Australia, and Canada, offering an indirect statutory route to union recognition in return for limitations on the right to strike. In a similar vein the 1906 Royal Commission on Trade Disputes and Trade Combinations, despite a very narrow remit to examine the recent judicial decisions on strikes, recommended a set of positive trade union rights.[113] Both initiatives failed because of the context of the judicial onslaught then underway. Trade unions responded to a hostile judiciary by seeking negative immunities instead of positive rights, which only reinforced a form of state practice that emphasized indirect administrative action rather than the use of labor law to create industrial relations institutions. This first alternative path, of positive rights and a greater role for statutory regulation, reappeared in the 1960s, with the same outcome.

The second alternative was corporatism, which enjoyed a brief period of popularity immediately after the end of the First World War. However, the experience of class collaboration during wartime was artificial and could not be sustained by the relatively weak class organizations of business and labor after the war. The strength of class organization lay at the industry level, not the confederal level, and it was unclear what equivalent positive-sum class compromise was available for the construction of corporatist institutions. But this alternative, too, was rediscovered after the Second World War, though with scarcely much more success than in the 1920s.

What of the consequences of state intervention on organized labor? Clearly it had an impact on union strength and membership; the periods of greatest growth in union membership corresponded to the periods of greatest state intervention, particularly wartime. Union density doubled between 1892 and 1913, and then again between 1913 and 1920.[114] But union membership fluctuated wildly, much more so than the institutions of bargaining. The far more important impact was that of the form of state intervention on the organization, practice, and ideology of trade unions.

Clegg has argued that the most significant trend in union internal governance in the interwar period was a centralization of union structures.[115] Industry bargaining encouraged a centralization of unions, which directed resources toward relatively high-level bargaining, usually by professional negotiators, and forced the leadership of unions to police their members, limiting industrial conflict and preventing leapfrogging wage demands. The 1917 Trade Union (Amalgamation) Act further encouraged both a centralization and a concentration of trade unions, and it was followed by a wave of mergers (the peak of merger activity prior to the Second World War was 1918–24) as unions sought structures more appropriate to national bargaining. The shape of trade union structural reform during this period involved both a shift from loosely organized union federations to single unions and a greater centralization over resources within unions.[116] A diffusion of power upward, toward full-time union officials and professional negotiators and toward national officials, was the primary organizational response to the first system of industrial relations on the part of unions.

Heery and Kelly have argued that British trade unionism has gone through three organizational phases, based on the "servicing relationship" between unions and their members, since the Second World War.[117] The first form, "professional unionism," which developed in response to the rise of industry bargaining in the interwar period, was characterized by "reliance upon a cadre of professional representatives to service a largely passive membership, principally through the medium of collective bargaining."[118] This had a certain logic to it when unions and collective regulation were largely absent from the workplace, so that bargaining over production issues was rare and the focus of union activity was instead national-level bargaining over pay. It implied a limited role for lay representatives of unions, indeed a defensive reaction to "challenges from below," and considerable autonomy for professional negotiators.[119] In the long term this contributed to the split that opened up in the 1950s and 1960s between full-time union officials and lay trade union officials inside the workplace (known as shop stewards). The relative paucity of resources devoted to developing union capacities inside the firm created space for shop stewards to emerge in response to the plant-level demands of both workers and managers.

The most important effect of this first system of industrial relations, for future developments, was that trade unions gained recognition largely *indirectly*, through industry bargaining. As Bain has argued, "Employers' associations have many functions but, from the trade unionists' point of view, one of the their most important has been to act as relay stations for transmitting minimum terms and conditions of employment, including union recognition throughout an entire industry."[120] This had several effects. First, unions became dependent for recruiting new members on employers and the state, who, in effect, recruited members for unions. There were certainly exceptions, but overall this contributed to relatively weak recruitment capacities on the part of unions, which would lead to problems in the future. When industry bargaining collapsed, employers and the state would come to challenge the collective regulation of industrial relations and would seek a decentralization of industrial relations institutions to the workplace. But by that time trade unions were often ill equipped to recruit new members and retain existing ones.

Second, this industrial relations system reinforced the ideology of voluntarism. British unions seemed able to thrive without the raft of legislative rights provided to their American, French, or Swedish counterparts. Demands for a right to union recognition from employers, along the lines of that provided in the Wagner Act in the United States seemed redundant because industry bargaining had the same effect. In effect, the original trade union preference for negative immunities, which was a response to hostile courts, became translated into a myth of bootstrap voluntarism, according to which trade unions had triumphed over employer and state opposition by virtue of their own autonomous strength and resources.[121] This perception became most widespread and powerful within the labor movement (and much of the academic industrial relations community) in the late 1960s and early 1970s, as we shall see in the next chapter. Its result was that British unions consistently underestimated their debt to the state, and they failed to recognize the dangers posed by a withdrawal of state support for trade unionism and collective bargaining.

The third important long-term result of this set of industrial relations institutions was also related to the emphasis on immunities rather than positive rights.[122] Legal immunities for unions offer some protection from the state, primarily the judiciary, whereas positive rights can offer protection from the economic power of employers. In the absence of those rights—to organize, to gain recognition, to collectively bargain, to strike—trade unions must depend on their own economic strength to challenge employers.[123] In underestimating their dependence on the state, British trade unions also failed to recognize that, in seeking to protect themselves from the state, they were giving up the potential of winning state protection from employers.

By the middle of the 1960s, in the context of a mounting cacophony of concern about relative economic decline and rising industrial unrest, the reform of British industrial relations had returned to the top of the political agenda. The nature of the challenges facing the economy, and the form in which class conflict manifested itself, had changed dramatically. But the legacy of this first set of industrial relations institutions for the structures, practices, and "rationalized meaning systems"[124] of the main industrial actors proved profoundly important for the construction of Britain's next industrial relations system.

Donovan, Dissension, and the Decentralization of Industrial Relations, 1940–1979

Between 1890 and 1921 a set of industrial relations institutions, which can legitimately be collectively labeled a system, was put in place. This system was organized around industry-level collective bargaining between trade unions and employer associations. It encompassed limited mechanisms for the collective regulation of social relations in the workplace (though such institutions did develop in a handful of industries—newspapers, mining, and some parts of engineering, for example) and practically no multiindustry, or corporatist, bargaining. Legal regulation of collective action and collective bargaining was also limited, with labor law facilitating, generalizing, and providing some legal support for the voluntary system. As Wedderburn has argued, labor law was never abstentionist; rather, after 1906, it insulated industrial relations from judge-made common law and assigned primacy to collective bargaining.[1]

The main outlines of this system of industrial relations were clear soon after the end of the First World War. There followed a decade of labor weakness, when the institutions largely survived but ceased to expand beyond the core industries where they had been created prior to and during the war. But from the beginning of the 1930s, in part in response to accelerated competitive pressures in staple industries, industry-level bargaining once again began to spread, a process that was dramatically accelerated by the onset of the Second World War. The commitment of postwar governments to macroeconomic policies designed to maintain full employment stabilized this system, and trade unions and the British state mopped up those areas of the economy which had resisted collective regulation up to that point. By the 1950s, when Kahn-Freund was celebrating the maturity of Britain's system of collective laissez-faire, while the first system of industrial relations had become more formalized, and almost universal, it was, paradoxically, also on the verge of far-reaching transformation.

This industrial relations system had emerged in response to the long-term decline of Britain's staple industries, the growing interdependence and hence vulnerability of the national economy, and a greater propensity on the part of workers and their unions to strike. The industrial relations institutions that emerged during the early part of the twentieth century represented a particular class compromise between the growing strength of organized labor and the interests of employers in the declining staple industries. Collective bargaining was usually a second-best solution for employers, jealous of managerial prerogatives, but the form that bargaining took was shaped by employer responses to intense levels of competition under conditions of fragmented and dispersed ownership and long-term decline. The first system of industrial relations served to limit market competition and industrial unrest while leaving employers free to organize and manage the workplace as they wished. In Gospel's terms, employers pursued a strategy of "externalizing" industrial relations outside the firm.[2]

By the mid-1950s it was clear that the center of gravity of British industry had shifted from the old staples (though industries such as textiles and mining continued their slow, painful decline) to newer, more recognizably Fordist firms, for which the system of industry-level collective bargaining was at best irrelevant and at worst a hindrance to growth. The second system of industrial relations shifted attention from industry bargaining to the firm itself, "internalizing" industrial relations.[3] Once again, the restructuring of industrial relations institutions was a response to pressure from workers and their trade unions, heightened by postwar conditions of full employment (in contrast to consistently higher unemployment levels in the first half of the century). But again the particular form that the new institutions that emerged in this period took was shaped by a new industrial structure and a new set of challenges facing employers. A different set of industries with more capital-intensive firms and a more concentrated ownership structure was less concerned with wage competition than with improving the productivity of existing factors of production. The system of industry-level bargaining failed both to offer a mechanism for managing change in the workplace and to limit competition. Heightened international competition and the process of European economic integration limited the practicality of using domestic institutions to dampen market competition. Under these conditions, employers increasingly recognized that they could not modernize and reorganize the workplace without a new set of industrial relations institutions, and that unilateral action on their part would elicit worker resistance. The second system of industrial relations sought to create institutions to involve trade unions in economic restructuring inside the firm both to manage change and to limit resistance.

As Britain's comparative economic decline became apparent, and a discourse of economic crisis came to dominate political debate, the remarkable political and social consensus that had supported the old system of industrial relations for more than half a century collapsed, bringing with it new projects of industrial relations reform and reawakening judicial activism, with its traditional hostility to collective action in the economic sphere. Once again, an increase in the level of strikes, and a shift in their form, created the trigger for industrial relations reform.

In this context a second system of industrial relations emerged from its existence in a few scattered industries to become dominant throughout the economy in the course of the 1960s and 1970s. The core features of this second system were the institutionalization of collective regulation directly inside the firm, and the extension of formal joint regulation beyond pay, hours, and dispute procedures to the whole range of issues related to labor productivity. Thus this second system involved a decentralization of collective bargaining to the firm and workplace level, the development of more formal and extensive workplace capacities for trade unions, a shift in the scope of bargaining to include work practices, work organization, technology, and so on, and the construction of a raft of new individual rights at work. Ultimately, the logic of this system implied movement toward the creation of institutions of industrial democracy inside the firm, institutionalizing the collective regulation of work.

These were all elements that had been largely ignored in the system of industry bargaining, where social relations inside the firm were either left to unilateral regulation by the employer or informally negotiated in scattered areas where groups of workers were able to develop some degree of job control. Here bargaining was heavily dependent on conjunctural factors influencing the balance of class power. Once again, the British state played an important role in the construction phase of this new decentralized system of industrial relations, encouraging and generalizing changes in the regulation of the wage relationship and the management of industrial conflict, though this time legislation played a more important and direct role. The Royal Commission on Trade Unions and Employers' Associations, which reported in 1968, set the agenda of industrial relations reform with a basic diagnosis of the ills of the old system. While some of the report's specific prescriptions were challenged, it was profoundly influential, mobilizing opinion within unions and among employers, and creating political space for state reform efforts. During this period the state acted more directly than in the period preceding and immediately following the First World War to provide new rights at work, to encourage unions and employers to create new workplace institutions of industrial relations, and to extend what it considered "best practice" from a few firms and sectors to new areas of the economy, including the public sector.

In a fundamental sense, the second system of industrial relations was a failure. It never enjoyed the degree of political consensus of the first system, and it collapsed following the "Winter of Discontent" wave of strikes and subsequent electoral victory of the Conservative Party, led by Margaret Thatcher, in 1979. The industrial relations reform project was undermined by wage restraint policies that made reform hostage to economic crisis management, and by resistance on the part of a group of employers for whom the institutionalization of trade union power inside the firm was vastly more threatening than the system of industry-level bargaining had ever been.

That said, there has been too little recognition paid to the extent to which many of the institutional elements of the second system of industrial relations did take root; the central locus of industrial relations regulation did shift downward to the firm, a dense network of workplace industrial relations institutions did appear, the focus of collective bargaining did expand to include the organization of work, and substantive legal regulation of work became embedded in the framework of labor law. This set of changes in turn set the scene for the Thatcherite project of industrial relations reform, which built upon and accelerated the decentralization of industrial relations but encouraged a shift from collective to individual regulation of social relations at work. Without the intervention of the second project of reform, the third, Thatcherite project would have been quite different.

And what of the impact of this period on the trade unions? They were the big losers of this period, cast as the villains of the piece, responsible for economic decline and political sclerosis. Events in this period initially reinforced the voluntarist ideology of the labor movement. But it is worth noting that an alternative path was possible in the first half of the 1960s, a branching point, which would have led toward a quite different system of industrial relations, one embodying a legal framework of positive collective rights at work, implying a new relationship between law and industrial relations institutions. This alternative was rejected in the second half of the 1960s, in the context of incomes policies and punitive legislation. Nevertheless, it reappeared two decades later, to become the dominant trade union response to the Thatcherite project of industrial relations reform, and the intellectual core of its Blairite successor.

THE HIGH POINT OF COLLECTIVE LAISSEZ-FAIRE

The Second World War and immediate postwar settlement saw a reinforcement of the collective laissez-faire, industry-level bargaining system of industrial relations, with the state once again playing a leading role in its extension. Gospel has estimated that by 1945 there were about five hundred national institutions in which employer associations negotiated with trade unions.[4] Milner's study of the coverage of collective pay-setting institutions shows that overall coverage by national collective agreements jumped from somewhere between 49 and 52 percent in 1940 to 71–73 percent in 1950, and then stayed at roughly that level until the second half of the 1960s. Of the 20 percentage-point increase between 1940 and 1950, roughly half came from an expansion of collective bargaining and half from an expansion of statutory wage-setting, primarily in low-wage industries.[5] The importance of industry bargaining and state substitutes for collective bargaining can be seen in the fact that the overall coverage of collective pay-setting agreements was a good 30 percentage points higher than the level of trade union density during this period; the institutions of the first system of industrial relations had spread the influence of collective regulation well beyond the unionized labor force.

The expansion of the public sector, through both the nationalization of key industries and the enlargement of public services, particularly local government, healthcare, and education, contributed to the spread of the industry bargaining model; in almost every case, Whitley industrial relations structures were introduced. Nationalization had the effect of centralizing decision-making in industries that had previously been under fragmented private ownership. In the coal industry, for example, the National Coal Board took over 1,470 collieries owned by eight hundred mining companies.[6] The resulting structures permitted genuine national bargaining, ensured that comprehensive consultative machinery was created, and led to the extension of collective bargaining to white-collar and even some managerial employees.[7] During the early decades after the Second World War, successive governments treated the public sector as a "model employer" understood to mean "that governments, as direct employers, could set the standards for employment policy and practice within Britain. . . . The practice of 'good' employment was presumed to be a precondition for stable and orderly industrial relations."[8]

Some features of the last decades of the first system need to be highlighted because of their importance for industrial relations reform in the second period. Once again, war provided an opportunity for the state to encourage, and on occasion impose, collective bargaining where it did not already exist, an opportunity that was made more likely by the presence of the Labour Party as part of the wartime coalition government, and a former general secretary of the transport workers' union, Ernest Bevin, as minister of labour and national service. The general secretary of the TUC, Walter Citrine, argued that in "wartime there was no room for the unorganised person" and pressed for the extension of collective agreements to entire industries, widening the scope of the trade boards, and establishing collective bargaining machinery in unorganized industries.[9] Either direct government pressure or the indirect effects of wartime provisions did expand the scope of collective bargaining. Bevin used the Essential Work Orders, whose primary purpose was to control labor supply in essential war industries, to encourage collective bargaining (as a condition of limiting the mobility of labor), and fifty-five new joint industrial councils or their equivalents were set up during the war.[10] Wartime provisions also encouraged the spread of workplace industrial relations institutions (such as shop stewards and works committees) in engineering as part of an agreement between employers and unions, brokered by the government, to create joint production consultative advisory committees. Thus the model of decentralized industrial relations, powerful shop stewards, and two-tier collective bargaining (industry and plant levels) that so influenced the royal commission's 1968 report was itself in part a product of earlier state action under wartime conditions.

The Second World War also saw the return of the familiar quid pro quo of prohibition of industrial conflict in return for compulsory arbitration, established by Order in Council 1305. This procedure made strikes and lockouts illegal, and referred disputes to the minister of labour. If they were not settled using voluntary machinery and conciliation, the minister could refer them to a National Arbitration Tribunal, whose award was binding. Employers were required to observe "recognised terms and conditions" (meaning a relevant industry agreement), and the award of the tribunal was incorporated into the contract of the workers concerned. Thus, without the strike weapon, unions could now take employers to arbitration against their will and have "recognized terms and conditions" imposed on the employer. Compulsory arbitration, or the threat of it, was especially valuable to white-collar unions, for whom striking was difficult. White-collar unions in engineering and shipbuilding won recognition and bargaining machinery, and the National and Local Government Officers' Association (NALGO) finally won a national JIC in 1943.

Compulsory arbitration was important for postwar industrial relations because Order 1305 remained in effect until 1951, when it was replaced by Order 1376, which dropped the prohibition on strikes and lockouts but continued to provide for compulsory arbitration during peacetime. If a union or employers' association thought that the terms and conditions of employment were not being observed by an employer, it could have the issue referred to the Industrial Disputes Tribunal under Order 1376, which could then make a binding award. Once again, a case could be referred to the tribunal only if all voluntary machinery had been exhausted. In 1958 Order 1376 was abolished, but its main provisions were subsequently incorporated into Section 8 of the 1959 Terms and Conditions of Employment Act. While somewhat weaker than Order 1376, Section 8 once again permitted a claim to be made, now to the Industrial Court, if an employer was not observing the terms of a relevant industry agreement.

Two points are important to make about these two orders in council and the 1959 act.[11] The first is that they explicitly had the goal of bolstering industry bargaining, because a union (and it was overwhelmingly the union side that used the procedure) could use the arbitration procedure only in industries where there were recognized terms and conditions, which meant where industry bargaining existed. Thus, this was an extension procedure that served to allow unions to sweep up the smaller employers who were not abiding by, or effectively undercutting, industry agreements. The 1959 act was primarily used by unions representing manual workers in engineering and construction.[12] It served to mop up nonfederated firms and bring them under industry agreements. Second, this extension procedure created an indirect form of trade union recognition because employers who refused recognition could have industry standards imposed on them. Under those circumstances it often made more sense to recognize and bargain with unions, and employers were also more likely to join the relevant employer organization so that they could at least influence industry bargaining.

Just as the 1896 Conciliation Act had provided legislative cover for the extensive role of Board of Trade officials in encouraging union recognition and the creation of industry disputes procedures prior to the First World War, so Order 1305 provided an opportunity for government officials to use their statutory duty to intervene in industrial disputes to encourage union recognition and collective bargaining during and after the Second World War.[13] Ministry of Labour regional industrial relations officers sought to preempt strikes, and when they intervened "they would typically not only secure observance of recognized terms and conditions but also urge the virtues of union recognition and of establishing joint negotiating machinery."[14] This explains why both the leadership of most trade unions and the main employers' associations generally supported Orders 1305 and 1376, despite the ban on strikes contained in Order 1306; the legislation served to protect and extend industry bargaining.[15]

The end of the Second World War and the first period of extended governmental power for the Labour Party did not bring any radical departures in industrial relations legislation, itself an indication of the strength of the political consensus still surrounding the first system of industrial relations. Apart from the modification of the extension procedure and the 1946 repeal of the 1927 Trade Disputes and Trade Unions Act, the main piece of industrial relations legislation was the 1945 Wages Councils Act. Wages councils replaced trade boards as a hybrid form between statutory wage regulation and voluntary bargaining. The architect of the wages councils, Ernest Bevin, the wartime minister of labour, intended them to become the statutory basis of the industrial relations system, filling the gaps where voluntary bargaining machinery did not exist. Just as in 1918, when legislation had permitted trade boards to be created, not simply where wages were very low, but also where voluntary collective bargaining machinery did not exist, a purpose thwarted by the Treasury in the 1920s, so the 1945 Wages Councils Act once again expanded the conditions under which wages councils could be created to include circumstances where "voluntary machinery is not and cannot be made adequate or does not exist or is likely to cease to exist or be adequate."[16]

Thus the extension procedures and statutory minimum-wage machinery were examples of the now familiar role of the British state in creating or encouraging industry bargaining institutions rather than directly regulating outcomes. In some industries this required a more direct state role in the construction of industry-wide wage floors where unions were too weak and employers too divided to enforce them. An effective hierarchy thus existed during the final decades of the industry-level bargaining system: voluntary collective bargaining covered industries where labor and employers were sufficiently organized; an extension procedure provided an additional enforcement mechanism for industry agreements; and wages councils, which mimicked collective bargaining, operated in industries where industrial actors were too weakly organized to create voluntary bargaining.

The potential importance of these statutory mechanisms was reduced, however, by the macroeconomic policy stance adopted by postwar governments. The policy of demand management with the goal of achieving and maintaining full employment was largely successful until the 1970s,[17] and full employment dramatically increased the bargaining power of workers and their unions. Thus the effect of compulsory arbitration and wages councils was swamped by full employment, as unions had less need of them.[18] Macroeconomic policy prevented (until the 1980s) a decline in union power and influence after the Second World War similar to the decline after the First World War. The question, of particular relevance to the period since 1997 when a new Labour government took power, but unanswerable for the 1950s and 1960s, is whether legislation of this kind *would have worked* in the absence of full employment and a climate of industrial relations in which public policy favored collective bargaining.

In light of the radical Conservative project of industrial relations reform that emerged in the 1970s, and was then put in place after 1979, it is important to emphasize the degree to which a political consensus existed around the first system of industrial relations until the end of the 1950s. Just as the term "Butskellism" was coined to refer to the convergence in Conservative and Labour economic policy, so Smith has argued that the 1940s and 1950s were a period of "industrial Butskellism."[19] The Conservative Party's major postwar industrial statement, The *Industrial Charter*, strongly endorsed collective laissez-faire, and successive Conservative governments until the mid-1960s rejected calls from their own backbenchers for legislative curbs on strikes. The public value of both strong trade unionism and collective bargaining was not questioned in this period.[20] Indeed, in 1951 it was argued that the "Conservative Party regards the existence of strong and independent trade unions as an essential safeguard of freedom in an industrial society. It must therefore be the purpose of a Conservative government to strengthen and encourage Trade Unions."[21]

INDUSTRIAL RELATIONS INSTITUTIONS UNDER PRESSURE

Almost as soon as the early postwar accounts of British industrial relations were written, lauding their maturity and stability, the first system found itself in trouble, buffeted by changes in the broader economy, which were manifested in growing levels of strike activity and the consequent weakening of the political consensus around that set of industrial relations institutions. The period from the mid-1950s through the end of the 1970s saw a series of developments within the British political economy, including changes in industrial structure, occupational change, accelerated economic restructuring, and a new economic role for the state. This set of changes cannot be captured by the notion of a simple transition from competitive capitalism to Fordism (though that was one component of change), not least because British Fordism never fit the ideal-typical model of Fordism. Rather it was the combination of this set of developments—interacting with each other—that increased levels of class conflict, changed the interests of a section of the employer class, and created pressures that the first system of industrial relations was ill equipped to handle. As we shall see, these developments all pointed to lacunae in the industrial relations institutions inherited from the first half of the twentieth century, and it was those lacunae which state industrial relations projects sought to remedy from the late 1960s onward.

The British economy experienced an acceleration in the process of industrial restructuring in the 1950s and 1960s, which "followed, and in some cases completed, the structural transformation of the economy which had begun in the 1920s."[22] The economic center of gravity had moved away from the old staples, which tended to be characterized by extensive growth emphasizing the addition of new factors of production (rather than the improved productivity of existing factors of production), reliance on wage competition, export dependence, and an industrial structure characterized by large numbers of relatively small producers. On the one hand, these industries themselves restructured, with firms becoming larger and ownership more concentrated. To take the example of the textile industry, in 1951 12.8 percent of the labor force worked in establishments employing one thousand or more people, a figure that had risen to 31.8 percent by 1978.[23] On the other hand, the new growth industries—vehicle assembly, light engineering, consumer durables, synthetic fibers, food processing, pharmaceuticals, oil refining, and other chemicals—were more capital intensive, labor costs were a smaller proportion of their total costs, and they were less dependent on export markets.[24] Firms in these industries were characterized by a more micro-Fordist form of growth, meaning that growth was achieved not by the addition of new inputs but by the more efficient use of existing ones: intensive rather than extensive growth. This was a period of rapid and sustained productivity growth, driven by technological change, the shift from batch to continuous-process production, and the methodology of time-and-motion studies and scientific management.[25] Keeping wages low became less important than ensuring high levels of productivity and avoiding strikes.

Across British industry average firm size and industrial concentration rose, driven in large part by an intense wave of mergers between 1959 and 1973.[26] Between 1948 and 1976 the one hundred largest manufacturing firms more than doubled their share of net manufacturing output while family ownership of large firms declined, and the output share of the three largest in each average industry firms rose from 29 percent to 42 percent between 1951 and 1973.[27] By the end of the 1960s industrial concentration had surpassed that in Germany and the United States.[28] In short, British industrial structure was transformed.

Industry-level bargaining was of limited value to these firms. In fact, the extension mechanisms (Order 1376 and the Terms and Conditions of Employment Act) posed problems for firms trying to develop internally consistent pay policies across their workforce; groups of workers could use compulsory arbitration to align their wages with industry standards even if that distorted internal pay scales, a problem made worse for industrial conglomerates operating in multiple industries and hence subject to multiple sets of industry standards.[29] The trade unions were certainly convinced that Order 1376 was abolished as a result of pressure from nonfederated employers.

Industry-wide procedures were not designed to manage change internal to the firm, and their existence inhibited the development of firm-level procedures. Thus from the 1950s onward growing doubts about the value of employer associations, and criticism of industry bargaining, were voiced by larger firms. As Samuel Courtauld, of the giant textile firm Courtaulds, put it: "Employers are not by any means always well represented by their existing associations, many of which are quite out of date. They were created long since to meet conditions quite vanished, but they are very difficult to replace or reconstruct."[30] The difficulty of replacement or reconstruction also hints at the important role that the state would later come to play in that process. Within the engineering, rubber, and chemicals industries' bargaining mechanisms there were efforts to deemphasize across-the-board pay increases and leave more room for firm-level bargaining, and a number of large firms either left national employer associations or loosened their ties with them, including Esso, Shell, BP, Alcan, Cadburys, GEC, and British Leyland.[31] The result was that during this period a growing number of firms seemed prepared to buy productivity improvements through improved wage levels, and this implied both a decentralization of bargaining to the firm and an expansion of the scope of bargaining to include work practices, work organization, and technology.

This came to be known in the 1960s as productivity bargaining, providing firms with predictable, controllable wage costs and hence control over wage drift, and removing work practices that employers considered inflexible and restrictive.[32] The classic example, made famous by the report of the royal commission in 1968, was the agreement reached at the Fawley oil refinery in 1960. The refinery was owned by Esso, which was both foreign owned and nonfederated.[33] The agreement provided for a pay increase combined with a reduction in overtime, resulting in an overall increase in take-home pay of 31 percent, in return for changes in working practices including the relaxation of job demarcations, more flexible work time, and the loss of some job breaks. These resulted in productivity improvements that more than covered the wage increase.[34]

Industrial relations institutions were implicated in the shift in industrial structure and growth regime in another manner as well. Sisson has argued that the dominant system of multiemployer industry-level bargaining in Britain differed significantly from bargaining at the equivalent level in much of continental Europe. Because collective bargaining was embedded within a voluntarist, "common law" framework, which privileged procedural rules over substantive ones and prevented those rules from being legally enforceable, British employers were unable to "neutralise the workplace."[35] The freedom from substantive collective bargaining rules, and from legislation, that British employers enjoyed was double-edged. It gave employers remarkable flexibility, but paradoxically, "the price of this freedom is that the trade union and, perhaps more importantly, its members in the workplace also have few limitations imposed upon them."[36] Flexibility for employers during times of labor weakness became vulnerability during periods of labor strength. As the pace of restructuring led to resistance from workers faced with either job loss or the impact of technological change on work, firms now faced sharply higher levels of industrial conflict. For example, in the automobile industry the number of strikes increased sixfold between 1950 and 1964, with an equivalent increase in the number of workers involved,[37] and throughout manufacturing the proportion of strikes over "working arrangements, rules and disciplines," rather than simple wage increases, rose dramatically.[38]

The degree of "job control" won by work groups inside the firm,[39] which was a major source of Britain's flawed version of Fordism,[40] posed particular problems for firms in industries seeking productivity agreements and made the necessity of regaining some control over the workplace by creating rules and procedures for managing change all the more crucial. This again implied the creation of industrial relations institutions that could, if not neutralize the workplace, at least permit negotiated change. Under these circumstances it is perhaps unsurprising that every major survey of managerial opinion during this period demonstrated support for, and a favorable image of, shop stewards, the main institution of workplace industrial relations.[41]

The British economy experienced not only a shift within the industrial sector but also deindustrialization and a major expansion of the service sector. Manufacturing's share of employment declined from its peak in 1955 (in absolute numbers, manufacturing jobs declined after 1966),[42] and an expansion of white-collar and service-sector jobs followed the growth of financial services and of technical, scientific, and professional employment. Employment growth was particularly large in financial and business services, health, education, hotels, and catering.[43] Overall, employment in the service sector rose steadily from a little over nine million at the end of the Second World War to fifteen million at the end of the period covered by this chapter,[44] so that it comprised 61 percent of total employment in 1981.[45] The importance of this shift for industrial relations reform was that the areas of employment expansion were often also areas of traditional employer resistance to trade union recognition and to any limitation on managerial prerogatives. In his report on recognition of white collar trade unions, prepared initially for the royal commission, Bain argued that roughly 45 percent of the workforce was employed in sectors where gaining recognition either was a problem or would be a problem were unions to seek recognition. This figured closely mapped onto the service sector, with the largest problem areas being distributive trades, insurance, banking and finance, catering, hotels, professional and scientific services, and miscellaneous services. White-collar workers had been successful in gaining recognition in the public sector and much of manufacturing, but Bain stressed that in both cases recognition had come as a result of either direct government action or indirect government action during wartime.[46]

Overwhelmingly, private-sector employers resisted recognizing trade unions for their white-collar employees (even when they recognized them for their manual employees), and for the most part unions were unable to force recognition. By the middle of the 1960s, when Bain was completing his report, there was evidence of greater success on the part of white-collar unions in manufacturing: the Association of Supervisory Staffs, Executives and Technicians (ASSET), later the Association of Scientific, Technical and Managerial Staffs (ASTMS), which organized scientific and technical workers, demonstrated an ability to grow rapidly using a combination of mergers with other unions and innovative organizing tactics.[47] Nevertheless, the general picture of employer resistance to service-sector unions remained accurate. The experience of the main banking union, the National Union of Banking Employees (NUBE), was fairly typical in this respect.[48] All the major banks set up staff associations to compete with NUBE and, with only a few exceptions, refused to recognize and bargain with the union.

Recalling the argument made in the last chapter, the achievement of trade union recognition in Britain was heavily dependent on industry bargaining, because recognition could be achieved indirectly through an employer association. In the service sector, industry bargaining was extremely limited, making recognition that much more difficult to achieve. Indeed, even the extension mechanisms were of little help, because they explicitly permitted claims to be made only where there were already recognized terms and conditions, in other words, where an industry agreement already existed. NUBE finally won recognition at the main high street banks as a result of an agreement to create national bargaining machinery, which followed a strike, the banks' own efforts to restructure their pay scales, and government intervention in the form of the 1963 Cameron inquiry.[49]

State economic management played an important contributory role in the collapse of the first system of industrial relations, interacting with and reinforcing the restructuring of the British economy described earlier, for two broad reasons. First, and unrelated to economic restructuring itself, the experience of a decade of full employment began to make itself felt. Tight labor markets and a social safety net provided a degree of labor decommodification that unbalanced the fragile class compromise that had undergirded the industrial relations settlement of the earlier period. In part this shift in relative strength made it easier for workers to resist change and make gains, permitting, in Coates's wonderful phrase, "do it yourself reformism,"[50] and in part it exacerbated a macroeconomic problem. A combination of Britain's international economic pretensions, the international interests of the City of London, and a bipartisan political fixation with maintaining the value of sterling, made Britain chronically vulnerable to currency crises.[51] British governments, both Labour and Conservative, chose to respond to this vulnerability with bouts of deflation and incomes policies that sought wage restraint.

Wage restraint policies of some kind, either voluntary or statutory, were in operation for practically the entire two decades after 1960.[52] The form of incomes policies employed by governments in turn encouraged decentralized productivity bargaining, because wage increases tied to productivity increases were often exempt from some varieties of incomes policy. The estimate that roughly six million people were covered by productivity agreements in 1969 was in part an artifact of efforts to circumvent wage restraint policies.[53] Incomes policies also had the effect of radicalizing trade unions, particularly public-sector unions. After being rejected by the membership on several occasions, the leadership of NALGO was able win support for affiliation to the TUC as a direct result of the 1961 "pay pause" and the creation of the National Economic Development Council (NEDC), which had TUC representation. Without affiliation, NALGO would have been subject to an incomes policy but would have had no voice in its formulation.[54]

A second aspect of state economic management that affected industrial relations reform was the shift from "arms length Keynesianism" to microeconomic intervention.[55] By the end of the 1950s it was clear that whatever temporary advantage the British economy had gained from being among the victors during the Second World War had disappeared, and relative economic decline was obvious. Both Conservative and Labour governments of the 1960s abandoned Anglo-Saxon Keynesianism, with its neglect of microeconomic intervention; instead, economic "modernization" and "planning," however incompetently operationalized and made hostage to wage restraint, became the watchwords of economic policy.[56] As Davies and Freedland have pointed out, once microeconomic intervention became considered acceptable, even desirable, a voluntarist industrial relations system with an abstentionist state made little sense. Collective laissez-faire was ideologically compatible with laissez-faire (and even Keynesian) economic policy, but not with economic planning. Governments were bound to start looking to labor law, and the whole range of industrial relations institutions, as adjuncts to microeconomic intervention.

Common to all these shifts in the British political economy was the inability of the existing set of industrial relations institutions to offer any help; indeed, they acted as obstacles to economic restructuring. Managing job loss and resistance to changes in technology and work organization could not be done at the level of industry bargaining, nor could productivity agreements be reached in the absence of workplace bargaining institutions. Existing union recognition procedures were indirect, operating through industry bargaining or an extension procedure. Neither were of much use in new areas of employment, precisely because these areas were not covered by industry bargaining. And, of course, industry bargaining was of no use in achieving wage restraint, at least not in situations of multiunionism, where several unions operate in each industry and many unions also operate in several industries. Rather, the challenges facing the British economy from the late 1950s onward suggested several avenues for industrial relations reform: the spread of workplace industrial relations institutions to manage change; an expansion in the scope of bargaining to include productivity issues; an expansion of legal protection for individual workers, to reduce resistance to restructuring; a more direct procedure to encourage union recognition; and some mechanism for permitting wage restraint.

As during the first period, the direct impulse for change in the industrial relations system was the level and type of industrial conflict. After declining from an immediate postwar peak, the level of strikes began to climb in the 1950s, reaching a peak in 1960, dropping back for the first half of the 1960s, and then reaching a new peak in 1970. The strike level remained elevated throughout the 1970s.[57] Cronin argued, on the basis of an analysis of British strikes up until the mid-1970s, that the strike wave of the late 1950s "belongs ideologically and in terms of union strategy to the interwar period while that of 1968–72 reflects more contemporary conditions,"[58] and Kelly has also suggested a generational effect, as strikes in the late 1960s and 1970s reflected the response of a new generation of workers, who had experienced a long period of relative job security and prosperity, to work intensification from employers seeking to restore profitability.[59] Distinctions in the form of industrial conflict are important. The strikes of the late 1950s were predominantly in manufacturing, involved manual workers, and were often unofficial. The figure of 95 percent of strikes being unofficial was widely cited, and given legitimacy by the royal commission. This kind of strike—firm based, in response to workplace grievances, without the sanction of the union leadership—was outside the ambit of the procedure agreements enshrined in the old system, so that existing industrial relations institutions neither removed the causes of strikes nor had mechanisms for handling them once they started.

Defining the problem of British industrial relations as unofficial strikes was tremendously important to the analysis of the royal commission and to the subsequent political projects of industrial relations reform. But the discursive construction of industrial relations crisis did not rest with the state or para-public entities alone. From the end of the 1950s onward, a quite specific narra-tive of "disorder" emerged from media representations of strikes.[60] Press cover-age had two primary effects. First, it emphasized the central role of shop stewards and local union officials in the spread of industrial unrest within the motor industry, reinforcing an argument that union leaderships had largely lost control over their lay officials, with deleterious consequences for productivity. Second, this narrative of industrial relations in the motor industry was ex-tended to represent British industry as a whole, so that the popular image of militant shop stewards, resistant to change and eager to engage in unofficial strikes, came to dominate discussion of national industrial relations reform.

In fact, whatever the adequacy of this representation of industrial unrest in the 1950s and 1960s, by the end of the 1960s the form of industrial conflict had already begun to shift, with the much greater involvement of white-collar workers and the introduction of large-scale, official public-sector trade union strikes, often in response to government incomes policies. Under these cir-cumstances, a public debate focused on the question of how to encourage trade unions to control their members was increasingly irrelevant. The Thatcherite industrial relations reforms of the 1980s, the subject of the next chapter, were a much more direct response to this kind of industrial conflict.

Accompanying the economic challenges to the old regulatory system, and prompted by them, came a weakening of the political consensus around it. The old system embodied a certain class compromise, based on the relative strength of business and labor and on the organization of the economy. That compromise unraveled in the two decades after the Second World War as growth faltered and labor became stronger, as a result both of decommodifica-tion and of ties to an actual or potential governing party.

Dissent over the class compromise emerged as a minority position within the governing Conservative Party in the 1950s and found particular expres-sion in a document, A Giant's Strength, drawn up by Conservative lawyers, which questioned the immunities in common law granted trade unions, and the absence of legislative limits on their actions.[61] But the most direct signal that a new compromise, and a new set of regulatory mechanisms, would be needed came from the return of judicial intervention into industrial relations in the 1963 legal decision in Rookes v. Barnard, which appeared to narrow significantly the immunity enjoyed by unions in trade disputes. The collective laissez-faire system was particularly vulnerable on the issue of trade union immunity for two reasons. First, it was vulnerable because a hostile judiciary could create liabilities faster than the legislature could provide immunities (and then each effort by a British government to pass legislation plugging a new hole in union immunity created an opportunity for a public debate about trade union power);[62] this was what led to the creation of the Donovan Commission in the first place. Second, trade union immunities could easily be discursively transformed into trade union *privileges*, with the resulting notion that unions were somehow above the law and needed to be brought within its ambit.

One of the reasons for the long-term stability of the first system of industrial relations was that judicial activism in labor law receded after the 1906 Trade Disputes Act, and the deep hostility of the British judicial system to collective organization and action on the part of workers was replaced by the more positive public policy presumption outlined in the previous chapter. The reappearance of judge-made law directly threatened collective laissez-faire, though it is unlikely that judges would have been so likely to act in the absence of widespread political and public disquiet with the industrial relations system. Historically, judicial activism in this area has waxed and waned with the level of threat posed by organized labor. In any case, it was *Rookes v. Barnard* that set in train the various state projects of industrial relations reform that dominated the decade after 1968.

THE DONOVAN DIAGNOSIS

The Royal Commission on Trade Unions and Employers' Associations, chaired by Lord Donovan, and usually referred to as the Donovan Commission,[63] was set up in 1965 as part of a quid pro quo between the new Labour government and the trade unions. The government promised limited legislation to restore the law to the pre-*Rookes* situation in return for a broad public inquiry into the state of industrial relations, which would provide cover for the change in law. But the royal commission was, more generally, a response to a growing drumbeat of concern with the power of trade unions; a mounting discourse of crisis surrounding the level of strikes had emerged from newspapers, popular books, and even entertainment.[64] The remit of the Donovan Commission was to investigate industrial relations with particular attention to be paid to their impact on industrial conflict and labor productivity, but the report was viewed almost entirely through the lens of what it proposed to do about unofficial strikes.

A mounting public perception of industrial relations crisis did not in and of itself suggest an obvious reform project, despite the shift in opinion within the Conservative Party in the direction of greater penal sanctions against strike action. The report of the Donovan Commission was central to the construction of a reform discourse; all reform projects for the following decade were viewed through the prism of the royal commission's diagnosis and prescription for reform, even when those reforms challenged its premises. The royal commission was being asked "to do nothing less than discover by rational inquiry what was the right normative order for industrial society for the future."[65] And while its report's conclusions achieved nothing like the political and social consensus of its 1894 predecessor, its impact on industrial relations reform was nevertheless profound. This was in fact the fifth royal commission to examine "the labour question" in some form since 1867, but it was the first since 1906, when the legal cornerstone of the first industrial relations system was laid.

The influence of the royal commission lay in the scale of its investigative endeavors, the amount of evidence it gathered, the expertise of those who wrote research papers for the commission, and the fact that its report articulated a strikingly original analysis of the development of British industrial relations, each of whose components formed part of a seamless garment that made it extremely difficult to pull apart. The report tied together numerous seemingly disparate aspects of industrial relations in one consistent argument, and it represented the high point of intellectual pluralism in the sphere of industrial relations. The critics of the royal commission were forced to argue on its intellectual terrain and were never able to construct an alternative analysis of British industrial relations; in other words, critics argued that the report did not do enough to address this or that problem, but nothing like an equivalent diagnosis of the ills of the British system of industrial relations appeared until the middle years of the Thatcher era. In this respect, the central role played by industrial relations specialists, both on the commission (Otto Kahn-Freund) and among its research staff (Hugh Clegg was research director, and research papers were written by Flanders, Fox, Bain, and McCarthy), shaped the final report and gave it its chief characteristics: a focus on industrial relations institutions themselves, and a respect for the limitations of legal sanctions in the regulation of class conflict. These emphases meshed well with those of George Woodcock, a member of the royal commission and general secretary of the TUC, whose objections to punitive legislation made it likely that any report recommending such legislation would generate a minority report and make the influence of any conclusions politically worthless.[66]

The report outlined the familiar symptoms of crisis within British industrial relations: poor productivity, restrictive labor practices, unofficial strikes, and wage drift with inflationary consequences. But in chapter 3, its intellectual core, the report laid out what the royal commission considered to be the root cause of these ills. The core of the argument contained in the Donovan Report was, briefly, as follows. Britain was characterized by not one but "two systems of industrial relations. The one is the formal system embodied in the official institutions. The other is the informal system created by the actual behavior of trade unions and employer's associations, of managers, shop stewards and workers."[67] The formal system referred to industry bargaining, which was increasingly irrelevant, used to negotiate wage minimums and dispute procedures, while real bargaining had shifted to the workplace, the locus of the informal system. Workplace bargaining was, in Flanders's famous words, "largely informal, largely fragmented and largely autonomous."[68] The shift was a product of full employment, which enhanced the local bargaining capacity of workers, and of the desire of managers to negotiate over changes in work organization, working practices, and the introduction of new technology while avoiding the inflexibility of formal agreements with unions. Multiunionism and weak trade union organizational capacities also contributed to the shift in bargaining level, as managers sought to enlist local union stewards as allies in managing conflict and change.

The problems arose because informal, fragmented, and autonomous industrial relations practices could result in a "tendency of extreme decentralization and self-government to degenerate into indecision and anarchy; the propensity to breed inefficiency; and the reluctance to change."[69] The two systems of industrial relations were poorly integrated because union officials had limited control or influence over shop stewards who were bargaining in the workplace, and employers' associations had similarly little influence over the practices of managers. This situation explained, according to the report, Britain's persistent industrial relations problems because the "formal and informal systems are in conflict. The informal system undermines the regulative effects of industry-wide agreements."[70] At the same time, the existence of industry bargaining encouraged firms to neglect taking responsibility for developing their own industrial relations policies and institutions. The absence of firm-level industrial relations institutions meant that change was not negotiated but instead led to conflict, and the absence of negotiated change contributed to poor productivity. Strikes were unofficial, and hence hard to either prevent or bring to an end, because of the absence of integration between different organizational levels of trade unions. In an almost Gramscian formulation of crisis, chapter 3 concluded "that the practices of the formal system have become increasingly empty, while the practices of the informal system have come to exert an ever greater influence on the conduct of industrial relations throughout the country; that the two systems conflict; and that the informal system cannot be forced to comply with the formal system."[71]

The goal of reform, in the view of the Donovan Report, should not be to attempt to choke off or reverse the decentralization of bargaining. This was firstly because it could not be done, as decentralization reflected the preferences of both managers and workers (and their workplace representatives) and secondly because the institutionalization of workplace bargaining had the potential to solve most of the ills that followed from existing practice. The report argued that the most modern, successful firms had shifted to a focus on the workplace for the very good reason that that was where economic change had to take place, and industry bargaining was largely incapable of negotiating change at this level. The royal commission noted that much of the innovation in industrial relations was coming from foreign-owned (often American) and nonfederated (not part of an industry bargaining agreement) firms. The example of the Fawley oil refinery, owned by Esso, was tremendously influential for the royal commission because it demonstrated dramatic productivity improvements as a result of negotiating change at the plant level. The report laid great store in the spread of productivity bargaining because it offered solutions to restrictive practices and, by tying wages more closely to productivity, it promised a more plausible mechanism for achieving noninflationary wage growth than incomes policies. Finally, more formal bargaining institutions in the workplace might be expected to regulate industrial conflict better than the current arrangements, in which trade unions had little or no control over their members and stewards. Thus, for the Donovan Commission, the problem was not the shift toward more Fordist forms of growth but rather the increasing dysfunctionality of the regulatory mechanisms of an industrial relations system designed to manage a different, earlier pattern of economic growth.

The goal then was "a reconstruction of voluntary collective bargaining"[72] to create institutions that could manage conflict while permitting economic restructuring to improve productivity. The task of the industrial relations system was to reduce worker resistance to economic change. In Flanders's famous phrase, managers "can only regain control by sharing it."[73] Only the creation of firm-level bargaining institutions would make it possible to overcome the entrenched opposition of work groups to restructuring. The royal commission's solution was to encourage the creation of permanent collective bargaining institutions inside the workplace and to link the old and new systems. Shop stewards were the linchpin of this reconstructed system, and the report argued that they needed to be both better integrated into their unions and better integrated into formal bargaining mechanisms. Two-tier bargaining was envisioned as the model, with industry bargaining still operating to set industry standards and provide a forum for discussing issues of general importance (such as training) while workplace bargaining took on the task of negotiating real wages, grievances, and working practices.

The major role in reform of the industrial relations system was reserved for employers and employers' associations, with a somewhat lesser role accorded trade unions (which were largely absolved from blame for the problems of the industrial relations system). The report argued that employers' associations, having created the industry bargaining system prior to the First World War, abdicated responsibility for its development in the interwar and immediate postwar period, leaving it to the state to encourage its spread. The royal commission now called on employers' associations to shift their emphasis from industry bargaining to helping smaller firms without dedicated industrial relations staff to develop workplace bargaining institutions and practices. Meanwhile employers were urged to recognize unions where they currently resisted them, especially white-collar unions, and to provide resources and facilities (such as the dues checkoff and time off for meetings) to encourage the development of workplace unionism and workplace bargaining. Trade unions were called on to recognize and formalize the role of shop stewards within their organizations, to specify the relationship between union full-time officers and stewards, to increase the number of the former, to help with workplace bargaining, and to find mechanisms for reducing interunion disputes.

What of the state? When it came to how to proceed with such a reconstruction of industrial relations, the Donovan Report saw a limited role for legislation, though not for the state. The royal commission was anxious to make the case against those who favored punitive action to prevent strikes, and nonintervention was used as a powerful talisman to ward off such action. Again and again, in regard to restrictive practices, unofficial strikes, and the legal enforceability of collective agreements, the report argued that punitive legislation was ineffective. Trade unions were not responsible for the conflict and had little control over the participants, so it made little sense to punish them. Thus the report anticipated the failure of efforts by the 1970–74 Conservative government to stop strikes and discipline strikers once they started. Sanctions could not be used effectively without the active participation of employers, and since the informal system was in part created by employers and their managers, they were unlikely to use sanctions made available by punitive legislation.

The report proposed the creation of an Industrial Relations Commission (IRC). Larger companies would have to register their collective agreements with the IRC, which could investigate the absence of agreements, gaps in the scope of what was covered in those agreements, and instances of nonrecognition of trade unionism, though no sanctions were attached to this latter task. In a strong statement of support for the value of trade unionism, it was argued that a "company will be failing in its public duty unless it can show that its employees are unwilling to join trade unions and be represented by them."[74] The royal commission also proposed legislation to prevent unfair dismissal. This legislation would have built on a growing body of *individual* labor law that appeared in the 1960s, providing for employment contracts, redundancy benefits, and so on.[75] All this legislation had the clear economic purpose of undermining worker resistance to economic restructuring.[76] Limited legislation was also recommended in order to reduce industrial conflict over trade union membership recognition, including a statutory right to belong to a trade union without penalty, and selective reintroduction of compulsory arbitration (similar to Order 1376). Finally, as a marker for an important debate in the second half of the 1970s, the royal commission addressed the issue of worker participation in management decisions, but while five of the twelve commission members were in favor of either voluntary or compulsory efforts in this direction, the majority opposed the idea, primarily on the grounds that the functions of managers and unions should remain separate.

The report of the royal commission was unanimous. There were a couple of inconsequential addendums and supplementary notes from members of the commission, but it was the "Note of Reservation" written by Andrew Shon-

field that received most attention,[77] primarily because it contained a fundamental critique of the main report and its recommendations. As such, it became a touchstone for those dissatisfied with the main report and urging tough
penal sanctions. In the note, and subsequently in an article in The *Sunday
Times*, Shonfield argued that the power of organized labor brought with it
responsibilities,[78] and that a voluntarist and state-abstentionist system of industrial relations was incompatible with the interests of a highly interdependent industrial society. Thus Shonfield recommended that the IRC have autonomous judicial authority to intervene in several kinds of industrial dispute
(those concerning union recognition, jurisdictional disputes, and so on), and
that it be able to investigate restrictive practices and ensure that bargaining
take place "in good faith." Collective agreements could, and should, also be
made legally binding.

The reasons for the influence of the Shonfield note should be of no surprise.
His intervention responded to the widespread demand that "something be
done" and that the wings of excessive union power be clipped. But it is important to notice that Shonfield's reservation was not based on an alternative
interpretation of British industrial relations and contained no rebuttal to the
argument of the main report that his remedies simply would not work, however desirable. Shonfield's Note rested on a somewhat abstract argument about
the nature of industrial society—an argument that in many ways prefigured
the academic interpretation of corporatism—rather than the more pragmatic
analysis of how industrial relations work, contained in the main report of the
royal commission.

The importance of the Donovan Report was that it traced all the myriad
symptoms of crisis and disorder to a root cause—dysfunction within the industrial relations system—rather than denouncing the behavior of workers, the
radicalism of unions, or the inevitability of class conflict in a capitalist society.
As such the report argued that it was impossible to treat the symptoms without
reconstructing the industrial relations institutions themselves; as currently
constituted these institutions created perverse incentives for industrial actors.
Each alleged problem of British industrial relations—poor productivity, unofficial strikes, wage inflation—was traced to the organization of the industrial
relations system itself, so that the report provided, in Wedderburn's formulation, "its crushing weight of evidence in favour" of institutional reconstruction
rather than penal sanctions.[79]

The Reaction to the Donovan Report

The key principles enunciated by the royal commission in 1968 echoed those
of the 1894 royal commission: the value of voluntarism and of union "organi-

zation." Over and over again the argument was made in the report that the core of the British system of industrial relations is, and must remain, voluntarism, and that every proposal for reform must be weighed against its implications for undermining the voluntary system.[80] Members of the commission were uncomfortable even about recommending legislation to protect against unfair dismissal, for fear of its impact on existing dismissal procedures that were the result of collective bargaining, and their report suggested that, on the advice of the IRC, firms or industries could be exempted from the legislation if they could demonstrate adequate voluntary procedures. The report was equally forthright in arguing that since "collective bargaining depends upon the existence, strength and recognition of trade unions,"[81] unions provide a public good, and employers needed to recognize them, strengthen them, and work with them. Trade unions were crucial to the reform process because without them workers would simply resist change.

Thus far one can see continuities with the past, and much of the reaction to the report stressed this continuity, especially the rejection of a greater juridification of industrial relations. In fact, the report marked an important break with the past in two respects. First, it proposed a reconstructed industrial relations system, one that placed far more emphasis on firm-level institutions than the earlier system, and one that sought to extend the scope of collective regulation beyond dispute procedures, wage minimums, and hours to include the organization of work. Second, the royal commission did envisage a significant expansion in the role of the state in encouraging this process of reconstruction, but not primarily through legislation. Its report endorsed the extension of labor law to include a new set of individual rights at work, and it recommended the creation of the IRC, which would have a proactive role in identifying areas where reform was necessary and encouraging the reconstruction of industrial relations. As Davies and Freedland have pointed out, an IRC constituted along the lines set out in the Donovan Report could have been deeply interventionist, but, true to earlier practice, the intervention would have been administrative rather than legislative.[82] The role of the state was, not to create de novo a set of workplace-level industrial relations institutions, but to use its intervention in industrial relations (through the IRC) to encourage "best practice": the recognition of trade unions and the construction of particular industrial relations institutions and particular types of bargaining. It has often been pointed out that the "two systems" analysis put forward by the royal commission was primarily a description of "mass production operatives in large engineering firms" and that significant areas of the British economy (particularly the public sector) were still dominated by industry-level bargaining.[83] But it was precisely the goal of the commission's report to use the state to extend this form of industrial relations from where it was developing naturally to the rest of the economy. The report identified a series of economic problems, diagnosed them as originating in the industrial relations sphere, and sought to generalize successful institutions and practices that were already emerging.

One final point about the report of the Royal Commission is worth making. The logic of the argument that punitive legislation would not work to solve Britain's industrial relations problems had the effect of cutting the intellectual ground from under arguments in favor of legislation that might directly strengthen trade unionism. Once the report denied the efficacy of legislation penalizing workers and unions, it was difficult to then justify more positive legislation. This argument was bolstered by the TUC's evidence to the royal commission, which, for reasons explained at the end of this chapter, chose to assert an extremely voluntarist position that trade union strength was entirely unrelated to state encouragement and support, and therefore the TUC requested practically no additional positive legislation.[84] By the early 1970s organized labor was more prepared to consider legislation directly supportive of trade unionism, but its concern in the second half of the 1960s that it not open the door to punitive legislation helped ensure that the royal commission's recommended legislative agenda would be limited.

The Donovan Report completely misread the political mood. The House of Commons debate on the report,[85] and the press coverage, were dominated by the discourse of crisis, in which an "epidemic" of strikes threatened the British economy. It was a discourse that the Labour prime minister, Harold Wilson, obsessed by currency speculation and the value of sterling, largely internalized.[86] The report was evaluated almost entirely through the prism of how it dealt with strikes, and in this respect it was judged to be too timid, in effect a surrender to the unions. Whatever its analytical strengths, the royal commission's report did not offer a politically feasible prescription, at least not for an already weakened Labour government. The report was also not entirely convincing in its solution to the problem of how to achieve wage restraint; arguing that inflationary wage settlements would disappear as the industrial relations system was reconstructed along new lines was unlikely to offer much political relief to governments of any political stripe. In any case, the debate over Donovan rapidly morphed into the political conflict over the Labour government's white paper *In Place of Strife*; the discourse of crisis overwhelmed discussion of the merits of the report. Nevertheless, it is important for understanding the legacy of Donovan to note a certain disconnection between the political debate and the reaction of the main industrial actors.

The political and public debate, while superficially about the economic implications of industrial relations reform, was more fundamentally about its political and constitutional implications.[87] Discussion of the royal commission's report took place within a framework in which the core conflict was defined as being between the state and the labor movement (over the relative power of each) and further animated by the demand that the state be seen to do something to limit "excessive" union power. The result was constitutional conflict, not class conflict.

Reaction from unions and employers, on the other hand, was much less hostile. In a joint response to the royal commission's report,[88] the TUC and the main employers' organization, the Confederation of British Industry (CBI), broadly welcomed the report, applauded its voluntarist emphases, and agreed, among other things, on the need to provide more facilities for shop stewards. Both the TUC and the CBI were concerned that the report did not acknowledge the advantages of industry bargaining (the CBI, in particular, stressed the economic rationale of industry bargaining, that it reduced both leapfrogging wage agreements and destructive wage competition), and the TUC argued that government incomes policies were one of the causes of unofficial strikes, but overall union and employer reaction was positive. This should come as no surprise, given the shifts within the British political economy outlined earlier in this chapter. As Sisson and Purcell have argued: "most managements implicitly accepted the central core of the Donovan Commission's analysis. While managements had the appearance of control in the workplace the reality was very different or threatened to become very different."[89] Just as the first system of industrial relations was organized around a class compromise in which the institution of industry-level bargaining permitted negotiation over wages, limits on industrial conflict, and managerial control of the workplace, so the Donovan Commission was suggesting a new form of class compromise in which managers and unions would create firm-level institutions to negotiate economic change and bring some order to the workplace.

The report of the Donovan Commission inaugurated a period of state experimentation in the reform of industrial relations. These experiments are often seen as bypassing, going beyond, or simply ignoring the analysis and recommendations of the commission's report. But if one recognizes that the goal of the report was to point the way toward the reconstruction of industrial relations so as to decentralize and extend the scope of collective regulation, then, to a remarkable degree, its central elements were implemented, though through a greater degree of state intervention than the royal commission intended. Indeed, after the disastrous failures of *In Place of Strife*, and the 1971 Industrial Relations Act, this project of reform became the industrial relations policy of the 1974–79 Labour government.

Reforming the Industrial Relations System

The decade following the publication of the Donovan Report saw three different governments, and three projects of industrial relations reform. This was the most intense period of state intervention in industrial relations since 1918–21 when the state took the lead in generalizing the Whitley system of industry bargaining. However, the post-Donovan period saw far less political consensus around industrial relations than the earlier period. Furthermore, the emphasis of the first two post-Donovan reform projects on controlling strikes in narrowly coercive ways overwhelmed the broader task of reconstructing the system of industrial relations. Wedderburn pointed out soon after the publication of the Donovan report that if one's goal was the integration of the "two systems" of industrial relations, that goal could be achieved either by strengthening workplace institutions or by greater state regulation of collective action and collective bargaining.[90] The former was the preferred route of the royal commission, but the latter played a much bigger part in the reform efforts that followed. In all three projects, legislation came to play a greater role than envisaged in the Donovan Report. But it would be a mistake to miss the core consistency of state policy during this period. All these projects were similar in that they recognized the need to strengthen trade union capacities inside the firm—union "organization," in other words, remained crucial to the success of industrial relations restructuring—and all of them shifted the focus of attention away from industry-level bargaining to the construction of new regulatory mechanisms inside the firm.

The reform of the industrial relations system had been largely put on hold during the mid-1960s in anticipation of the Donovan Commission's recommendations, but two developments during the 1960s are worth briefly mentioning in order to avoid the perception that legislative reform of collective regulation was the sole avenue of state intervention in industrial relations.[91] First, demonstrating both a continuity with and an acceleration of prior practice, the 1960s saw a remarkable degree of ad hoc intervention in industrial disputes. In every strike of any scale government ministers became involved, either in a personal capacity, acting as mediators, or, in larger disputes, setting up commissions of inquiry.[92] Reading the annual reports of the TUC, or the diaries of Barbara Castle, who was secretary of state for employment and productivity between 1968 and 1970,[93] one comes away with an overwhelming sense that the state was intimately involved in the management, indeed often the micromanagement, of industrial conflict. This reflects a more urgent concern with the macroeconomic implications of wage agreements, a somewhat more interventionist stance by the Labour governments of the 1960s in comparison with their Conservative predecessors, and the growing inability of existing industrial relations institutions to manage conflict. In this context the state became the arbitrator of last resort. And though state intervention of this kind was reactive, it nonetheless followed a logic similar to that of the early decades of the twentieth century in that governments sought not only to prevent or contain conflict but also to use conflict to create new industrial relations institutions.

The second development was the construction of a body of individual labor law, something that had long received only limited attention from the state, reflecting the preferences of both employers and unions for the collective regulation of labor contracts through bargaining rather than legislation. But the mid-1960s saw a slew of new individual rights at work: the Contracts of Employment Act (1963), the Industrial Training Act (1964), the Redundancy Payments Act (1965), and the National Insurance Act (1966). Two related points are worth noting about this legislation. First, governments took the lead in the passage of this legislation rather than waiting for consensus and a request for action from employers and unions. Second, state action was an explicit response to a perception of the requirements of economic modernization. Much of this legislation emerged out of the new planning process set in train by the creation of the National Economic Development Council. It sought to promote labor mobility to facilitate economic restructuring, and to solve collective action problems (particularly in the provision of industrial training). But above all, the object was to reduce resistance to change,[94] and, in the words of the Organization of Economic Cooperation and Development (OECD), "improve industrial relations so that there would be less friction when structural changes resulting from improved technology, methods of production, changes in demand etc. took place."[95] Thus the breach of collective laissez-faire involved in greater statutory regulation of the individual employment contract was an attempt to construct new industrial relations institutions to better enable economic modernization, particularly by undermining collective resistance.

Of the three major state reform projects that followed the publication of the Donovan report, the first two can be dealt with quickly because both failed as a result of massive trade union resistance. They are interesting more for what they tell us about the goals of reform than for their institutional legacy, though both shaped trade union ideology in important ways. The Labour government responded to the Donovan report with a white paper, *In Place of Strife*, in January 1969. The proposed set of reforms were, first and foremost, a political response to the widespread perception that the government had to "do something" in the context of the continuing weakness of the British economy and the high level of industrial conflict. But intellectually, the reforms were also designed by the paper's principal author, Barbara Castle, to be both "a charter of trade union rights"[96] and a coherent socialist industrial relations response to new economic conditions; economic modernization required the integration of industrial relations into broader mechanisms of social and economic planning. In that respect collective laissez-faire was clearly inconsistent with the evolution of state economic intervention.

In Place of Strife followed Donovan closely in proposing to create a Commission on Industrial Relations (CIR), which would register all collective agreements and could intervene in cases of employer refusal to grant union recognition, but it added measures to directly regulate industrial action by requiring strike ballots and permitting the state to impose a "conciliation pause" where strikes were deemed unconstitutional (in terms of the relevant trade unions' rules; this was aimed at unofficial strikes) or inadequate joint discussion had taken place. While five of the eight main new elements proposed in the white paper were derived from the Donovan recommendations, public attention was concentrated on the limits on strikes, which contradicted the Donovan approach. In April 1969, in an effort to show toughness toward the unions, Wilson proposed a short industrial relations bill, the core of which would create a new statutory right to belong to a union, the power to impose a CIR recommendation of union recognition on an employer, and a new power of the state to impose a settlement in strikes arising out of interunion disputes and to impose a twenty-eight day conciliation pause in unconstitutional strikes. This was a straightforward quid pro quo: union recognition for limits on strikes. The TUC rejected it, the Labour government lost the support of its own backbenchers, and Prime Minister Harold Wilson backed down and accepted the political fig leaf of a greater commitment from the TUC to settle disputes itself.[97] Insofar as the fate of In Place of Strife was viewed through the prism of a constitutional conflict between the state and the labor movement, the state was deemed the loser, and the Conservative Party led by Edward Heath won the 1970 general election.

The new Conservative government passed the Industrial Relations Act (IRA) in 1971. It was a comprehensive reconstruction of industrial relations that replaced all existing trade union law, repealing the 1906 Trade Disputes Act, the cornerstone of collective laissez-faire, along the way.[98] It was modeled explicitly on elements of U.S. labor law, particularly a trade union recognition procedure, a new category of "unfair labour practices," and a state-imposed cooling-off period during industrial disputes. Its very comprehensiveness made the legislation immensely complicated, but its essence was similar to that of the previous Labour government's short industrial relations bill: union recognition in return for limits on strikes. The legislation offered a statutory union recognition procedure that would operate through the CIR. There were then restrictions on union legal immunities during strikes: interunion disputes were not covered by the immunity, nor were secondary disputes. A new National Industrial Relations Court (NIRC) could also decide that certain actions were "unfair labor practices," and the government received emergency powers to deal with legal strikes if they were damaging to the economy or community, through imposing a sixty day cooling-off period and ordering a strike ballot. Collective agreements were deemed to be legally enforceable unless explicitly stated otherwise in the agreement. This provision was aimed at creating binding dispute procedures that would encourage the negotiation of no-strike agreements. Thus strikes were to be reduced in three ways: by narrowing legal immunity to exclude a range of types of strike, by giving the state emergency powers to intervene in disputes, and by trying to encourage unions and employers to police their own agreements. One might add that in introducing a right of protection from unfair dismissal for the first time in British labor law, and thereby building on the body of individual rights at work mentioned above, the Conservative government was also seeking to reduce strikes by providing a legal remedy for certain types of dismissal.

Barbara Castle had believed that a more organized capitalism required a more regulated industrial relations system. Edward Heath's government, paradoxically, appeared to believe that its economic project of deregulation, and a return to a more arms-length relationship between state and market, also required greater state regulation of industrial relations. Diametrically opposed economic philosophies generated similar industrial relations projects. More so than *In Place of Strife*, though, the IRA demonstrated a very real tension between individual rights, of both employers and individual workers, and the collective rights (or at least immunities) necessary to accommodate regular, stable collective bargaining arrangements.[99]

The Conservative legislation assumed that trade unions would register under the act in order to receive the benefits of the statutory recognition procedure, that employers would take advantage of the legislation to reconstruct their industrial relations, and that, most fundamentally, rank-and-file trade unionists were more moderate than their leaders. All these assumptions proved to be false. Once again trade unions rejected the legislation, and for the most part refused to register under the act.[100] Trade union opposition to this and the earlier Labour government proposal was in part a result of simple opposition to their coercive elements, but it also reflected a recognition that any system of industrial relations that put the onus on unions to control their members, given the limited organizational power of unions, would tear them apart. Employers also proved largely unwilling to provoke industrial conflict through the use of the legislation, and the legal enforceability of collective bargains was neatly sidestepped by the insertion of so-called TINA-LEA ("this is not a legally enforceable agreement") clauses into agreements. The NIRC proved to be a lightning rod for trade union resistance, making martyrs of the trade unionists whom it imprisoned. Even the sole use of the emergency powers, in the 1972 rail dispute, failed. Overall, the IRA appeared to be a stunning confirmation of the Donovan Commission's justification for why using penal sanctions to modify the behavior of industrial relations actors would not work. And in the end, industrial relations policy was trumped by economic crisis and the perception that reconstructing collective bargaining practices was less pressing than achieving wage restraint. By the end of 1972 the IRA was being quietly ignored by the government in an effort to gain trade union cooperation for a new iteration of incomes policy.

THE INDUSTRIAL RELATIONS POLICY OF THE 1974–79 LABOUR GOVERNMENT

In 1974 a Labour government was returned to power with an ambitious agenda of industrial relations reform that cleaved closely to the spirit of the royal commission's report, though it envisaged greater use of legislation to achieve its goal: the formalization, extension, and decentralization of the institutions of the collective regulation of industrial relations. The labor movement was intimately involved in drawing up the industrial relations reforms (though unions did not receive all that they wanted from the reforms), in part as a result of the desire to repeal the IRA, but also in part as a result of changes within unions that encouraged a new generation of union leaders to contemplate the decentralization of authority within union organizations, toward shop stewards, and to rethink union strategy, which included a greater willingness to contemplate positive legislation to embed collective rights and industrial democracy. While the Donovan Commission was not directly responsible for the organizational shifts within unions, nor for the greater militancy of union members and their leaders, its analysis of the power vacuum inside the firm and its call for trade unions to shift resources to the workplace level meshed well with the preferences and strategic rethinking of several key union leaders, including Jack Jones of the Transport and General Workers Union (TGWU) and Hugh Scanlon of the Amalgamated Engineering Union (AEU).

The legislative strategy envisaged by the TUC and the Labour Party in advance of the 1974 election had three stages: first, repeal of the IRA, which was achieved by the 1974 Trade Union and Labour Relations Act (TULRA) and a 1976 act amending the 1974 legislation (the earlier legislation was passed when Labour was a minority government, and it was amended after Labour achieved an overall majority); second, the provision of new individual and collective rights at work, embodied in the 1975 Employment Protection Act (EPA); third, legislation on industrial democracy to extend the scope of collective regulation, for which a Committee of Inquiry on Industrial Democracy, headed by Lord Bullock, was set up, though no legislation on the subject ever appeared.

The first step was relatively straightforward. It entailed reenacting the immunity provisions of the 1906 Trade Disputes Act, and the TULRA also sought to close some of the loopholes that had allowed judges to narrow immunity, and to limit the recourse of employers to injunctions against trade union strike action. In both cases, the Labour government was trying to exclude common law and judicial intervention in industrial relations to return to the long period of judicial passivity preceding *Rookes v. Barnard*. That effort failed. The result of the TULRA and its 1976 Amendment Act was to restore collective laissez-faire with regard to the right to engage in collective action. It is worth noting that not only was this simply a restoration and not an advance, but that neither the labor movement nor the government gave serious consideration to using the legislative opportunity provided by the need to put something in the place of the repealed IRA to create a positive right to strike. Reliance on negative immunities remained the path whereby strike action was rendered legal.

In the area of industrial action, the state demonstrated no spirit of innovation. The innovation in this project of industrial relations reform came, as in the construction phase of the first system of industrial relations seventy years earlier, in the area of collective bargaining. The EPA did provide and extend a set of rights at work. In this respect the legislation worked hand in hand with separate legislation concerning race and sex discrimination, provision of rights to maternity pay, protection from dismissal for pregnancy, and so on. The general right to protection from unfair dismissal, which had been an important element of the 1971 IRA, was retained. Workers also received some minor rights such as a right to time off to look for work, and to a written explanation for dismissal.

But the main emphasis of the EPA, and the focus of analysis here, was the goal of formalizing and extending collective bargaining. In this regard, it is important to note that all but one of the measures were designed to operate at the level of the workplace, encouraging the decentralization of collective regulation, and that, in contrast to the period of collective laissez-faire, legal regulation was given a major role. As Davies and Freedland have argued, collectively this legislative package has "some title to be regarded as a grand plan for the promotion by legal means of the system of collective bargaining."[101]

There were three elements to the effort to strengthen and decentralize collective bargaining. First, like its predecessors, *In Place of Strife* and the IRA, the Employment Protection Act created a statutory right to trade union recognition. Where an employer denied recognition to a union, that union could approach the newly created Advisory, Conciliation and Arbitration Service (ACAS), which was explicitly charged with promoting collective bargaining, and request that it investigate, conciliate, and, if necessary, issue a ruling on the legitimacy of the claim for recognition. But, as discussed below, the enforcement of any ruling was indirect, operating in a similar way to the compulsory arbitration provision of Order 1376. That is to say, an employer could not be forced to grant recognition. Rather, if an employer refused to follow ACAS's recommendation to grant recognition, the Central Arbitration Council (CAC) could change the terms and conditions of employment for employees at that firm.

Second, the EPA provided a whole set of largely individual rights designed to encourage and improve collective bargaining. These included government funding for shop steward training, a right to time off for stewards to engage in union activities, a right that relevant information be disclosed ahead of collective bargaining, and a right of consultation over layoffs. As Wedderburn argued at the time, this could be described as "building a 'collective right to associate' out of the bricks of certain 'individual' employment rights."[102] This use of individual rights at work to underpin collective rights was a significant innovation in British industrial relations. From the end of the 1980s, it became an increasingly central component of the strategy of the labor movement for post-Thatcherite industrial relations reform, as the next chapter will indicate. ACAS was charged with constructing Codes of Practice—the first two covering facilities for stewards in the firm and information disclosure—which had some legal force, in that they could be used during arbitration proceedings.[103] Thus a combination of legal rights, identification of best practice, investigation of industrial conflict, and persuasion were the tools that ACAS was empowered to use to fulfill its statutory duty of promoting collective bargaining, which was thereby deemed to be in the public good.

The right of recognition and measures to encourage and extend collective bargaining all operated at the level of the firm or workplace; they were expected to either create decentralized bargaining institutions if they did not exist or to strengthen them if they already existed. Their implications for industry bargaining were likely to be indirect. But the third element of the EPA did create a new procedure for the extension of collective bargaining. Schedule 11 of the EPA permitted a worker to make a claim to ACAS that an employer was observing terms and conditions that were either less favorable than "recognized terms and conditions or, where . . . there are no recognized terms and conditions, the general level of terms and conditions."[104] This extension procedure was similar to the 1959 Terms and Conditions of Employment Act, except that it included the provision that a claim could be made even if there was no relevant industry agreement between an employers' association and one or more trade unions. Under those circumstances, the employer was expected to apply the "general level" of terms and conditions for comparable employees in the same trade or industry. In other words, instead of operating solely as a buttress to industry bargaining, Schedule 11 permitted the extension of collective bargaining into new areas, such as private services. And in fact, Schedule 11 was used far more extensively than the 1959 Terms and Conditions of Employment Act, and the great bulk of claims made were under the "general level" heading rather than the "recognised terms and conditions" heading. In practice, the statutory procedure was used primarily by white-collar unions (ASTMS, AUEW-TASS, and APEX), and the large general unions, particularly the TGWU.[105] The logic of the extension procedure in the EPA was quite different from that of its predecessors; it provided a mechanism to drive employers to the bargaining table and grant recognition to trade unions in sectors of the economy that had not seen collective regulation during the heyday of collective laissez-faire.

In a similar vein to the extension procedure, legislation on wages councils was also modified in order to make their repeal easier if voluntary collective bargaining institutions existed. Whereas ten wages councils, covering around 400,000 people, had been abolished between 1945 and 1968, fourteen councils, covering approximately 600,000 people, were abolished between 1969 and 1979.[106] A new intermediate institution, between a wages council and voluntary collective bargaining, was also authorized, the Statutory Joint Industrial Council, though none was ever created.

The industrial relations legislation of the 1974–79 Labour government had a clear and coherent logic. It sought to retain the emphasis on the collective regulation of industrial relations that had marked the first system of industry bargaining, but in keeping with the conviction that economic restructuring could be negotiated only within the firm, it dramatically shifted attention from industry bargaining, which it largely ignored, to the construction and reinforcement of collective regulation within the firm. The resources and capacities of workplace labor representatives were increased, and supplemented by mechanisms to enable unions to gain recognition in areas of the economy where they had previously proved unable to persuade employers of either their strength or their utility to the firm. Even if some of the means differed, this legislation was the kind of experiment recommended by the Donovan Commission. Central to this reform project were measures to encourage trade union recognition by individual employers. In contrast to the industry-level bargaining system of the earlier period, trade union recognition was the "fulcrum" of the emerging decentralized industrial relations system, upon which firm-level collective bargaining rested.[107]

The Trade Union and Labour Relations Act and the Employment Protection Act reflected, in crucial respects, the labor movement's interpretation of Donovan. That is not to say that employers, or even a majority of employers, opposed the decentralization and reinforcement of collective bargaining. That process went ahead, and in the decade and a half following Donovan, a system of decentralized collective bargaining, with a panoply of workplace institutions of collective regulation, became deeply implanted into British industrial relations, as the next section will demonstrate. But the particular trade union interpretation of how this system would come about had implications for how it was received by employers, and for the long-term fate of this second system of industrial relations.

For example, the new provisions contained in the EPA were heavily marked by the unions' distrust of penal sanctions, and reinforced by the experience of the IRA, and the labor movement's profound antipathy to the judiciary. As such, ACAS was given few sanctions, and the awards of the CAC on union recognition, extension of bargaining, and disclosure of information all operated indirectly. The result was that noncompliance with the legislation from a relatively small number of employers had few costs, which encouraged resistance to it and discredited the legislation even in the eyes of its supporters.

The Grunwick case played an important part in demonstrating the impotence of ACAS.[108] Grunwick was a small photo-processing firm in London, whose employees went on strike seeking recognition of the white-collar trade union APEX in 1976–77. The employer resolutely refused recognition and did not cooperate with ACAS. The House of Lords overturned the ACAS recommendation in favor of union recognition on the grounds that a proper survey of employee views was made impossible by the firm's noncooperation, thereby legitimizing the strategy of resistance. ACAS increasingly found that noncooperation on the part of employers prevented it from issuing recommendations.[109] By the time that a new Conservative government was elected in 1979, ACAS itself was saying that it could not operate the recognition provisions of the EPA,[110] and the trade union movement shed few tears when the statutory recognition and the Schedule 11 extension procedures were abolished.

The influence of the labor movement on this set of industrial relations reforms also shaped their reception and impact in another way. State intervention in the first period had encouraged employers' associations and trade unions to construct collective bargaining institutions at the industry level. Insofar as unions were strengthened, it was indirectly, through the transmission of union recognition to members of the employers' association, and through the opportunities that regularized bargaining afforded unions to make gains. Employers were under no obligation to cede some portion of their managerial prerogative to collective regulation with union representatives in the firm. The Employment Protection Act sought to change bargaining practices by directly strengthening trade unions inside the workplace. In other words, new institutions and forms of collective bargaining were to be by-products of stronger labor organization. This was the sense in which Jack Jones, general secretary of the TGWU, famously described the legislation as a "shop stewards charter."[111] The deliberate and direct strengthening of organized labor within the firm was quite different, and potentially more threatening to employers, from the indirect effects of state intervention in the first period: every workplace now became a site of potential struggle over the degree and scope of collective regulation.

More threatening still to employers was the third stage of industrial relations reform, industrial democracy. While the Labour government did set up the Bullock Committee to make recommendations on the form that industrial democracy might take in Britain, the committee was sharply divided and issued majority and minority reports, corresponding to the labor and business sides respectively, and no legislation on the subject ever made it to the statute book. The separate reports indicated that by the second half of the 1970s there had been an almost complete collapse in the social consensus around industrial relations reform. To a certain extent, it is possible to see the debate over industrial democracy as a sideshow to the main business of industrial relations reform; the Donovan Commission had been dubious of industrial democracy's place in British industrial relations, and even the labor movement was a late convert, with the TUC being willing to propose statutory labor representation on boards of directors only in the context of debate about how a future Labour government should respond to the industrial relations reforms embodied in the IRA.

Nevertheless, industrial democracy did fit the economic logic of the second system of industrial relations; indeed it would have been its logical end point. The second system of industrial relations extended collective regulation in three directions: horizontally, to new sectors of the economy; vertically, to the workplace; and qualitatively, to expand the scope of collective regulation so that it could include bargaining over the process of economic restructuring. Productivity bargaining was where the emphasis of the Donovan report lay, but there was no good reason why the negotiation of nonwage issues, and the linkage of wage to nonwage issues, should be limited to work organization, work practices, and technology. Corporate planning was intimately tied to economic restructuring, and insofar as this period saw an attempt to create institutions that would reduce the resistance of workers to economic change, participation in corporate decision-making was the obvious next step. Had proposals for industrial democracy contemplated the creation of entirely new forms of worker representation—works councils elected directly by employees with a statutory duty to cooperate with management, along the lines of those in Germany, for example—one could speak of some distinctively different project of industrial relations, not least because it would have implied competing representational structures. But the proposals made in the majority report of the Bullock Committee were much less radical. They involved a simple extension of joint regulation to a range of aspects of corporate planning without the creation of any new "substructure," to use Kahn-Freund's word.[112] Thus the method of selecting labor representatives to be appointed to the board of directors of a firm would be determined by a "joint representative committee" of those unions currently recognized, so that the "link between board-level representation and collective bargaining could hardly have been more strongly asserted."[113] In this respect, the form of industrial democracy envisaged would have been part and parcel of the wider project of expanding the scope of collective regulation, and of shifting attention to the negotiation of economic change.

EVALUATING INDUSTRIAL RELATIONS REFORM

Any evaluation of the industrial relations of the 1970s inevitably focuses on industrial conflict, incomes policies, and a series of set-piece battles between the labor movement and the state. This period is understood to represent a failure of industrial relations; certainly the period of the Social Contract between the 1974–79 Labour government and the trade unions, and the "Winter of Discontent" of 1978–79, traumatized both the Labour Party and the unions, setting in motion the transformation of the party into today's New Labour Party and permitting Margaret Thatcher's Conservative Party to win power on a platform of industrial relations reform. Nevertheless, as the remainder of this chapter suggests, while industrial relations reforms during this period can be considered a political failure, they were an institutional success, and it is this process of institution-building that needs attention if one is to understand the shape and outcome of the future reform efforts that created the third system of industrial relations after 1979. For that reason, this chapter passes over the well-known story of failed incomes policies and public-sector strikes to examine the emergence of decentralized industrial relations institutions, primarily in the private sector.

This period saw a marked increase in the degree of state intervention. Efforts to limit and control strikes were the most trumpeted and visible elements of those interventionist efforts. Less visible, but much more important and successful, however, was the effort to reconstruct Britain's system of industrial relations, retaining the first system's emphasis on the necessary role of trade unions and permanent collective bargaining institutions in the regulation of relations between business and labor, but shifting away from industry-level bargaining toward the workplace, which was the site of conflict over the process of economic restructuring, and simultaneously expanding the scope of collective regulation to include the organization and nature of work.

In the second system, state intervention operated through legislation, incomes policies, and, once again, its management of public-sector industrial relations (for example, general agreements in local government in 1969 and the health service in 1971 recognized shop stewards[114]), and it encouraged a decentralization of bargaining *indirectly* through strengthening the capacities of trade unions inside the firm. The British state did not, for the most part, create this new set of industrial relations institutions; as the Donovan report noted, they were already being constructed in some firms and some sectors of the economy. Instead the role of the state during this period was to accelerate changes in industrial relations practices that were occurring naturally, and to spread those changes from a few advanced sectors to the rest of the economy. This required that the state overcome resistance to this evolution, particularly from trade unions. Whereas in the early decades of the twentieth century it was employer resistance to trade unionism and collective actions problems facing employers in highly competitive industries that required the attention of the state, in this period it was the trade unions that initially needed to be persuaded of the virtues of decentralized collective bargaining. As the sectoral conferences organized by the TUC after the Donovan report was published demonstrated, it became clear that unions were heavily invested in industry bargaining;[115] again and again, union representatives articulated concern with the implications of decentralized bargaining and defended the practice of industry bargaining. Decentralization stretched already thin organizations, threatened established lines of authority, and raised the specter of fragmentation and wage competition between union members. Industry bargaining had also permitted individual firms to neglect the development of personnel policies, and employer responses to Donovan also emphasized the economic virtues of industry bargaining.

Thus both employers and unions had fixed costs embedded in the industrywide bargaining system, particularly unions, whose organizational structures—inherited from the earlier period—were often centralized, and relied on cadres of professional negotiators and full-time officials.[116] The state could reduce the costs to unions and employers of decentralizing bargaining, and spread those costs more widely through the economy. Providing a right of union recognition at the firm level (which required a demonstration of strength inside a firm), giving new rights to unions in firm-level bargaining, and requiring employers to provide resources for, and therefore effectively subsidize, union activity inside the firm, all encouraged trade unions to shift their attention to the firm and to create firm-level bargaining institutions. In 1968 trade unions certainly largely resisted the "two systems" analysis of the royal commission; by the end of the 1970s it was practically hegemonic within the labor movement.

By the end of the 1970s there had been an unmistakable shift in the physiognomy of the British industrial relations system as a "new industrial relations system had emerged in Great Britain,"[117] such that a system of industry bargaining with a few pockets of decentralized bargaining had been transformed into one where two-tier bargaining was the norm, and the central locus of industrial regulation was inside the firm. Alongside a decline in industry bargaining, a set of firm- and workplace-level industrial relations institutions had emerged to regulate decentralized bargaining. At the same time, firm-level bargaining became increasingly extensive and formalized, going well beyond terms, conditions, and dispute procedures to encompass bargaining over a wide range of work organization issues.[118] Whether labeled productivity bargaining, new technology bargaining, or flexibility bargaining, it is clear that by the end of the 1970s management had ceded its right to unilaterally organize the workplace.[119]

In raw institutional terms, these new institutions and practices became embedded within the wider industrial relations system in a remarkably short amount of time. The essence of this second reform project was that trade unions were to be enlisted in the process of economic modernization through their representation in firm-level bargaining institutions. It was a decentralized system of industrial relations incorporating the collective representation of workers. Evidence for the period up until the early 1980s shows that British industrial relations did decentralize across the economy, that trade unionism spread well beyond its traditional strongholds, into new sectors and among new categories of workers, and that firm-level institutions and union capacities did grow significantly. Industry-level bargaining retained an important role in collective bargaining, but the real growth in new bargaining came at the level of the firm or workplace. Indeed, in a 1978 survey of manufacturing employers, Brown noted a decline in multiemployer bargaining and a large rise in single employer bargaining, especially among larger firms and those with foreign ownership. Only about one quarter of firms in Brown's sample considered that industry-level bargaining was the main locus of pay bargaining.[120] A similar shift in importance, from the industry to the workplace or firm level, was repeated across the economy. A 1980 survey found that 56 percent of firms considered that the workplace and firm levels of bargaining were more important for pay determination than industry or regional bargaining for their manual employees, while 78 percent considered them more important for their nonmanual employees.[121]

The focus of this section is the private sector; it was industrial relations failure in this sector, manifested in the scale of unofficial strikes in manufacturing, that initiated the Donovan Commission and framed the prescription for reform that emerged by the end of the 1960s. In the public sector, the first system of industrial relations still reigned supreme, with widespread implementation of the Whitley model of national bargaining, national pay scales, extensive arbitration machinery, and limited local, workplace trade union development.[122] However, by the middle of the 1970s, industrial relations developments in the public sector were evolving in a direction parallel to those of the private sector. This was the product of state pay policy: incomes policies that fell most heavily on public-sector workers generated rank-and-file resistance, and the introduction of bonus schemes and incentive payments for manual employees after 1967. This required workplace institutions to monitor the operation of the schemes; in 1969 a general agreement recognized shop stewards in local government, with a similar agreement in the health service in 1971. Public-sector trade unions then authorized shop stewards and began training and electing them. By the end of the 1970s such decentralized institutions were widespread in the public sector.[123]

Trade union membership and density accelerated through the end of the 1970s, reaching its twentieth-century peak of 13.4 million and 55.4 percent in 1979.[124] This expansion involved both a saturation of union membership among manual workers in manufacturing and rapid growth among white-collar workers, who accounted for two-thirds of total union growth in the decade 1969–79. Fully half of all union membership growth came from the public sector. Thus trade unionism not only grew in its areas of traditional strength, but it became more widely diffused across the economy. The statutory recognition procedure accounted for only a small proportion of this total,[125] partly because of the limitations of the procedure, but partly because it was simply swamped by one of the two or three greatest periods of trade union growth in British history.

Shop stewards, the most visible symbol of the second system industrial relations, also saw a rapid growth in numbers, from about 90,000 in 1961 to approximately 317,000 in 1980.[126] By the end of the 1970s shop stewards had spread well beyond their traditional concentration among manual workers in manufacturing, to become widespread in the public sector and as representatives of manual workers in private services and white-collar workers in manufacturing. This was accompanied by a formalization of steward organization, with big increases in the numbers of full-time stewards, more formal elections of stewards, and time off for steward training.[127] Inside the workplace there was also the development of institutions to manage interunion relations, such as joint shop steward committees. There was similar expansion in the spread of other workplace industrial relations institutions: closed shop agreements became both more common and significantly more formal,[128] and the dues checkoff spread rapidly, particularly in the public sector (where it was almost universal by 1980) and among manual workers.[129] The diffusion of both the closed shop and the dues checkoff had the effect of permitting a shift in the role of shop stewards, from recruiters and dues collectors to negotiators and grievance officials.

It should be unsurprising, therefore, that trade unions engaged in a parallel decentralization of authority within their organizations.[130] Decentralization took place in different ways, depending on the previous structure, and for different reasons, responding both to internal debates and contests over power and to the external requirements of managing the decentralization of bargaining, but the trend across the labor movement was clearly in the direction of decentralization.[131] The best example of this process was the TGWU, where there was strong support for decentralization from Jack Jones, who became general secretary in 1969. The union shifted the emphasis of its bargaining from national agreements to firm bargaining, dramatically increased the number of shop stewards (while the number of full-time officials fell), incorporated stewards onto negotiating bodies, and expanded the scope of "reference-back" procedures. This latter reform gave affected trade union members the right to accept or reject collective agreements, curtailing the high degree of autonomy previously enjoyed by full-time officials.[132]

In a similar vein, Heery and Kelly argue that "professional unionism" gave way to "participative unionism" after the mid-1960s, only to be transformed into "managerial unionism" in the 1980s and 1990s. "Participative unionism" is understood as involving a "shift in the servicing relationship, such that the task of the [union] bureaucracy came to be identified as one of fostering relatively self-sufficient workplace trade unionism. The membership came to be seen in activist terms, capable of formulating and prosecuting its own interests."[133] Both the description of internal union organization and the timing of the heyday of "participative unionism" identified by Heery and Kelly map well onto the broader shifts in the institutions of industrial relations outlined in this chapter.[134]

Nevertheless, for all its institutional success, this system of industrial relations failed, primarily because it achieved neither the political consensus nor the stable class compromise of the earlier system. Britain's economic problems proved intractable to governments of the 1960s and 1970s, and incomes policies of various types were in operation more or less continuously from 1961 to 1978. Decentralizing industrial relations could only weaken the capacity of governments, employers, and unions to control wages. A series of incomes policies were implemented, some with the force of law, others as voluntary, policed by trade unions. These policies hit the public sector particularly hard, because it was here that they were most easily implemented. The 1974–79 Labour government persuaded the TUC to operate a voluntary policy, in part in return for the legislation outlined above, for three years. The TUC finally refused another year of wage restraint, and the policy collapsed in a wave of strikes in the so-called 'Winter of Discontent' of 1978–79, which led directly to the election of the Conservative government of Margaret Thatcher in 1979.

The "Winter of Discontent" highlighted the contradiction embedded within the state project for industrial relations reform in this second period. The project sought to simultaneously centralize wage regulation through incomes policies and decentralize bargaining institutions and trade union structures. Decentralization made it impossible for union leaders to deliver wage restraint, while near continuous incomes policies overwhelmed efforts to create stable bargaining structures inside the firm. In seeking to use the industrial relations system to manage macroeconomic crisis, the British state doomed its reform project.

Industrial relations reform was also undermined by the resurgence of judicial activism. The hostile position of much of the judiciary was nicely captured by Lord Denning's remark that "when parliament granted immunities to the leaders of trade unions, it did not give them any rights."[135] The Trade Union and Labour Relations Act, in responding to the return of judicial intervention in industrial relations in *Rookes v. Barnard*, had attempted to squeeze the genie back into the bottle and restore broad immunity to those engaged in collective industrial action. This time it failed. The 1975 House of Lords ruling in *American Cyanamid v. Ethicon* dramatically reduced the threshold for obtaining a temporary injunction to stop a strike.[136] Subsequent rulings were essentially new policy departures,

> thinly disguised by an expanding legal framework which embodies substantial scope for restraining industrial action. The development of narrow and difficult distinctions and the gratuitous qualification of the statutory language by concepts of reasonableness, directness and remoteness have enabled the courts to assert a high level of discretion and control over the circumstances in which industrial action may be lawfully conducted.[137]

Furthermore, judicial oversight of ACAS had the effect of preventing it from acting, or appearing to act, as a neutral third party charged with the promotion of decentralized collective regulation of industrial relations. A series of court cases encouraged the narrow legal regulation of industrial relations, and tended to privilege individual rights rather than providing the legal space for ACAS to encourage collective regulation.[138] As noted above, this ultimately led to an admission from ACAS that it could not carry out its statutory mission.

The second project of industrial relations reform was clearly a political failure, in that it never achieved broad political legitimacy. It lacked the degree of autonomy from political control by the state that its predecessor had enjoyed. Corporatism, and the relationship between wage restraint policies and the political linkages between the Labour Party and the trade union movement, politicized industrial relations. At the same time, macroeconomic policy was deeply implicated in the material conditions underlying the second system of industrial relations because of the importance of full employment. This mean that a return to higher levels of unemployment was always one possible alternative path: a means for employers to regain power in the workplace without having to share it.

The new Conservative government elected in 1979 was elected in large part because of the perceived failings of this system, and it came to power determined to abandon it and create a quite different set of industrial relations institutions and practices. The question of social consensus, or the degree to which a class compromise existed between employers and unions around this set of industrial relations institutions, however, is more difficult to examine.

Employers were divided and ambivalent about the extension of union power directly into the workplace. The surveys that we have from this period suggest quite strong support for decentralized collective bargaining with union representatives inside the firm.[139] Over and over again, surveys have demonstrated that employers tended to be supportive of the activities of shop stewards and the closed shop because they stabilized industrial relations and offered the opportunity to tackle conflicts that originated inside the firm. As Batstone put it, there is "a long history of management support for stewards."[140] One of the main themes of research on shop steward development in the 1970s was not that stewards were imposed on employers but rather that employers took the lead in encouraging and deliberately fostering them, as part of what Terry has termed "reform strategies."[141] In one sense this should come as no surprise, since the development of informal, irregular workplace bargaining, promoted by managers and work groups, was precisely what the royal commission argued had been happening spontaneously without any help from the state. Initially, at least, it was trade unions that were dubious about the decentralization of collective bargaining, for fear that they lacked the resources and strength to bargain at the firm level. Managers were the "true disciples" of the Donovan report, and the prime movers behind the reconstruction of British industrial relations along the lines laid out in the report.[142]

That said, one would expect employer support for decentralized collective regulation to be greater in industries with a legacy of either strong trade unions or powerful work groups, where new workplace industrial relations institutions might provide mechanisms for overcoming resistance to the negotiation of economic restructuring. In industries where unions had proven too weak to gain recognition, and where managers still enjoyed a high degree of unilateral managerial prerogative, the Labour government's legislation in the mid-1970s posed a very real threat. It gave workers and unions rights that might lead to the imposition of collective regulation on a reluctant employer. Thus the first system of industrial relations solved a set of collective action problems for employers while not directly strengthening unions, and while keeping union influence over firm-level decisions limited, whereas in this second period, unions were directly strengthened, and managerial prerogatives were directly challenged. As noted above, for employers who saw little to be gained from the new class compromise embedded in decentralized collective regulation, the industrial action around the attempt to gain union recognition at the Grunwick Film Processing Laboratories in 1976–77, and the inability of ACAS to impose recognition on the employer, demonstrated that resistance to trade unionism and government legislation was a viable strategy. And the collapse of efforts, under the auspices of the Bullock Commission, to create institutions of industrial democracy marked the end point of union encroachment on traditional managerial prerogatives inside the firm, showing that there were clear limits to employers' willingness to share power in order to regain control.

Nevertheless, this project of industrial relations reform initially failed because it was unable to achieve a degree of political consensus, rather than because of employer opposition. The main elements of the reform effort were widely adopted by employers because they appeared to respond to the problem of how to manage economic change inside the workplace. However, for the Conservative Party and, increasingly, important sections of the Labour Party, the second system of industrial relations was instead judged in more political terms, by its failure to either reduce industrial conflict or encourage wage restraint, thus weakening the political legitimacy and economic competency of the state.[143] The Thatcherite reforms, and the new set of industrial relations institutions that they ushered in, were, again initially, aimed at reducing the strike level and controlling wage inflation, rather than dismantling the institutions of collective regulation within the firm. Any more fundamental reconstruction of the industrial relations system would have had to confront those employers who were quite comfortable with, and in some cases had spearheaded, the innovations of the 1960s and 1970s.

However, as the next chapter will demonstrate, as time went on economic restructuring encouraged a shift in the interests of many employers, and support for a distinct third system of industrial relations appeared. But if the industrial relations reforms of the 1970s ultimately proved too fragile to survive the onslaught of structural economic change, and too vulnerable to employer and state hostility in the 1980s and 1990s, they did, paradoxically, create the preconditions for this third system, the core of which is decentralized industrial relations but without the collective representation of workers.

The Debate over Rights-Based Industrial Relations: A Missed Opportunity?

The 1960s saw a highly visible public debate about the direction of British industrial relations. Barely noticed at the time, however, was a parallel debate within the labor movement, which pitted traditional voluntarism against an alternative rights-based approach that would have entailed a significant juridification of British industrial relations. In many ways, it revisited the debate at the end of the nineteenth century around compulsory arbitration, which was discussed in the previous chapter. This internal debate was about, and its outcome was shaped by, the relationship between trade unionism and the state. It was one of those rare moments of historical fluidity, in which an alternative direction was possible. In the event, debate over an alternative direction was overwhelmed by a combination of the balance of power within the trade union movement, the legacy of the first system of industrial relations, and the actions of the state. The result was to reproduce and reinforce voluntarism, and to permit organized labor's critics to dominate the discursive construction of crisis.

It was the abolition of Order 1376, more than the *Rookes* decision, that stimulated a debate within the union movement about the industrial relations system and the role of labor law. Among the growing body of white-collar unions, Order 1376 provided a route to recognition that they had lacked because of the absence of indirect recognition through industry bargaining, the resistance of employers to recognition, and the resistance of many of their members to taking strike action to achieve recognition.[144] The banking industry provides perhaps the best illustration of the problems facing white-collar unions, as the banks created barely independent staff associations to compete with financial-section unions, and refused industry bargaining. NUBE had used the threat of compulsory arbitration to gain recognition at Barclays Bank, and the abolition of that mechanism galvanized the union to seek alternatives.[145] Similarly, the Clerical and Administrative Workers Union and the Union of Shop, Distributive and Allied Workers (USDAW) had used Order 1376 but found that they could not use its successor, the 1959 Terms and Conditions of Employment Act, because it operated only where an industry agreement already existed.

From 1960 until the publication of the Donovan report, demands from white-collar unions for new mechanisms to gain recognition from employers, and for a more comprehensive system of labor law, were regularly debated at the annual meetings of the TUC and the Annual Conference of Unions Catering for Non-Manual Workers. Motions from NUBE, ASSET, and others called for a variety of solutions, ranging from the reimposition of Order 1376, through the incorporation of ILO Conventions 87 and 98 into British law, to consideration of some equivalent to the U.S. Wagner Act.[146] Remarkably, considering the TUC's evidence (see below) and the final recommendations contained in the Donovan report, the evidence that a large number of individual unions contributed to the Donovan Commission also called for a set of trade union rights, including a right to recognition and to bargaining, to be enshrined in British law.[147] ASSET probably went furthest in calling for ILO conventions to be translated into a comprehensive charter of rights at work, and for company law to be amended to force employers to recognize unions, bargain in good faith, disclose information, make company unions illegal, and provide protection from unfair dismissal. In oral evidence, the general secretary of ASSET, Clive Jenkins, also spoke favorably of the recognition procedure contained in the Wagner Act.

The TUC, however, showed little interest in this movement. It was still dominated by large unions that already had recognition, and had the strength and propensity to strike if need be. In a telling speech at the 1960 TUC conference a NUBE delegate pleaded with "the great unions. . . . Please, for pity's sake, do not run away with the idea that because you on your shop floors and in your factories have 100 per cent organisation the Movement is all right and will continue to thrive and prosper."[148] The TUC's evidence to the Donovan Commission was an almost classic statement of collective laissez-faire. It argued that the role of the state in industrial relations was a "second best" solution and that in general the "Government stands aside. Its attitude is one of abstention, of formal indifference."[149] The voluntarist argument was made in a crucial passage, worth quoting at some length:

> The fact that trade unions in Britain have succeeded through their own efforts in strengthening their organisations and in obtaining recognition, not relying on the assistance of Government through legislation, is one of the most important factors sustaining their strength and independence. Trade unions have not been given privileges; they have fought for what they have achieved. If they had been granted privileges, if their organisation had been sustained and strengthened by Government action, it might well be logical to argue today that trade union function would also be the responsibility of Government; the right to bargain had been granted by Government and Government could take it away. Trade union strength has been developed without the help of any external agency.[150]

This statement represents the apogee of a particular interpretation of industrial relations on the part of the British labor movement, one in which union strength was entirely the product of autonomous resources and capacities, independent of the state or employers. The TUC understood that new legislation on recognition would come at the price of limits on strikes, and did not believe that the quid pro quo was worth it. Pure voluntarism seemed preferable to explaining why some forms of state intervention were appropriate and others were not; it had the merit of internal consistency.[151] The experience of incomes policies also intervened, because as early as 1965, when the TUC raised the possibility of the reintroduction of some form of compulsory arbitration, the Labour government had linked the issue to pay policy.

It is also worth noting that when the TUC (and many individual unions) did consider the problem of recognition, it preferred to tinker with existing machinery rather than to contemplate entirely new forms of legislation, such as those modeled on U.S. labor law. The first system of industrial relations exerted a certain ideological path dependence as British unions tended to focus on *indirect* mechanisms for achieving recognition: amending the Fair Wages Resolution or the Terms and Conditions of Employment Act; reintroducing Order 1376. In fact, when NUBE complained about its inability to bring the main banks to the bargaining table, one of the TUC's suggestions was to consider requesting a wages council for the banking industry! The results of these existing, or well-known, mechanisms could be more easily predicted than more comprehensive legislation.

In any case, the pressure for a new framework of labor law came to an abrupt end by the end of the 1960s, overwhelmed by union opposition to incomes policies and growing evidence from the political sphere that any legislation was likely to have a large punitive component.[152] Motions at the TUC annual conference rapidly became hostile to state intervention of any kind. *In Place of Strife* and the IRA poisoned trade union views of the potentially positive role of legislation for the next two decades. While the TUC endorsed the extension of rights for workers and unions in the Employment Protection Act, it retained its mistrust of legal sanctions and sought an indirect recognition procedure. It is, of course, impossible to know whether, had unions embraced a different approach that embedded rights to organize, to recognition, to bargain, and to strike in labor law, they would have been in a better position to resist the assault of the 1980s. But it was certainly the case that, two decades later, when the catastrophic impact of Thatcherite industrial relations reform on trade union strength had become clear, it was a rights-based approach that emerged from within the labor movement as the dominant strategy for renewal.

Recall from the previous chapter that Summers argued, in a comparison of Britain and the United States, that the demand for immunities is the response of a labor movement that sees the judicial apparatus of the state as the main threat to its existence, while a rights-based approach is sought by a labor movement that sees employer hostility as the main threat.[153] During this second period of the reconstruction of industrial relations, British unions still believed that the courts posed a greater danger to their activities than the business class. Indeed, the ideology of voluntarism was *reinforced* by the events of the 1960s and 1970s. In fact, the spread of workplace trade unionism after 1960 was heavily dependent on employer support, including facilities and resources provided by employers to unions. As Brown has put it, "it was fair-weather trade unionism. It was bargaining on the cheap."[154] The belief that unions could rely on their own industrial strength was to prove nearly fatal after 1979.

CHAPTER FIVE

The Decollectivization
of Industrial Relations, 1979–1997

INTRODUCTION

In 1979 13.3 million people belonged to trade unions, the highest level ever reached in Britain, for a union density of 55.4 percent. The influence of industry-level bargaining and the wages councils meant that approximately 85 percent of the working population were covered by collective pay-setting mechanisms.[1] Firm-level industrial relations institutions such as union shop stewards, the closed shop, and joint consultative committees were deeply embedded in the workplace, extending the reach of collective regulation to the shop floor. The influence of the labor movement extended into public policy through a dense network of tripartite institutions, privileged access to the Labour Party, and the norm that governments of either party would consult regularly about issues of social and economic significance. And alongside collective representation and collective regulation, the scale of collective action was as high as it had ever been; indeed, a plausible case could be made that strikes had brought down two elected governments, those of Edward Heath in 1974 and Jim Callaghan in 1979.

By the end of 2001, after eighteen years of consecutive Conservative rule, and more than four of a "new" Labour government, union membership had declined by 40 percent to 7.6 million, and density had fallen below 30 percent of the workforce.[2] The collapse of industry-level bargaining and abolition of the wages councils had taken the coverage of collective pay-setting mechanisms to under 35 percent, which was the lowest level since the early 1920s. These figures also represented the smallest gap between union density and the coverage of collective regulation since the First World War.[3] More than one-third of workplaces had no union members, no worker representatives, no formal structure of employee representation, and no collective consultation of any kind.[4] The institutions of tripartism had been largely dismantled, and the labor movement was reduced to ad hoc lobbying of government, even when the Labour Party, the party it founded, returned to power. Finally, strike levels since the mid-1990s have been the lowest since records began being kept in 1891.[5] The authoritative series of workplace industrial relations surveys concluded cautiously that the changes that have taken place "in the structures and conduct of British industrial relations can reasonably be regarded as a transformation"[6] and that "so great were the changes that it is not unreasonable to conclude that the traditional, distinctive 'system' of British industrial relations no longer characterized the economy as a whole."[7]

In place of a system of industrial relations organized around a dominant role for collective regulation, powerful trade unions, and two-tier bargaining over not simply terms and conditions but also the organization of work is the unmistakable architecture of a third system, characterized by the wholesale decollectivization of industrial relations. This includes the emasculation of collective representation, collective regulation, and collective action, a more significant role for legal regulation of the labor market through the provision of statutory individual, not collective, rights at work; unilateral regulation of the workplace by the employer; and the individualization of social relations between employer and employee. The simultaneous decline in union membership, union recognition, and collective bargaining means that collective bargaining between unions and employers is no longer the dominant system of industrial relations. In its place, we see the growing dominance of workplaces where management sets the terms and conditions of employment unilaterally, in some cases after consultation with employees but with only minimal constraint from trade unions, national or industry-level agreements, or legislation protecting individual workers.

The period since the Conservative election victory in 1979 has been marked by a sharp break with the past. The main difference between the first and second systems of industrial relations was the *locus* of joint regulation—industry or workplace—but they shared the emphasis on the public policy good of trade unions and collective bargaining. The third system has dropped both of these elements. What began in 1979 as an effort to fence in unions, reduce their capacity to damage the economy, and narrow their strategic options, while freeing the hands of employers, has become an individualized system of industrial relations, based on the absence of collective representation for workers in the majority of the economy and on the collapse of linkages between unions and collective bargaining *inside* the firm, and unions and collective bargaining *outside* the firm in what remains of the unionized sector. In the latter case, what is emerging is something close to a de facto enterprise unionism. The result is that even on those scattered islands of collective regulation, overwhelmingly located in older firms, in an ocean of individualized industrial relations, trade unions lack effective sanctions, existing largely at the sufferance of employers.

How did so rapid a transformation come about, and why did this particular form of industrial relations emerge in turn-of-the-century Britain? The lesson of the ill-fated *In Place of Strife* proposal and the 1971 Industrial Relations Act appeared to be that the autonomous strength of labor, a strength based in large part on the consent and active participation of employers, was immune to the exercise of state power. That conclusion was clearly wrong.

The eighteen years of Conservative government industrial relations reform saw the most sustained assault on trade unionism among advanced capitalist countries in the postwar period. While there are other cases of severe union decline—France and the United States come to mind—in the last two decades of the twentieth century, none have been so rapid nor so thoroughgoing, and in no other country was the labor movement apparently so strong just prior to decline.

Part of the reason for this turnaround, as I have argued in previous chapters, is that the British labor movement was more vulnerable, and more dependent on state resources and state practices, than conventional accounts recognize. The ideology of voluntarism and the legacy of collective laissez-faire gave trade unions a false sense of security, and masked the degree to which the institutional configuration of British industrial relations had been constructed by the state. Thus the removal of state support for collective regulation, and dismantling of the institutions of the first and second system of industrial relations, profoundly weakened the labor movement.

By any measure, British trade unions were powerful industrial and political actors by the end of the 1970s. Yet, the fragility of that strength, and its reliance on the particular economic and political conjuncture of the 1970s, must be recognized to understand the crisis of British trade unionism since then. Unions in the 1980s were captives of weaknesses inherited from past choices, with the result that, for all their numbers and influence, they remained deeply vulnerable to attack from employers and the state. The manner in which unions grew after World War II, the conditions under which their growth took place, and the choices that they made during a period of strength formed a legacy that made British trade unionism singularly ill equipped to face the economic conditions of a globalized post-Fordism and the political conditions of a hostile state. Furthermore, trade unions had failed to respond to the economic crisis of the 1970s with any strategic reassessment, relying instead on a schizophrenic oscillation between strike action and political incorporation. The "Winter of Discontent" strike wave in 1978–79 only made clear what should have been obvious, that the expansion of unionism in the 1960s and 1970s was a response to a particular economic and political conjuncture rather than a secular growth of union organizational power.

The argument of this chapter is threefold. First, the form of industrial relations that emerged in the 1980s and 1990s reflected a wave of economic restructuring that constructed a peculiarly British variant of post-Fordism. As the interests of employers changed in response to new economic conditions, increasing numbers sought to construct industrial relations institutions that not only avoided trade unions and collective bargaining but shunned collective representation and collective regulation of any kind. There is little or no evidence that employers used their greater freedom in the management of social relations in the firm to create nonunion forms of collective regulation, such as works councils or collectivist human resource management; the individualization of social relations was the goal and result of employer strategy.

Second, the role of the British state was central to this process of institutional restructuring. State action overcame resistance to the decollectivization project, from both workers and employers; it created the conditions in which employer preferences could be translated into practice, and it gave employers the confidence to contemplate sundering existing relationships with their employees and restructuring workplace institutions. More directly, the state withdrew crucial resources that had propped up the second system of industrial relations and, particularly in the public sector, itself constructed new industrial relations institutions.

Third, the impact of this class project has been more than a weakening trade unions and the encouragement of the emergence of a third system of industrial relations. It has led to a fundamental strategic reconceptualization on the part of the British labor movement. The legacy of industrial relations policy over the last two decades has been to change the way in which trade unions think about their relationship with the state; this ideological shift may be the most profound implication of the British state's role during this period.

This chapter focuses on the Conservative industrial relations project and its impact on industrial relations institutions and labor movement strategy. But the Conservatives lost power in 1997 and were replaced by a "modernized" Labour Party, which often preferred the label "New Labour." This government was reelected in 2001, so that there is every reason to expect at least eight years of a Labour government. The concluding chapter examines the record of these two Labour governments. It will argue that this current Labour government is best understood as a consolidation of, rather than a radical departure from, Thatcherism—implying that the third system of industrial relations will enjoy some longevity.

EMPLOYERS AND THE CONSTRUCTION OF A BRITISH POST-FORDISM

The second system of industrial relations lasted a scant decade before state policy sought to reverse it, or, more accurately, to redirect industrial relations in a radical new direction. The Conservative victory in 1979, and the project of industrial relations restructuring that the Conservative government subsequently pursued, followed from the experience of the 1970s (which is one reason why it was felt that no new royal commission was needed to legitimate change). That experience was interpreted to indicate a trade union movement that was too powerful, both politically and economically.[8] Politically, so the argument went, its ties to the Labour Party and corporatist endeavors by governments of both parties had given unions a quasi veto over public policy and led, ultimately, to the unions bringing down two governments. Economically, strikes and entrenched workplace power had contributed to inflation, a bloated public sector, poor productivity, and weak competitiveness. The public sector was a particular area of concern because, unlike the strike waves that had ushered in the first two systems of industrial relations, the most salient strikes at the end of the 1970s were large public-sector strikes, in both public services and the nationalized industries.

But the Conservative critique went deeper than a focus on the 1970s; it was, in fact, a critique of the entire postwar political economy of Britain, as managed by Labour and Conservative governments. The argument has been nicely characterized by Gamble as "the free economy and the strong state," implying the need for state intervention to remove the obstacles, to "unwind the coils of social democracy and welfarism," in Gamble's wonderful formulation, to let loose the functioning of a free market.[9] Foremost among these obstacles were trade unions and the collective regulation of industrial relations. More broadly, this view identified Keynesian demand management, the goal of full employment, the mixed economy, powerful trade unions, and a rigid labor market as the central problems of the British economy and proposed monetarism, price stability, privatization, and labor market deregulation as the solutions. Now, this set of policies did not need to be a response to the particular set of economic conditions inherited by the Conservatives in 1979. Its analysis was ahistorical, arguing from first economic principles, and from a notion of the rights that inhere in property ownership rather than an actually existing political economy. Rarely was a claim made that industrial relations reform was necessary because of the particular conditions of post–oil crisis Britain.

This raises the question of whether the industrial relations projects of the 1970s and 1980s were simply different political responses to the same set of economic conditions—a Labour and a Conservative form of industrial relations regulation, if you like—or whether they were different political responses to different economic conditions. One could argue that the goal of industrial relations reform in both the 1960s and 1980s was to improve productivity. What differed were the social relations employed to achieve that goal. The second system of industrial relations sought to overcome the resistance of British workers to workplace restructuring using the tools of collective bargaining with the hope that change could be negotiated, and power shared. The third system sought to restore unilateral managerial control in order to permit the imposition of work reorganization.

It is a difficult question to answer, and clearly some of the problems associated with economic restructuring in the 1950s and 1960s—deindustrialization, the search for productivity improvements—remained in this third period. But by the end of the 1970s the older problems of the British economy had become qualitatively more significant, and a new set of problems had emerged. The second system of industrial relations was transitional; it was, in retrospect, the last gasp of Fordist regulation, whose failure opened the way both for more profound economic restructuring and for a different approach to managing that restructuring process. Across the advanced capitalist world, mass production regimes, which relied heavily on circuits linking productivity gains to an expansion in domestic demand, and relatively rigid deployment of labor and capital within forms of work organization that were difficult to change rapidly, faced a generalized crisis.[10] The scale of that crisis and the range of alternatives varied, depending on the organization of the economy and the particular sets of political-economic institutions available to manage change. What emerged then were distinct national post-Fordisms.[11] They shared a commitment to a regulatory framework that achieved supply-side flexibility, but the manner in which this was achieved varied.

In retrospect, British Fordism was not only flawed but short-lived. For all the reasons adduced by scholars, and discussed in previous chapters, a combination of social factors (the organization and practices of managers and workers) and economic ones (the size and form of the domestic market, the level of technological sophistication, the interests of financial capital, and the external vulnerability of the British economy), the effort to construct a durable form of British Fordism quickly collapsed. The emphasis on the interlocking and interdependent nature of institutions contained within the Varieties of Capitalism theoretical framework helps us understand this failure. British governments in the 1960s and 1970s tried a range of institutional reforms in the sphere of industrial relations but never seriously tackled the reform of corporate governance, or the financial system, or the training regime.[12] Industrial relations reforms alone were never going to be sufficient to shift the trajectory of British capitalism, yet policymakers were far too willing to believe that the root of all economic problems lay in the industrial relations system. As noted in the previous chapter, the effort to create institutions of industrial democracy was the logical end point of an alternative regulatory framework for the British economy, and its failure closed off that route.

Under these circumstances, it is no surprise that supply-side flexibility was eventually achieved in Britain in a quite different manner, one associated with unilateral managerial control, the decollectivization of social relations, and labor market deregulation. What has been termed "hyperflexibility" in the British case was a natural, though certainly not inevitable, variant of post-Fordism.[13] In the absence of a commitment to a difficult and much more thorough reshaping of the regulatory institutions of the British economy, accentuating the operation of market-oriented institutions was a more straightforward route. There was no such commitment from the ruling Conservative Party or the main employer organizations. Without alternative financial institutions, or legislation underpinning alternative structures of corporate governance, employers were faced with the choice of continuing with the industrial relations institutions they had (often only recently) constructed in agreement with trade unions, or seeking a return to unilateral control of the firm. We shall see in this chapter how state policy interacted with these different strategies.

Ironically, it was the Labour government elected in 1997, not the Conservatives, that made the most explicit link between broader economic restructuring associated with post-Fordism and the need to reform industrial relations institutions. Blair has repeatedly argued that what might have been justifiable during the postwar boom is no longer appropriate: "The labour market today is completely different in substance from what it was in the early part of the twentieth century. It is light years away from that, but distant even to what it was ten or fifteen years ago, never mind forty or fifty years ago."[14] Globalization, deindustrialization, new technology, and the feminization of the labor force have created new conditions for economic success, requiring that "we must be adaptable, flexible and open to change . . . [that] we will change jobs often and change the nature of our jobs even if we keep them."[15] Thus new economic conditions in turn require new sets of social relations inside the firm.

The main elements of economic restructuring will be familiar to comparative political economists. The first system of industrial relations was constructed as the British economy became truly nationally integrated. The third was constructed as international economic integration became more significant after the collapse of Bretton Woods, the creation of much larger speculative currency markets, an acceleration in the dynamic of European integration, and the expansion of inward investment to Britain. This is not new: a long-standing feature of British capitalism has been the export orientation of manufacturing industry and the international bias of the financial sector.[16] But the period since 1979 has seen a significant increase in the internationalization of the British economy. One study estimated that on average 54 percent of the manufacturing activity of British multinationals is now located outside Britain, and over a third of the leading firms in manufacturing are subsidiaries of foreign-owned firms while another third are British-owned multinationals.[17] A very high proportion of British firms' employment is located overseas, and in comparison with other countries, British multinationals are more service oriented.[18] The numbers employed in manufacturing industry by British subsidiaries of foreign companies, after remaining constant at 12–13 percent for most of the 1980s, rose sharply to 18.6 percent in 1994,[19] while the proportion of private-sector workplaces owned by foreign firms also doubled between 1980 and 1998 to 13 percent, with most of the rise coming in the 1990s.[20] Britain became the second most popular location of foreign direct investment after the United States.[21] In 1989 over half (54 percent) of manufacturing workers employed by foreign multinationals in Britain were employed by U.S. firms, 18 percent by European Community firms, and only 4 percent Japanese firms.[22] An additional incentive for foreign firms has been government regional development policies that provide incentives for investment in areas

with relatively high unemployment. It has been estimated that foreign investment projects receive three-quarters of development assistance.[23]

There have also been important shifts in industrial structure and the composition of the labor force, though here again these have been largely a continuation of long-term trends in the British economy. The employment share of
industry in Britain peaked in 1955 and declined in absolute numbers after
1966. The scale of the changes since 1979 is nonetheless astonishing. Between
1979 and 1996 employment in manufacturing fell by 44 percent (or 3.2 million). By 1996 manufacturing employment as a proportion of the total workforce was 15.8 percent, down from 28.9 percent in 1979. Meanwhile employment in the service sector increased by 25 percent, accounting for two-thirds
of total employment in 1996.[24] Parallel, and related to deindustrialization, has
been the rise of small firms. Reliable time series data on firm size are hard to
find; however, it is clear that since 1979 there has been a growth in employment by small firms and a sizable decline in employment by very large firms,
reversing postwar trends. Between 1979 and 1989 the share of total employment in firms employing fewer than fifty people rose from 33.6 percent to 42.3
percent, while the share of firms employing over five hundred people fell from
42.8 percent to 34.2 percent.[25] A different series focusing on manufacturing
between 1985 and 1994 shows a similar trend, with the share of employment
in local units employing fewer than fifty people rising from 21.6 percent to
26.3 percent, and that in firms employing over five hundred people falling
from 35.5 percent to 26.2 percent.[26]

The composition of the labor force has also changed in important ways.
The feminization of the labor force has been a marked feature of the period.
Between 1979 and 1996, women increased their share of total employment
from 39.9 percent to 46.3 percent, and if one excludes self-employment, which
doubled over this period to 13.2 percent of total employment, by 1996 women
comprised almost half, 49.5 percent, of employees.[27] More dramatic than the
feminization of the labor force has been the collapse of secure, full-time jobs
and their replacement by various forms of atypical work. Part-time jobs increased their share of total employment from 18.5 percent in 1979 to 24.8
percent in 1996; indeed more than four-fifths of the increase in female employment during this period was accounted for by the increase in part-time jobs.
By the middle of the 1990s fully 38 percent of those in employment were self-
employed, working part-time, or on temporary contracts.[28]

Further evidence of an acceleration in post-Fordist restructuring can also
be seen in the spread of "flexibility," whether negotiated or not. It is important
to make a distinction between productivity bargaining in the 1960s and the
kind of flexibility agreements (and flexibility that was unilaterally imposed on
workers in the absence of agreement) that emerged in the 1980s. Productivity
agreements in the 1960s were primarily about gaining worker acquiescence to
new forms of technology and work organization, in many cases those associ-

ated with mass production, which often had little to do with flexibility;[29] increasing productivity in this way did not require substantive labor flexibility. In the 1980s, by contrast, employers were more likely to seek flexibility in the deployment of labor, in hiring and firing, in work time, in pay determination and employee evaluation, and in the kinds of tasks and skill sets expected of workers. And a series of studies have shown evidence of very significant changes in working practices in the course of the last two decades. Ingram found, for the 1980s as a whole, that three-quarters of collective bargaining groups introduced changes in working practices, and that there was an acceleration in the signing of these flexibility agreements as the decade progressed.[30] The great bulk of flexibility agreements appear to have centered on changes in working practices. Beatson's exhaustive study of labor market flexibility, covering numerical flexibility, flexibility in working time, functional flexibility, and wage flexibility, found strong evidence to conclude that the labor market had become more flexible in the fifteen years prior to 1995.[31] Finally, it is worth noting that most of these trends accelerated in the 1990s and were thus not a short-term or one-off effect of the deep recessions that hit the British economy early in the 1980s and again early in the 1990s.

Of course, the processes of international integration, deindustrialization, demographic change, and flexibility affected all advanced capitalist economies, yet as noted above, when faced with the resultant economic pressures, different countries responded in different ways. It was the *interaction of international and domestic economic developments, played out on a field of national institutions*, that generated the specific strategies pursued by the state and private industrial actors in Britain. Many of the distinctive institutional features of British capitalism—the absence of employer coordination, the absence of long-term relationships between industrial and financial capital, and the absence of the capacity for coordinated wage bargaining—had the effect of encouraging a response to any intensification of international competitive pressure through cost reduction and low-wage/low-skill strategies.

This has obvious implications for industrial relations. As Heery has pointed out, a social partnership model of industrial relations needs large firms, dominant in their markets, able to pursue high-quality, high value-added strategies, to thrive.[32] The British economy, characterized by smaller firms in competitive markets, pursuing cost-reduction strategies, was more likely to produce social conflict than social partnership. The role and value of trade unions and collective regulation are less clear under these circumstances.

The significance of the economic shifts noted above has primarily been their effect on the interests of employers. As the internationalization of the British economy and demands for flexibility increased, so have employers sought different relationships with their employees. The ability to respond rapidly to international competition strengthened the existing firm-centric focus of the second industrial relations system. But the greater importance attached to flexibility in this period undermined the collective basis of that system of industrial relations, because employers increasingly wanted to differentiate in the terms and conditions of their employees. This made collective bargaining for large groups less attractive to employers. In the second period, employers sought to buy out restrictive practices in the workplace, and they used collective bargaining as a mechanism for achieving that goal. In this period, they were more likely to seek an individualization of their relationship with their employees, rendering collective representation problematic.

The speed with which employer attitudes toward trade unions and collective regulation turned to hostility is remarkable.[33] Until at least the mid-1970s the bulk of employers seemed committed to making Donovan work—working with trade unions to reach collective solutions to the problems posed by economic restructuring. The same could not be said by the end of the 1980s. A great deal of this was a reflection of the new kinds of firms being created by economic change. The series of workplace industrial relations surveys, thus far spanning the period 1980 to 1998, have demonstrated that the transformation in industrial relations was for the most part a result of the differences between the industrial relations practices of dying and new firms, rather than of changes in the practices of continuing firms,[34] and Machin has argued that in the private sector the key variable in explaining changes in union strength, more important than compositional factors such as firm size, ownership, and level of part-time work, is the age of the workplace. Union recognition rates are much lower in workplaces that have been set up since 1980, and that effect becomes more marked over time.[35]

Evidence for increased employer hostility to collective regulation is available from both what employers say and what they do. What they do—the industrial relations institutions and practices that have emerged in the last two decades—will be discussed in some detail later in this chapter, but a flavor of the shift in attitudes can be offered here. Poole and Mansfield's survey of managerial attitudes in 1980 and then again in 1990 showed a reinforcement over time in the "unitarist preferences" of managers, with increases in a proclivity for no collective representation at all, or for consultation alone in place of collective bargaining, and a sharp drop in informal contacts with union representatives in the workplace.[36] The 1998 Workplace Employment Relations Survey found that 72 percent of managers expressed a preference for consulting directly with their employees rather than bargaining with unions,[37] and showed a collapse in the proportion of managers who strongly recommended union membership to their employees.[38] It is important to recall, as foreign as such a fact may seem early in the twenty-first century, that this hostility to collective regulation is of recent provenance and that, for the previous half century at least, large numbers of employers actively supported collective bargaining with trade unions for the benefits that it could bring.

Finally, on the subject of employer attitudes, we can turn to the proceedings of the House of Commons Employment Committee's investigation into "the future of trade unions" in 1994. Convened to provide a survey of the state of British industrial relations after a decade and a half of Conservative rule and the passage of the sixth major package of industrial relations legislation, the committee invited written and oral evidence from trade unions, employers' organizations, and particular firms.[39] In contrast to the 1894 and 1968 royal commissions, and to the work of the Whitley Committee, The *Future of Trade Unions* report followed rather than preceded industrial relations reform, serving to place the developments of the previous decade and a half within a new understanding of the role of trade unions and the appropriate regulatory institutions within the firm. The report celebrated individualized industrial relations and marked out a terrain in which trade unions should exist primarily outside the firm, as providers of individual services to workers rather than as collective bargaining agents.

Reading the transcripts of the oral evidence, one cannot but be struck by the hostility of the employers' organizations to collective regulation and the inability of their representatives to find positive things to say about trade unions.[40] The Institute of Directors called for further legislation to remove "the special legal privileges trade unions still enjoy," to ultimately return labor law to the situation *before* the 1906 Trade Disputes Act.[41] It argued that the central role of trade unions should be the provision of services to individual members and that collective bargaining should be replaced with individual contracts negotiated between employer and employee. The Confederation of British Industry was scarcely less radical, also arguing that if unions were to survive, "more emphasis on the role of the individual rather than collective representation" would be necessary.[42]

An Activist State and the Construction of Crisis

There can be little question but that there has been a metamorphosis in the way in which British employers think about the regulation of class relations. But to what extent has the British state played a part in this metamorphosis, and has its role been simply to facilitate employer preferences or to shape them? The remainder of this chapter will examine the industrial relations policies of Conservative governments after 1979, and their impact on the institutional architecture of British industrial relations, in some detail. Here I want to point to the broader importance of the state during this period. The role of the state in the construction of the third system of industrial relations differs from its role in the earlier two periods. In the 1900s and 1910s, and again in the 1960s and 1970s, the state was encouraging the development and spread of industrial relations institutions that were already appearing in leading sectors and firms; its efforts were with the grain of industrial relations evolution. After 1979 the British state encouraged a sharp break with, and a reversal of, an established set of industrial relations institutions and practices. It sought, at a time of historically unrivaled labor movement strength and influence, and the deep implantation of collective forms of regulation, to weaken trade unionism and encourage unilateral managerial regulation of the workplace, and the individualization of industrial relations. For this reason, the role of the state was more significant, more direct, and more coercive. Labor law took on a more central role than the administrative measures of previous periods.

As we will see, the decision to pass facilitative legislation, which permitted employers to choose whether to challenge collective regulation rather than forcing employers to change their relations with their employees, played an important part in ensuring limited resistance to Conservative industrial relations legislation. It is also the case that, for the most part, employers were not opposed to the direction of this legislation, certainly the first two packages of legislation in 1980 and 1982. There is also plenty of evidence that elements of the legislation were implemented at the urging of employers' organizations.[43] Conflict between the government and employers over industrial relations was limited. But it is also true that state policy was usually ahead of the demands of the bulk of employers; that is to say, employers tended to approve legislation once enacted, but the legislation itself was not driven by active, enthusiastic lobbying from business. That became more and more true as the 1980s progressed and the intent of legislation shifted, from its initial goals of limiting the circumstances under which legal strikes could take place, to the broader decollectivist transformation of industrial relations. The consultative papers issued by Conservative governments prior to legislation were likely, from 1984 onward, to elicit concerns from employers about the disruption of established industrial relations. Yet, once the proposals were implemented, employer concerns tended to disappear. In the evidence to the House of Commons report mentioned above, employers' organizations professed themselves satisfied with all the existing legislation. Thus, the state prodded employers in particular directions, and it shaped how employers thought about the acceptable limits of their ability to change their industrial relations practices.[44] As time went on, the words and actions of Conservative governments gave employers confidence that their efforts to resist trade unions and collective bargaining would be aided and encouraged by state action; by making strikes less likely and more costly to workers and trade unions, the British state changed the calculus facing employers as they considered changing their industrial relations practices.

It has been suggested that this period saw a "managerial renaissance," and that phrase captures both the confidence and the experimentation of the last fifteen years or so.[45] But it is hard to imagine such a renaissance in the absence of confidence in the support of the state. Dunn and Metcalf have argued, for example, that the real importance of Conservative industrial relations legislation lay in encouraging the "slow build-up in management confidence to resist unionization."[46] At base, state action in this period changed the discourse of industrial relations, and hence the way in which industrial actors thought about the regulation of class relations. The conclusion to a summary of changes detected in workplace industrial relations surveys in the period since 1980 is worth quoting at length in this regard:

> the government's programme had a more pervasive and deeper impact. This was to undermine the foundation of the system of collective representation and joint regulation. Clearly the institutional fabric of collective relations was destroyed to a large extent. But equally important was that the widespread assumption that voluntary joint regulation was a desirable basis for employment relationships was abandoned by swathes of managers and employees. If this change had not occurred, the crumbling of the institutional structure could not have happened on the scale that it did.[47]

In discussing earlier periods, I have argued that royal commissions played an important role in shaping public discourse about industrial relations in ways that provided the state with greater legitimacy to intervene to construct new industrial relations institutions. This was all the more important after 1979 because state policy entailed such a reversal of what had gone before. And yet in this case no royal commission was involved, and no officially apolitical, academic survey of industrial relations was necessary to build legitimacy for the abrupt reversal of public policy that was to follow. The reason was the industrial conflict of the 1970s, and particularly the strike wave of 1978–79, the so-called Winter of Discontent, or, more accurately, the manner in which that set of events fed its way into public discourse. Colin Hay has argued that crises are "constituted in and through narrative" and that narration has the capacity to portray particular events as symptomatic of some more general crisis.[48] In this respect, "Thatcherism as a state project, though conceived long before, was born in the context of crisis during the winter of discontent."[49] As this suggests, the restructuring of industrial relations was at the core of the Thatcherite state project.

As Hay and others have demonstrated, the British media were responsible for the selection of events and their primary narration. Images of rotting garbage lying uncollected in the street and dead bodies left unburied because of public-sector strikes were seared into public consciousness such that a quarter century later the threat of minor public-sector strikes could evoke comparisons; the Winter of Discontent is the dominant form in which any public-sector strike threat is still discursively constructed in Britain.[50] The media also played a central role in linking these images to notions of overly powerful trade unions, ignoring the very real sense in which strikes during this period reflected the *weakness* of British trade unionism and the loss of control by union leaders over their members. Yet media hostility to trade unionism was hardly new in Britain in the late 1970s. Edward Thompson's study of letters sent to the *Times* of London during strikes demonstrates a series of recurring themes with regard to trade unionism since at least the 1880s; strikes have brought regular bouts of "moral panic," which contribute to the sense of crisis and demand state action.[51] But these have never led to state projects as intent on restricting trade unionism as that which followed the election of 1979. It was the Conservative Party that played the central role in "secondary narration," in linking the Winter of Discontent to a broader meta-narrative of crisis and state failure that undermined broad public support for trade unionism and collective bargaining, creating the ideological conditions for the third system of industrial relations. As Stuart Hall argued at the time, "the crisis has begun to be lived in *its* [Thatcherism's] terms."[52] Thus no small part of the role of the British state in the construction of the third system of industrial relations was ideological, to provide a rationale—for both business and the wider public—for the legislative program that was to follow.

One final general comment about the form that state action took in undermining the second system of industrial relations and constructing a new set of institutions concerns economic policy. The broad economic shifts associated with post-Fordism were not purely exogenous to politics; most were actively encouraged by post-1979 governments, both Conservative and Labour, with the effect of accentuating their impact on the British economy. The paradigm shift from Keynesian demand-side policies prioritizing the maintenance of full employment began in 1976 under a Labour government. The emphasis on low inflation was the centerpiece of Conservative macroeconomic policy and was subsequently institutionalized in the granting of operational independence to the Bank of England by the New Labour government one week after taking power in 1997. Deindustrialization was also indirectly encouraged by the high value of the pound sterling in the early 1980s, when recession contributed to a collapse of manufacturing jobs, and again in the late 1990s as Britain remained outside the Economic and Monetary Union and the pound was overvalued in relation to the euro.

The election of the Conservatives in 1979 also meant that the loss of state economic capacity in the international economy was actively promoted in government policy. From the removal of exchange controls in July 1979 to the refusal of Britain to accept the social chapter of the Maastricht Treaty in December 1991, the policy of successive Conservative governments was to deregulate economic activity so as to encourage domestic entrepreneurs and lure foreign investment to Britain. The European policy of the Conservatives can be in part explained by divisions within the party and the attempt to ride public antipathy toward European integration. But there was an objective basis to Britain's refusal to accept European social policies. The British government clearly attempted to position Britain as a relatively low-wage, deregulated economy that could attract foreign investment, by both European firms shopping for a liberal regulatory environment and non-European firms seeking access to the European Union but without the costs—financial and regulatory—of other European countries. The Department of Trade and Industry produced a prospectus aimed at inward investors that marketed Britain's "quality people at low cost" and argued:

> Unlike most continental countries, employment regulations are largely on a voluntary basis with no requirements for works councils and mandatory union agreements, while single-union agreements are relatively easy to negotiate. There are also fewer restrictions on both recruitment and dismissal.[53]

It was certainly the case that, as the *Economist* put it in 1993, "Britain comfortably comes bottom in surveys of EU employers' perceptions of the stringency of employment protection regulations."[54] Thus high unemployment, labor market flexibility, deindustrialization, and international economic integration were not only refracted through the institutional structure of the British political economy but were accelerated and intensified as a result of state action.

The Instruments of Conservative Industrial Relations Policy

Despite the much more explicit use of legislation to shape industrial relations practice, it is still necessary to take an expansive view of state action in order to understand the scope of government policy and influence during the period between 1979 and 1997. As the previous section suggested, the state played an important role both in the narration of crisis, which itself permitted the mobilization of state power to restructure industrial relations, and in influencing the manner in which post-Fordist economic pressures were transmitted to the British economy; higher unemployment, accelerated deindustrialization, and closer international economic integration were encouraged by state macroeconomic policy, and all contributed to the demise of the second system of industrial relations. In a similar fashion microeconomic policy, which deregulated the labor market, reduced the insulation from the market enjoyed by workers, in turn encouraging different behavior on the part of employers, managers, and workers themselves.

The restructuring of the public sector in Britain after 1979, and the collapse of corporatist institutions (and with it the indirect influence of trade unions on public policy), were also crucial parts of the project of industrial relations reform that were achieved either through administrative action alone or through legislation whose impact on industrial relations was indirect. Nowhere is this more true than in the privatization of the nationalized industries and the decentralization, and creation of market surrogates, in what remained of the public sector. There was little or no legislation that sought to directly

alter the institutions of public-sector industrial relations, but the wider restructuring of the public sector dramatically changed industrial relations practice.

Less tangible, but still important, were such factors as the handling of major
strikes and the impact of policing during those strikes. Certainly a case can
be made that the government's victory over the mine workers' union in the
1984–85 coal strike, in which the Coal Board was prevented from reaching a
compromise settlement by the government and policing prevented aggressive
picketing from spreading the strike, had an important demonstration effect
for both trade unions and private-sector employers.[55] In the same vein, it is
impossible to measure the impact of the industrial relations "climate," to
which state policy surely contributed, on the behavior of employers, unions,
and workers. Conservative governments after 1979 made it clear that collective bargaining was no longer considered a public policy good, and that they
would support employers who sought new relationships with their employees;
in some cases (the replacement of collective bargaining with personal contracts, for example) legislation legalized employer practice after courts had
ruled against that practice. In short, it seems certain that the climate of industrial relations fostered by the state gave employers the confidence to experiment with new industrial relations institutions and practices of their own. As
the authors of one of the most comprehensive studies of Conservative industrial relations legislation put it: "Employers were thus given the encouragement and the power to execute a similar policy in the workplace and, when
appropriate and necessary, sufficient confidence to use the anti-union legislation."[56] Finally, though less active in the 1980s and 1990s than in the previous
two decades, the judicial system played a complementary role to government
action through the issuing of injunctions to halt industrial action.

Nevertheless, a distinctive feature of this third period of industrial relations
reform was the extent to which successive packages of legislation sought to
directly restructure industrial relations. When a piece of legislation did not
appear to achieve the goals set for it, the response was further legislation, to
"add another layer of cement" rather than to seek nonlegislative solutions or
to change the goals themselves.[57] Conservative governments after 1979 had
learned two key lessons from the failure of the 1971 Industrial Relations Act,
which translated into the different forms that post-1979 legislation took. The
first lesson was to move slowly, adding new pieces to the architecture of a new
system of industrial relations "step-by-step" so that resistance on the part of
the labor movement was more difficult than it would have been if the whole
system had been visible at the start. The rolling nature of the legislation, with
each piece building and extending the pieces that went before, made resistance at each point more difficult.

The second lesson was to make the legislation facilitative. While Conservative hostility toward trade unions was clear, the main aim of government policy was not to prescribe a particular model or form of industrial relations

but to remove restrictions (either in the form of legislative obstacles or in the capacity of trade unions to resist) on the right of employers to choose the industrial relations arrangements that they deemed most appropriate. Whereas the 1971 Industrial Relations Act created a set of criminal liabilities for noncompliance—thus focusing attention on the role of the state in the enforcement of the legislation—the legislation of the 1980s and 1990s created only civil liabilities. It was up to employers to choose whether to use the new legislation. This both minimized employer resistance to the legislation, because employers were not being forced to change their industrial relations practices, and prevented the creation of trade union martyrs around which the labor movement could mobilize support. This approach was wonderfully summarized by Norman Tebbit, secretary of state for employment in 1981 and 1982:

> If necessary I will surround every prison in this country with police—and if needs be the army. I am willing to seal them off with barbed-wire barricades. Under no circumstances will I allow any trade union activist—however hard he tries—to get into prison under my legislation.[58]

That said, by the end of the 1980s Conservative policy had become increasingly concerned not so much with eliminating abuses of collective bargaining and the collective representation of workers, and permitting employers to deal with their employees as they wished, as with encouraging an individualization of industrial relations in which trade unions and collective bargaining had a limited role. Conservative ministers urged unions to get out of the business of collective bargaining and instead offer individual services to their members, and government white papers called on employers to reconsider their industrial relations practices and stressed the merits of individual contracts, promising to support "the aspirations of individual employees to deal directly with their employer, rather than through the medium of trade union representation or collective bargaining."[59] Thus the permissive nature of industrial relations legislation should not detract from the fact that decollectivization was an explicit state strategy between 1979 and 1997.

The role of legislation after 1979, and the willingness of the police and the judicial branch of the state to enforce that legislation, do mark a ratcheting up of the level and nature of state intervention compared with previous efforts to act as midwife to a new set of industrial relations institutions. That should be no surprise given the strength of the labor movement and the deep implantation of collective regulation. A strong state was indeed a prerequisite for the construction of a "free economy" in this regard.

Conservative industrial relations legislation was both pragmatic—a response to changing conditions and opportunities—and ideological: it was ideological in its content, direction, and coherence but pragmatic in its timing and the manner in which it sought to achieve its aims. There were six major pieces of Conservative industrial relations legislation, each one comprising several parts and addressing multiple themes, along with sundry other pieces of legislation that impinged on industrial relations. The main legislative packages came at regular intervals between 1980 and 1993 and were the 1980 Employment Act, the 1982 Employment Act, the 1984 Trade Union Act, the 1988 Employment Act, the 1990 Employment Act, and the 1993 Trade Union Reform and Employment Rights Act.

Making sense of this mass of legislation requires an intellectual road map. In 1979 Friedrich Hayek published a three-volume examination of labor law, *Law, Legislation and Liberty*, and as Wedderburn has pointed out, the ideological nature of Conservative industrial relations legislation can be seen in its congruence with (and the government's public enthusiasm for) the arguments and principles enunciated by Hayek.[60] In effect, *Law, Legislation and Liberty* provided an intellectual blueprint for Thatcherite industrial relations reform. Arguing that employment contracts were no different from other contracts, that trade unions should enjoy no legal privileges, and that their sole legitimate role was to act as friendly societies rather than collective bargaining agents, Hayek provided a map of the terrain of future Conservative industrial relations legislation. As noted above, this analysis was ahistorical, derived from principles of private property and free market economics; thus the industrial relations reforms of the 1980s would have been as appropriate to the 1900s and 1950s, and would have been justified by reference to the same principles. Wedderburn has articulated the main principles that derive from Hayek's analysis. They provide a means for categorizing Conservative legislation. They are the disestablishment of collectivism; the deregulation of employment law; the treatment of trade unions as unique organizations requiring extensive government regulation, with priority given to the rights of individual members *against* the union itself; and enterprise confinement, meaning that where unions operate, their influence should be confined to the firm and not extend beyond it.

Dunn and Metcalf have offered a somewhat different, but compatible, categorization of Conservative industrial relations legislation under the headings of responsibility, voice, and exit. Voice and exit are relatively self-explanatory, in that they emphasize the reform of trade union internal governance structures and the elimination of institutions, beyond individual preference, that encourage union membership. By responsibility, Dunn and Metcalf mean measures both to make trade unions responsible for their actions and to limit the influence of collective regulation:

> If the first preference [of Conservative legislation] is to legislate collective bargaining out of existence, diminishing unions to harmless friendly societies and workers' advice bureaus, then, should that prove too difficult, the fallback position is to cordon off union enclaves and prevent them contaminating the existing non-union sector

and new-born enterprises . . . if legislation stops the spread of collectivism among market rivals, individual unionised companies and their employees have to face up to the costs of trade unionism in an increasingly non-union world.[61]

If these were the broad goals of Conservative industrial relations legislation, what were the specific measures? The legislation was too wide ranging for any summary to be exhaustive,[62] but the main elements of the legislation will be examined in the following sections. These sections will proceed topically rather than chronologically. The legislation returned repeatedly to topics already addressed in previous legislation, but it is worth noting that over time legislation tended to shift from encouraging certain kinds of industrial relations behavior to enforcing it, and that legislation came to focus more and more on issues of the internal governance of trade unions and the rights of union members vis-à-vis their unions.

Industrial Action

In Britain, the legality of industrial action has depended on the provision of immunity from civil and criminal liability, so Conservative legislation first sought to narrow the conditions under which industrial action was protected by immunity. A distinction was made between primary and secondary (or sympathetic) action, and the latter lost all immunity. Similarly, the definition of a trade dispute (for which protection existed) was narrowed so as to cover only immediate terms and conditions of work. So, for example, a strike by telecommunications workers against the privatization of British Telecom was not protected, but a strike over some deterioration in working conditions that followed from privatization might be protected. Mindful of the impact of mass "flying" pickets in the mining strikes of the 1970s, picketing was also restricted to permit only the picketing of one's own place of work, and to limit the number of pickets.

From 1984 onward industrial action was protected only if a ballot was held in advance. This requirement became progressively more highly regulated. Initially, workplace ballots were permitted on the grounds that participation in postal ballots was lower, but from 1993 only postal ballots were allowed. Legislation determined the wording of ballots, the time limits on the use of ballots, and even required that employers be allowed to know the names of those balloted, creating the potential for intimidation.

Legislation also required that unions act to prevent unlawful industrial action on the part of their members or be liable to pay compensation. This culminated in the 1990 Employment Act with the position that all industrial action was presumed to be endorsed by the relevant union unless explicitly repudiated by the union. And if repudiated, the employer could then selectively dismiss individual strikers, putting unions in an almost impossible position.

Finally, union members and (from 1993) even third parties to a dispute could take a union to court if they believed that the action was not legal. Unions were prevented from disciplining members who acted as strikebreakers, and a commissioner for the rights of trade union members (CROTUM) and a commissioner for protection against unlawful industrial action (CPUIA) were created to provide help to union members and members of the public who sought to challenge the legality of industrial action.

Three general points should be made about the legislation on industrial action. First, it sought to limit such action to the workplace where the dispute arose, and to a narrow range of strictly economic issues. The requirement that separate ballots be held for each workplace further undermined broader types of collective action. And postal ballots individualized participation on the assumption that a worker would respond differently to the likelihood of a strike when sitting at home filling out a ballot than when voting at a workplace meeting, surrounded by colleagues. In all these areas, industrial action was partially decollectivized. Second, firms were not under any obligation to challenge the legality of a strike if they did not wish to. Thus, the law gave employers new powers to challenge unions if they wished but did not force them into conflicts. It was only at the end of the 1980s that union members and later members of the public were able to challenge the legality of strikes, and, unsurprisingly, this disturbed many employers who feared that their efforts to settle disputes would be undermined by dissident unionists or outraged customers. Third, the balloting procedure became extremely highly regulated, such that a "rigid statutory template" was imposed on trade unions.[63] Unless these enormously complicated regulations were followed, trade unions opened themselves up to liability for industrial action.

Trade Union Governance

Prior to 1979 (with the brief exception of 1971–74, when unions were expected to register under the Industrial Relations Act) governments had operated on the presumption that union autonomy in internal governance procedures was more important than external regulation. After 1979 this position was reversed. A high priority was given to enforcing a certain form of democratic process within unions. This priority followed, first, from the conviction that trade unions were unique organizations, quite different from other voluntary organizations by virtue of their capacity to impede market relations, and so deserving of special attention from the state, and, second, from the belief that ordinary trade union members were naturally more moderate than their leaders, and certainly more moderate than shop stewards and other union activists. The legal regulation of strike ballots, and the creation of CROTUM, were part of this emphasis on external regulation. Legislation also required that key national positions within trade unions, including the principal executive committee (whatever its exact name) and the union president or general secretary, be elected every five years (eventually insisting that postal ballots be used).

In a challenge to trade union funding for the Labour Party, in 1984 it was required that any trade union with a political fund should ballot its members every ten years on whether they wished to continue to support such a fund. No equivalent legislation was introduced to give company shareholders a vote on business contributions to political parties; trade unions were regarded as unique organizations. Finally, under the heading of internal union governance, the ability of unions to discipline their members, or limit their actions, was restricted by legislation. So, for example, the right of a union to exclude or expel someone from membership was removed. This particular provision undermined the TUC's 1939 Bridlington Agreement, which had sought to minimize multiunionism through collective agreement on separate spheres of influence for each union.

External Support for Trade Unions and Collective Bargaining

As previous chapters have argued, the institutions of collective regulation of industrial relations have in part depended on support of one kind or another from both the state and employers. Legislation in the 1980s and 1990s largely removed any form of state support, and it limited the statutory duty of employers to provide support for unions and collective bargaining. In 1980, both the short-lived statutory union recognition procedure and provisions for unilateral arbitration were abolished. It will be recalled that unilateral arbitration, which had existed in one form or another for most of the forty years after the outbreak of the Second World War, had been a mechanism for the extension of collective bargaining, permitting unions to sweep up firms that refused to participate in industry bargaining agreements. The Fair Wage Resolution was also rescinded. Successive pieces of legislation after 1979 also chipped away at the closed shop—a mechanism for preventing free riding by employees where unions were recognized—until finally outlawing it altogether in 1990. Written authorization from each employee for union dues to be automatically deducted from a paycheck by employers was also now required at least every three years.

Conservative legislation also minimized the effects of the 1975 Employment Protection Act by limiting the range of duties for which employers were required to give time off to union officials and by reducing the requirement that union officials be paid for time undertaken for union training. In 1993 government financial support for union training was also phased out. In all these cases, the prior assumption had been that good industrial relations depended on well-trained and resourced union officials in the workplace, and that the state and employers should, in effect, subsidize these activities. This was reversed after 1979, thereby pushing the cost exclusively onto trade unions themselves.

Finally, collective bargaining lost its imprimatur as a public policy good in itself. This occurred symbolically in 1993 when ACAS's statutory duty to encourage collective bargaining was removed. This was the formal end to a public presumption in favor of collective regulation that had existed since the end of the 1890s, though government practice had been different since 1979. Another provision of the 1993 Trade Union Reform and Employment Rights Act went further, in permitting employers to provide financial inducements to employees to opt out of collective bargaining agreements and adopt "personal" (individual) contracts. Previously it had been accepted that such action would discriminate against union membership and hence be illegal. But a crucial distinction was drawn between union membership, which remained protected against discrimination, and a trade union as collective bargaining agent, which was not. This provision chimed well with the growing discourse in the early and mid-1990s that emphasized the role of trade unions as providers of individual services to members rather than as collective actors, representing collectivities of workers in their relationship with an employer or group of employers. As such, it epitomized the decollectivist logic of the third system of industrial relations.

Employment Rights and the Labor Market

Conservative legislation had somewhat contradictory goals for the labor market. On the one hand, it had a strongly deregulatory emphasis. Protection from unfair dismissal was watered down by removing the burden of proof from employers and increasing the length of service, from six months to two years, before employees came under the umbrella of unfair dismissal legislation. The wages councils, Britain's only form of statutory minimum-wage legislation, first had their powers reduced, so that young employees did not come under their remit and they could set a base minimum wage only in their industry, and then, in 1993, were abolished, leaving Britain as the only European Union country with no statutory minimum wage. Nevertheless, measures to deregulate the labor market were relatively few in Britain for the simple reason that legislation had never played much of a role in regulating employment relations. The legacy of collective laissez-faire meant that trade union strength was the main obstacle to a flexible labor market.

On the other hand, several pieces of legislation provided new employment rights, which acted in the opposite direction, partially reregulating the labor market. This apparent contradiction is resolved by noting that the bulk of the new employment rights came to Britain courtesy of European directives. Thus the 1993 Trade Union Reform and Employment Rights Act contained provisions to comply with the European Community (EC) Pregnant Workers' Directive, the EC Proof of Employment Directive, the EC Health and Safety Framework Directive, and the EC Acquired Rights Directive.[64] As we shall see in the next chapter, when a Labour government was returned to power in 1997, European Union directives became an increasingly important source of reregulation of the labor market, though directives were usually implemented in a minimalist fashion and over the protests of the Labour government.

PUBLIC-SECTOR INDUSTRIAL RELATIONS REFORM

Explicit industrial relations legislation was not alone in shaping the construction of a new set of institutions for the regulation of class relations. Developments in the public sector were of particular importance. Trade unionism and collective bargaining had grown very rapidly in the public sector from the mid-1960s, with the extension of such workplace industrial relations institutions as shop stewards to the public sector, though the bulk of collective bargaining remained at the industry level, primarily because of the centralization of the nationalized industries and public services. In addition, public-sector workers began to exercise their industrial muscle in the 1970s with strikes, not just in traditionally conflictual industries like mining, but in health care, education, and local government. During the construction of the first and second systems of industrial relations, the state had used the public sector as a "model employer," to provide a demonstration to private-sector employers of those industrial relations practices preferred by public policy. Thus the creation of Whitley councils in public services after the First World War, and the trade union facilities and collective bargaining structures introduced into industries nationalized after the Second World War, were archetypes of what successive governments hoped private-sector employers would emulate.

Thatcherite governments after 1979 had a radically different vision of public-sector industrial relations. The public sector embodied everything that the Conservatives considered dysfunctional about British industrial relations: centralized, inflexible bargaining; industrial strife; overly powerful trade unions. Thus reform of public-sector industrial relations had a high priority. After 1979, state policy shifted from using the public-sector as a model employer to importing private-sector best practice to the public sector. In other words, the public sector was now to learn from and emulate the private sector, not vice versa.[65] Nonetheless, the reform of public-sector industrial relations, for the most part, took place indirectly as a result of the wider restructuring of the public sector. That is to say, the state rejected the possibility of legislation specifically designed to change public-sector industrial relations—for example, banning strikes in essential public services was frequently mooted but never implemented—and instead relied on exposing public-sector managers, trade unions, and workers to market forces, in the expectation that this would lead to changes in industrial relations institutions and practices. The Conservative government followed two paths here. On the one hand, it reduced the size of the public sector in the belief that market forces would impose different industrial relations practices on the newly privatized firms. On the other hand, for those industries and services which remained in the public sector, market surrogates were introduced, and public-sector industrial relations were reorganized.[66]

In the first half of the 1980s the emphasis of government policy lay in the appointment of public-sector managers who would be prepared to undertake tough restructuring tasks and carry them through in the face of union opposition, in a willingness by the government to fight strikes, and in tight control of public-sector pay. From the mid-1980s onward the emphasis shifted toward transferring large sectors of the public sector to private hands, encouraging surrogates for market competition within the remainder of the public sector, and encouraging the introduction of "best practice" from the private sector, which tended to mean decentralization of bargaining and a range of types of flexibility. This latter phase saw quite dramatic effects on industrial relations, through both the impact of privatization and the restructuring of bargaining relationships within the public sector.

In the early 1980s government policy toward the nationalized industries centered on the appointment of tough "macro managers"—Michael Edwards at British Leyland, Ian MacGregor at British Steel—who would be prepared to break with what the Conservatives saw as a somewhat cozy relationship with the trade unions and undertake the restructuring necessary to bring nationalized industries closer to profitability.[67] This imperative became more important as certain industries were targeted for privatization and therefore had to be made attractive to investors. Strikes at British Rail and British Leyland over flexible work time were endured and won by management. The government appears to have been an important actor in some of these disputes, despite protestations that managers had autonomy, in order to encourage management to resist concessions.

This was certainly the case in the most important strike of the decade, the mine workers' strike in 1984–85. There is a vast literature on this strike, but it is clear that the Conservative Party, stung by defeat at the hands of the miners in 1972 and 1974, prepared extensively for the likelihood of a strike and was not prepared to contemplate a settlement that did not entail the defeat of the National Union of Mineworkers (NUM).[68] This strike was in many ways the defining moment for Conservative industrial relations policy, and a microcosm of the range and scope of state action employed in the restructuring of British industrial relations; even the intelligence services were drawn into the conflict.[69] Once the mine workers had been defeated, the coal industry was privatized, and mine closures and layoffs have to all intents and purposes eliminated the industry. At the time of the strike, the NUM had 180,000 members employed in 170 pits. By the time Arthur Scargill retired from leadership of the NUM early in 2002, membership was estimated at 3,000, with only 13 pits remaining, all privately owned.[70]

As the example of coal suggests, most important for public-sector industrial relations was privatization and the restructuring of the public sector. The list of privatized industries included gas, electricity, water, steel, telecommunications, coal, and rail. The total number of people working in the public sector fell by one-third, from 7.4 million in 1979 to 5 million in 1998, with the great bulk of the decline resulting from privatization as the workforce of the nationalized industries fell by 83 percent, from 1.8 million to less than one-third of a million.[71] It is difficult to generalize about the industrial relations practices of newly privatized firms. There has been a wide range of practice, and it is clear that the managements of some privatized firms have proved more hostile to trade unions than others. There has been very little explicit derecognition of trade unions in privatized firms, not least because unions tend to be well entrenched with large memberships. There have been exceptions, such as some of the regional water companies where privatization, and the subsequent changes in collective bargaining, led to a large decline in union density, primarily as white-collar employees were shifted from collective bargaining units to personal contracts.[72] Union recognition has also been challenged in the electricity supply companies and British Telecom through the replacement of collective bargaining by personal contracts among managers. Whereas unionization during the second period treated in this book tended to shift up the managerial hierarchy, increasingly including supervisory and lower levels of management staff, during this period it appears that employers sought to seal off management and supervisors from unionization by measures designed to integrate them more closely with the firm.

There was also a widespread move toward rationalized bargaining, meaning either "single-table bargaining," where all represented unions in a firm negotiated simultaneously with management, or an outright reduction in the number of recognized unions. Additionally, in practically every case privatization has resulted in the end of national bargaining and instead a decentralization to either regional centers or different business groups.[73] Additionally, privatization has almost always been followed by broad-ranging flexibility agreements, including multitasking and performance-related pay.

Restructuring of the public sector itself has gathered pace since the late 1980s and has emphasized attempting to give greater autonomy to local units of the public sector—hospitals, schools—while also injecting some form of competition into the public sector. This process began in local government with "contracting out" and then "compulsory tendering." It forced public-sector unions' employees to compete with private contractors for the provision of certain services. The most important forms of restructuring came in the National Health Service, where after 1991 its constituent parts were allowed to become self-governing "trusts." That process was complete by the end of the 1990s, before a new Labour government tried a different reform approach. The evidence, once again, was that outright union derecognition was rare—though some ambulance services did it—but that the trusts used their auton-

omy from local government control to "rationalize" their bargaining arrangements and move toward single-table bargaining. Movement toward local pay
determination was initially slow because employees were at first allowed to
retain national terms and conditions, but there have nonetheless been widespread changes in pay structures and job evaluation.

A distinctive feature of privatization and public-sector restructuring is that
they simultaneously acted as *antistrike strategies*. The Ridley Plan, drawn up in
1978 by a group of backbench Conservative MPs (then in opposition), had
explicitly identified privatization as the surest strategy to avoid strikes in the
public sector.[74] Faced with strikes in the rail industry in 1995 and in the Royal
Mail in 1996, the Conservative response was to accelerate the former's privatization and lift the latter's monopoly on small-letter carrying. Furthermore,
the decentralization of collective bargaining in the National Health Service
(NHS) and railways made *national* strikes in these industries extremely difficult. Instead, strikes are more likely to be local and confined to one hospital
trust or one railway company. Thus, changes in the ownership and organization of the public sector have clearly had industrial relations goals as well as
broader economic ones.

Finally, in the public sector, pay determination for increasing numbers of
public-sector employees has been removed from collective bargaining and
placed instead under the auspices of pay review bodies (PRBs), which make
pay recommendations based on broad comparability criteria, though their recommendations are not binding on the government. Whereas PRBs established
prior to 1979 were used for groups that did not engage in collective bargaining
(doctors, dentists, the armed forces, and highly paid state officials), those established after 1979 involved groups that had previously had collective bargaining rights. This practice was used for those groups with whom there were
disputes over pay but for whom there was broad public sympathy, in effect, as
a measure of depoliticization. Thus in 1983 nursing staff and midwives joined
doctors and dentists in a pay review body, and in 1986 the government abolished the Burnham Committee system of collective bargaining for teachers
and in 1991 placed them within a pay review body. As a result almost one
million people were removed from collective bargaining, increasing the number covered by PRBs by two-thirds.[75]

THE COLLAPSE OF CORPORATISM

Britain lacked the density of corporatist institutions, and their importance
in wage restraint policies, of the well-known northern and central European
countries. Nevertheless, in the course of the 1960s and 1970s, a range of tripartite institutions were created in the search for collaborative solutions to economic decline and in abortive efforts to introduce a measure of economic
planning. In addition, the labor movement found itself with plentiful access

to politicians and other state officials after the Second World War. This was true both when the Labour Party was in government, for obvious reasons, but also during periods of Conservative rule. The search for wage restraint ensured that any government would need to involve trade unions in public policy.

Tripartism, and union access to government, came to an abrupt halt after 1979. Government efforts to deal with what was seen as the corporatist bias of British policymaking were straightforward to implement and clear-cut in their effects. High-level contacts between the TUC and Conservative governments were very limited. When meetings took place, they were with more junior government officials, and the TUC recorded many fewer "successes" as a result of the meetings.[76] The destruction of tripartite bodies was particularly serious for the trade unions. As Mitchell has pointed out, "The election of Mrs. Thatcher led to a serious and systematic decline in the TUC's access and influence" as the tripartite bodies of greatest importance to the trade unions—the Manpower Services Commission and the National Economic Development Council, probably the most potent symbol of the postwar "British Consensus"—were first weakened and then abolished.[77]

Corporatist arrangements at other levels of government were also reduced because of changes in state structure. The British state has always been centralized, but there existed, nonetheless, education and health services that operated at the level of local government. These services afforded political space for elected local councils to conduct industrial relations in their areas of competence as they wished. Since many of these local councils were controlled by opposition parties, they might differ from the national government in their attitude toward trade unions. In the course of the 1980s and 1990s central government largely eliminated that political space. In addition to stringent spending caps on local authorities, schools and health services were encouraged to opt out of local government control and manage their own industrial relations, and the putting out to tender of various public services was first encouraged and then required. Not only did this drastically reduce the ability of trade unions to find safe havens from the impact of central government industrial relations policy, but it also eliminated most of the political resources of the trade unions that had not already disappeared with the Labour defeat in 1979, and inhibited the development of distinctive local and regional industrial relations systems.

JUDICIAL ACTIVISM

While the 1980s and 1990s were not a period of judicial activism to compare with the decade leading up to the *Taff Vale* decision or the late 1950s and early 1960s, the courts did nonetheless play a supportive role in the Thatcherite industrial relations reform project. One implication of the much greater weight of statutory regulation of industrial action has been that there has been greater scope for the issuing of temporary, or interlocutory, injunctions, enjoining action on the part of a trade union.[78] These injunctions could be issued after brief hearings, on the grounds simply that an employer's case against the union's action might have merit. Once issued, and the action stopped, the injunction alone was usually sufficient. It was extremely rare for employers then to pursue the case in order to get compensation. Thus of 201 legal actions against unions between 1980 and 1995, 166 were injunctions of this type, and further legal action was taken in only 9 cases.[79] The fact that about one-third of these injunctions concerned strike ballot provisions speaks to the manner in which the complexity of the law surrounding industrial action has made injunctions an important weapon in an employer's armory. It is also worth noting that whereas the Court of Appeals tended to send cases arising out of the industrial relations legislation of the 1974–79 Labour government to the House of Lords for judicial interpretation, it did not feel the need to do the same for cases arising out of Conservative legislation in the 1980s.[80]

Judicial action, the collapse of corporatism, restructuring of the public sector, and legislation limiting the ability of trade unions to take industrial action, regulating their internal governance procedures, removing external supports for unions and collective bargaining, and deregulating the labor market were the main mechanisms by which Conservative governments sought to reconstruct the industrial relations system between 1979 and 1997. There were other measures that had a primarily symbolic importance. In a few high-profile cases, most notably a case involving the Government Communications Headquarters (GCHQ), collective bargaining rights were removed from government employees. Margaret Thatcher argued with regard to workers at GCHQ that "there is a basic conflict between the structure of trade unions and loyalty to the state."[81] The main effect of action of this kind, beyond the effect on the workers themselves, was to demonstrate the legitimacy of union derecognition to employers. Another act of symbolic importance was the 1995 abolition of the Department of Employment and the dividing of its functions among several departments, with the Department of Trade and Industry getting the main industrial relations functions and the Department of Education, renamed the Department of Education and Employment, getting the training and employment functions. This marked an institutional recognition that employment policy now operated entirely on the supply side, through training programs. It also marked the first time since 1916 that the government official responsible for labor and employment was not of cabinet rank.[82]

From Industrial Relations to Employment Relations

What was the impact of almost two decades of Conservative state activism on the institutions and architecture of British industrial relations? The period since 1979 has seen the most far-reaching change in British industrial relations since the spread of industry bargaining at the beginning of the twentieth century. Purcell has powerfully described the outcome of this period of change as the "end of institutional industrial relations,"[83] referring to the collapse of the institutions of collective regulation. It is clear that those institutions, the core elements of the first and second systems of industrial relations, are in tatters; what is less clear is what, if anything, has been put in their place.

More profound, though, than institutional restructuring, has been the impact of change on the labor movement. There has been a quite fundamental, and potentially irreversible, shift in the balance of class power in Britain, with the shrinking, weakening, and hollowing out of trade unionism. The logic of collective organization and action differs for capital and labor.[84] While firms can benefit from some forms of collective action (as the spread of employer associations to manage industry bargaining attests), collective action is of more fundamental importance for workers. It is a prerequisite for the ability both to sanction employers and to articulate a distinct, unitary labor interest.[85] As such, the weakening of trade unionism, especially in the absence of alternative forms of collective organization, implies a change in the balance of class power in Britain. Moreover, the last two decades have also seen a remarkable shift in the ideology and strategic repertoire of British trade unionism. The result has been the greatest period of strategic innovation on the part of labor since the collapse of the Triple Alliance, a wholesale shift in the labor movement's conception of where labor's power resources are located. This in turn has involved a reformulation of strategy, involving, perhaps most strikingly, the end of British trade unionism's adherence to the ideology of voluntarism.

Flanders famously argued that "the tradition of voluntarism cannot be legislated against," yet the experience of the recent past suggests that indeed it can.[86] The apparently autonomous strength of British trade unionism has been overcome by a combination of the scale and scope of state activism, the willingness of governments to endure industrial conflict, and a raft of industrial relations legislation, alongside a withdrawal of support for collective regulation on the part of many employers and a period of profound economic restructuring. There is a great deal of debate on the role played by the state in effecting industrial relations change, in comparison to the impact of employer strategy and economic change. It is hard to separate out the effects of state action from those of economic restructuring and employer strategy, which all operated in the same direction. Many commentators see the specific impact of legislation as modest,[87] often overwhelmed by other factors.[88] In the course of this section I will identify areas where legislation is likely to have been most important in bringing about change. It is certainly not the case that the state acted alone, or that its actions were determinative; state autonomy is an implausible position in this case, and for the most part the importance of the state was in facilitating employer preferences and, over time, encouraging employers to consider restructuring their relations with their employees.

But it is also important both to avoid a narrow focus on legislation, taking instead an expansive view of what constitutes state action in the sphere of industrial relations—including economic policy, legislation, persuasion, demonstration, administrative policy, and the management of the public sector—and to avoid a narrow focus on declining union strength as the outcome to be explained. Industrial relations restructuring went much deeper than simply weakening unions. Furthermore, "change is almost entirely in the direction in which public policy was directed."[89] It is difficult to downplay the impact of the state when every measure of union strength peaks in 1979 before beginning a long decline that lasts until at least the election of a New Labour government in 1997. The broad economic forces of international integration, deindustrialization, and the feminization of the workforce all began well before 1979. It seems plausible that the deep recessions at the start of the 1980s and then the 1990s played an important role in weakening trade unions and permitting employers and the state to engage in a restructuring of industrial relations, but it is hard to explain both the continued decline of trade unionism and the continuation and, in the 1990s, acceleration of change in the *institutions and practices* of industrial relations without reference to the state. Certainly, in their evidence presented in the House of Commons investigation into the future of trade unions, employers "were unanimous in the belief in the efficacy of the 'step-by-step' developments since the changes have significantly increased the power of managers,"[90] and the Institute of Directors argued that the "reform of trade union law since 1980 has been outstandingly successful in ushering a new age of good industrial relations and it has proved popular."[91]

This section will first look at the evidence for the destruction of the old institutions of collective regulation and then survey the evidence for the emergence of new industrial relations institutions, starting with trade unions. Since 1979, British trade unions lost almost six million, or 40 percent, of their members, bringing union density below 30 percent. The decline in membership briefly stabilized between 1998 and 2000 before continuing, and even the small increases in membership at the end of the millennium were not enough to reverse the overall decline in union density.[92] If one looks instead at individual trade unions, decline has been almost universal, and it is very difficult to identify success stories. To be sure, some unions have suffered more than others, but it is striking that there is no clear, recognized "model" trade union that has managed to buck the general decline. Decline has been so great within traditional sectors of the economy that there has been a convergence in the union density rates of men and women, manual and nonmanual workers, and production and services. The big disparity in union density lies between the public sector, where density is slightly below 60 percent (though the size of the public sector itself has greatly shrunk), and the private sector, where density is now below 20 percent.[93]

Turning to evidence from the Workplace Industrial Relations Surveys,[94] a study of the period from 1980 to 1998 detected declines in every measure of union strength and concluded that "falls in union membership were themselves widespread, rather than confined to particular industries or types of workforce or of employer."[95] Trade union recognition fell even faster than union membership, so that recognition in the private sector halved during this period to 25 percent. In the 1950s and 1960s, the engineering industry formed the model for British industrial relations (and was especially influential for the Donovan Commission), with the strength of its unions and its decentralized institutions of collective regulation; by 1998 union recognition in engineering had fallen to 19 percent (from 65 percent in 1980) and was on a par with that for the hotel, catering, and distributive trades industry.[96] The great bulk of the fall in recognition came about as a result of changes in the composition of British industry, with firms that recognized unions being displaced by newer firms that did not. There was relatively little explicit derecognition of unions by firms, though it tended to occur in sectors characterized by high levels of industrial conflict or changes in ownership and was concentrated into a few years at the end of the 1980s and very early 1990s.[97] Derecognition was a strategy used by employers on "the weak, the apathetic, the peripheral, the inappropriate, and, exceptionally, the defeated."[98] What is more, while recognition has always been strongly associated with high rates of union membership, that relationship has weakened; the average union density at workplaces where unions were recognized declined precipitously between 1980 and 1998. The proportion of workplaces with union density between 75 percent and 100 percent declined from 67 percent to 31 percent, while the proportion with union density below 50 percent rose from 14 percent in 1980 to 39 percent in 1998.[99]

Related to the decline of union density where unions are recognized has been the disappearance of the closed shop: by 1998 the closed shop affected only 2 percent of workplaces.[100] The closed shop is one area where the government legislation, which outlawed the practice, clearly had a direct impact. Brown has argued that it was legislation removing immunity from industrial action to defend the closed shop that was primarily responsible for its elimination,[101] and Dunn and Metcalf cautiously estimated that between 1980 and 1990 the disappearance of the closed shop, by accentuating the free rider problem, was responsible for about one-third of a million of the decline in union membership.[102]

This period also saw dramatic changes in the scope and form of collective bargaining, though in this area, outside of the public sector, it is hard to identify the direct effect of legislation. The net result of these changes was that the coverage of institutions of collective pay-setting fell to levels unseen since the 1920s. Overall, the coverage of collective bargaining fell from 70 percent of employees in 1984 to 40 percent in 1998.[103] Once again the decline in coverage was especially precipitous in the private sector, and here collective bargaining was replaced with unilateral management determination of pay. Thus in private-sector manufacturing in 1984, collective bargaining was the main form of pay determination in 50 percent of workplaces (employing over twenty-five people), while in 1998 that had fallen to 23 percent, with management determining pay unilaterally in 72 percent of workplaces.[104] In 1998 collective bargaining took place in only 14 percent of private-sector service workplaces.[105] Collective bargaining did decline by more than 30 percentage points in the public sector during this period, from 94 percent of workplaces to 63 percent, but its demise was replaced, not with managerial determination of pay, but with external determination by central government, pay review bodies, or the like. It is also important to note that there has been a decline in the proportion of workplaces where unions are recognized that practice collective bargaining, from 86 percent in 1984 to 67 percent in 1998.[106] This raises the question of what the function of trade unionism is in those one-third of workplaces where recognition does not bring a voice in the determination of terms and conditions.

Another significant change in collective bargaining has been the collapse of two-tier and industry, or multiemployer, bargaining. In the second half of the 1980s alone, industry agreements were terminated (or the main firms in the industry withdrew from the agreement) in buses, banking, food retailing, the docks, newspapers, clothing and textiles, and, most spectacularly, engineering.[107] The collapse in trade union recognition in engineering was a direct result of the ending of multiemployer bargaining in that industry, as employers picked off poorly implanted unions that had depended on the industry agreement for their survival. While in 1984 multiemployer bargaining had been the main locus of pay determination in 41 percent of workplaces, that had fallen to 13 percent in 1998.[108] In the private sector multiemployer bargaining determined pay in under 5 percent of workplaces by 1998, and even in the public sector, long a bastion of centralized industry bargaining, the decline was from 82 percent of workplaces in 1984 to 39 percent in 1998.[109] Thus, the influence of collective bargaining has declined sharply since the early 1980s, and where it still survives, it is almost exclusively collective bargaining between a single employer and one or more trade unions.

While the coverage of collective bargaining has shrunk, and industry-level bargaining has largely disappeared outside the public sector, the form of bargaining even where it remains within the firm has also changed in important ways. The 1960s and 1970s saw an expansion of the scope of collective bargaining beyond basic conditions of work to include a range of substantive issues of work organization. This followed from the effort to enlist unions in improving productivity. By the end of 1990s it was "evident that there has been a very substantial decline in union representative involvement in the regulation of employee obligations and work organization" as the scope of bargaining once again shrank, leaving the organization of the workplace as a matter for unilateral managerial prerogative.[110] Furthermore, collective bargaining itself often took on a less formal character, resembling consultation rather than negotiation. Even where institutions of collective regulation of industrial relations remain, their character has changed.

It is not simply the strength and influence of trade unions that has been transformed since 1979. The internal governance of trade unions has also undergone change, in large part in direct response to the balloting legislation of Conservative governments. The effect of that legislation was "to impose a standard national template for choosing key national officials upon quite different national institutions and practices."[111] The direct election of the main decision-making bodies and individuals within unions by individual-member postal ballot "confirmed the demise of lower-level, intermediary bodies, in the election of PECs and General Secretaries."[112] The overall result of the balloting legislation for union elections and industrial action was to reduce membership participation, weaken the checks and balances acting on union leaders, undermine intermediate bodies, and accentuate centralizing and bureaucratizing tendencies. This encouraged the decollectivization of unions' internal governance itself, as collective decision-making bodies were supplanted with individual ballots and greater decision-making freedom for union leaders.[113]

These developments are consistent with Kelly and Heery's argument that the organizational form of British trade unionism has entered a new phase, distinct from the decentralized and "participatory" unionism of the 1960s and 1970s, which emphasized the involvement of lay activists in the running of the union. They describe the current phase as "managerial unionism," in which the union bureaucracy becomes "more managerial in its functioning, researching and monitoring employee needs, designing and promoting union services to match and planning the organisation, training and deployment of its own human resources to support service delivery."[114] Managerial unionism is not simply a return to "professional unionism" (characteristic of the first system of industrial relations) in that it focuses less on bargaining and more on recruitment, and it involves a centralization of power within trade unions away from both lay activists and full-time officials toward the leadership and research departments of unions.

Levels of industrial conflict have fallen dramatically in the last twenty years. In 1998 the number of working days lost to industrial disputes and the number of labor stoppages were the lowest since records began in 1891.[115] The strike rate in the second half of the 1990s was approximately 1 percent of that in 1979, and while strike levels have fallen throughout the OECD, they have declined considerably more rapidly in Britain than in the rest of the OECD.[116]

The Workplace Industrial Relations Surveys regularly asked managers in firms that recognized trade unions whether they had experienced any form of industrial action: in 1980 one-quarter of managers responded affirmatively, compared to 4 percent in 1998.[117] It is next to impossible to separate out the effects of legislation from broader economic forces acting in the same direction to make industrial action less feasible. Certainly the removal of immunity from secondary strikes has all but eliminated them. A study by MacKay suggests that employers were more likely to use the legislation in sectors that were traditionally more conflict prone. Thus injunctions sought against strike action clustered in printing and publishing in the mid-1980s, before becoming more common in the public services at the end of the 1980s.[118] There is also anecdotal evidence from trade union negotiators that employers threatened to use legal action against any possible industrial action in the course of bargaining.[119] The constant accretion of new legal regulations on the right to take industrial action made it extremely difficult for trade unions to keep up with what was and was not protected from legal challenge, which in turn made unions more cautious and contributed to the desire of union leaders to centralize control over deployment of the strike weapon. The shifting legal terrain meant that for the labor movement the "art of the possible became an increasingly futile pastime."[120]

However, the decline in strikes did not mean the elimination of industrial conflict; to a large extent it changed form and was displaced from collective action to individual action. The 1990s saw record numbers of individual cases brought before ACAS, with 1997 marking the sixth consecutive increase in these cases,[121] and work-related complaints to the Citizens Advice Bureaux doubled between 1983 and 1993.[122] In the absence of collective labor organizations capable of taking collective action, class conflict was itself individualized.

CREATIVE DESTRUCTION? THE EMERGENCE OF NEW INDUSTRIAL RELATIONS INSTITUTIONS

Overall, the core institutions of collective regulation were systematically dismantled in the two decades after 1979. Decollectivization manifested itself in the decline in trade unionism, the primary collective agent of workers; in both the decentralization of collective bargaining to the firm and workplace and its replacement by unilateral managerial determination of terms and conditions; in the weakening of collective decision-making structures within trade unions, and in the decline in collective action and its replacement with individual legal cases or complaints directed toward state agencies rather than trade unions.

What industrial relations institutions have replaced regularized collective bargaining between trade unions and employers or employer associations? There is a range of potential alternative institutions, all of which have been mooted as possible replacements for collective bargaining with unions. In the second half of the 1980s, in response to the arrival of several Japanese-owned firms in Britain and growing interest in "European" industrial relations, a great deal of attention was paid to nonunion but collective forms of representation, such as works councils or company councils. As the next chapter will demonstrate, arguments about the influence of European Union (EU) industrial relations developments were especially important in evaluating the new Labour government's approach after 1997. In search of a "Third Way" in industrial relations, the role of alternative (nonunion) forms of workplace representation was raised as one possible reform path.[123] Since neither Conservative nor Labour governments encouraged these industrial relations institutions, and employers consistently opposed their statutory imposition, they have proved extremely limited in their spread.

A second potential alternative, which Storey and Bacon have labeled the "new collectivism," represents one strand of human resource management.[124] The use of teams, group briefings, quality circles, and so on are collective mechanisms for managing industrial relations, but they are not representative in the sense that trade unions or elected works councils are. They operate at the discretion of management and are as much forms of work organization as industrial relations. There is more evidence of the development and spread of these institutions, but they remain a minority practice, as we will see below.

Finally, there are forms of the individualization of industrial relations. Here one can distinguish between procedural individualization, which simply refers to the removal of collective regulation and its replacement by unilateral employer determination of employment contracts, and substantive individualization, which refers to the differentiation of individual contracts to provide contracts tailored to each individual employee.[125] The argument of this section is that the dominant form of the emerging third system of industrial relations is individualization, though procedural individualization is more developed than its substantive variant.

A central theme of employers' organizations since at least the mid-1980s has been a preference for the individualization of industrial relations. As noted above, the radicalism of the broad goals outlined by employer associations is remarkable.[126] What has been most striking about the industrial relations practices of employers is their hostility toward the panoply of new forms of worker participation, works councils, quality circles, and other forms of consultation, indeed toward *collective* representation of any kind. Employers have consistently objected to EU proposals for statutory worker participation, arguing that employee consultation must be voluntary and flexible.[127]

Differences between industrial relations practice in foreign-owned and British-owned firms were much commented on in the 1980s, though, in fact, foreign-owned firms have always taken the lead in the import and diffusion of techniques and practices in Britain. In the 1980s Japanese firms were seen as the industrial relations innovators. Their importance lies less in their numbers than in their distinctive style of industrial relations. Beginning with the 1981 agreement between Toshiba and the electricians' union, Japanese firms have been associated with a package deal known as a "single union agreement" (SUA). The real innovation of SUAs, no one element of which is entirely new, lies in the package as a whole, which ties together most of the themes of new management practice in the 1980s. SUAs typically involve recognition of a single union; an agreement to exhaust all avenues of negotiation, mediation, and arbitration before recourse to a strike (often involving "pendulum arbitration"); a company council in which employees are directly represented alongside union officials; single status for all employees; and a comprehensive package of flexibility in which workers agree to a high level of functional flexibility. However, at the end of the 1980s this distinctive industrial relations package was still very rare,[128] and it appeared to run out of steam in the 1990s.[129] Overall, though studies have demonstrated some differences in the practices of British and foreign-owned firms,[130] it is questionable whether there are clear differences based on ownership. Just as there has been a convergence in industrial relations practice between public, recently privatized, and private sectors, so has there been a convergence within the private sector.

The best picture we have of the development of new industrial relations institutions comes, once again, from the Workplace Industrial Relations Surveys. The 1990 survey found very little evidence of new industrial relations. All forms of collective representation, including trade union representation and joint consultative committees, had declined since 1984, such that "the fundamental change over the period was the proportion of employees *without* access to a joint management-employee committee; that grew from 57 percent of employees in 1984 to 70 percent in 1990."[131] In its place, there was an increase in regular meetings between employees and management and in company newsletters, both clearly operating at the discretion of management. Thus the 1990 survey was skeptical that the old institutions of collective regulation had been replaced by new forms of nonunion collective or individual industrial relations. Its stark conclusion was that:

> Britain is approaching the position where few employees have any mechanism through which they can contribute to the operation of their workplace in a broader context than their own job. There is no sign that the shrinkage in the extent of trade union representation is being offset by a growth in other methods of representing non-managerial employee interests and views. There has been no spontaneous

emergence of an alternative model of employee representation that could channel and attenuate conflicts between employers and employees.[132]

The 1998 survey was more upbeat, identifying a significant rise in the spread of new industrial relations. This suggests that, while the main industrial relations development of the 1980s was the destruction of the old mechanisms of collective representation, in the 1990s that process continued but was accompanied by the partial construction of new mechanisms. The main findings of the 1998 survey in this regard were that the very large decline in the presence of trade union representatives in the workplace was partially offset by an increase in nonunion worker representatives, and that various forms of direct communication between management and workers, in particular problem-solving groups, briefing groups, and regular meetings, all became much more common, being present in between half and two-thirds of workplaces (employing over twenty-five people).[133]

Two clear conclusions concerning "employee voice" can be drawn from the 1998 survey. The first is that the last two decades have seen a sharp decrease in mechanisms of *union-only voice* and an increase in *nonunion-only voice*, where the latter includes the forms of direct communication between management and employees listed above. In continuing workplaces, union voice mechanisms tended to be supplemented with these other mechanisms to create a dual channel of communication, while new firms would only rarely have any form of union voice but were more likely to have nonunion voice. The second, and related, conclusion is that there was a steep decline in the presence of any form of *collective* representation—union, consultative committee, works council—but an increase in mechanisms of direct participation, through institutions created and controlled by management. These industrial relations institutions are likely to be much more fragile, less likely to survive an economic downturn or other crisis, than those based either on a strong trade union presence in the workplace or on legal requirements, such as continental European works councils.[134]

Turning more directly to the individualization of industrial relations, evidence is, understandably, more difficult to find. The most comprehensive study to date argues that while procedural individualization has been widespread, substantive individualization is still underdeveloped.[135] The evidence for this conclusion is that, in firms without collective bargaining, employment contracts remain standardized. Certainly, set against the Institute of Directors vision of individually tailored contracts, this suggests limited substantive individualization. But this may be an overly formalistic interpretation. The study does show that employment contracts provide for greater differentiation in terms of pay rewards and are more open-ended; that is to say, the employer can require more from the employee. Thus at least pay determination is increasingly based on individual performance, as evaluated by management. It is also worth noting in this context large increases in the proportion of workplaces using profit-sharing and share ownership incentive schemes.[136]

What then should one conclude about the restructuring of industrial relations institutions in Britain in the past two decades? The impact of the decline in trade union membership is particularly important for British industrial relations because of the absence of mechanisms for the extension of collective agreements beyond the workplaces where they are negotiated. Without legal extension, or extension by coordinated employer organizations, the decline in trade union coverage leads directly to a decline in collective bargaining coverage, as the exceptionally narrow gap between these two levels at the end of the 1990s demonstrates. As Brown, Deakin, and Ryan have put it: "although the decline of trade union membership may not have been exceptional in international terms, the implications of it are."[137]

Trade unions still organize around a third of British workers, one-fifth of those in the private sector. Yet trade unionism in these remaining sectors is quite different from the trade unionism of the 1970s. Hyman has suggested that unions and collective bargaining may constitute a "hollow shell" unable to mount an effective defense of employee interests. The fact that union membership is declining even in workplaces where trade union recognition has been granted, and that around one-third of workplaces where trade unions are recognized do not have collective bargaining "may mark a qualitatively different phase in the development of unionism."[138] This implies a fundamental shift in the function of trade unionism, and a more individualized relationship with workers.

The net effect of decollectivization on trade unionism has been to make trade union organizations within the workplace less able to rely on resources from outside the workplace, and correspondingly more dependent on the employer. A recent study has pointed to the increasing dependence of firm- or workplace-level committees on union officials from outside the firm.[139] As noted above, this suggests that where collective bargaining has been retained, its scope has narrowed, so that issues beyond pay are determined unilaterally by managers. Recall that one distinguishing feature of the second system of industrial relations was the extension of the scope of collective bargaining to include a range of issues related to the organization of work; this appears to have been reversed. The result has been that the "scope, status and influence of these organisations [firm-level union organizations] had, in all cases, diminished greatly. By implication, the extent of collective regulation had diminished."[140] The study concludes: "Thus what recognition means in practice is very much what the employer chooses it to mean."[141]

Almost two decades ago, Wolfgang Streeck suggested that, in a context of high unemployment, German works councils had a propensity to engage in "wildcat cooperation" with employers, gravitating toward more cooperative behavior.[142] The weakness of British trade unions, and the inability of workplace unions to develop resources and capacities independent of the employer, appear to be having a similar effect. Kelly and Heery's study of trade union full-time officials points out that, in contrast to the 1960s and 1970s, when union officials were more likely to try to moderate the action of shop-floor activists, today union officials try to encourage unions in the workplace to be more militant and less cooperative with employers.[143]

The question, as yet unanswerable, is whether British trade unionism has reached a tipping point; if so, its weakness is irreversible even in the climate of a less hostile government. The Workplace Industrial Relations Surveys suggest that while employer hostility to trade unionism played an important part in union decline in the 1980s, by the 1990s worker indifference played a larger part. Once unions come to approximate "hollow shells," workers are even less likely to envision benefits from union membership. Reversal of union decline will be difficult if only because of the steadily declining propensity of each successive cohort entering the workforce to become union members.[144]

The result is that a quite new system of industrial relations is emerging in Britain. What is being created is an economy in which a large majority of workers do not belong to unions and are not covered by any form of collective bargaining. There has been a massive *individualization* of the regulatory mechanisms governing industrial relations. The individualization of representation goes along with an employer preference for individualized terms and conditions as merit pay, flexible working time, and so on have spread. Overwhelmingly, employers have chosen not to replace collective representation by unions with alternative forms of collective representation, such as works councils or employee boards. In what remains of the union sector, the hands of unions are tightly tied by legislation, and unions have become more dependent on employers.

Contemporary Britain has three industrial relations sectors: traditional collective bargaining, which is largely limited to the public sector and large well-established firms; a much weaker form of collective regulation, relying on workplace union structures that are largely autonomous of the wider trade union and have come to approximate works councils without the legal footing, in older manufacturing firms and a few parts of the service sector; and the approximately two-thirds of the economy that has more or less sophisticated mechanisms of individual regulation. The issue is not simply the relative size of these sectors but the trajectory of change; collective regulation is stronger in declining industries, while newly created firms are much less likely to recognize unions than older ones have been. It is an open question as to whether developments in Britain are the harbinger of an industrial relations system appropriate to the twenty-first century or of "a free, unregulated labour market of the sort that predated the birth of collective bargaining 100 years ago."[145]

Trade Union Ideology and Strategy

The restructuring of industrial relations institutions has been the focus of this chapter. I want to end this chapter, however, by turning briefly to the parallel shift that has taken place in the ideology and strategic repertoire of the British labor movement. The legacy of the state project of industrial relations reform (and here the Labour Party, both in opposition and in government after 1997, has played a part almost as significant as its Conservative counterpart) includes its effect on the ideology and practice of the British trade union movement.

Trade unions began the 1980s with the ideology of voluntarism fully intact. They did not, for the most part, seek the juridification of either collective or individual rights at work. If anything, union attachment to voluntarism had been reinforced by the impact of the struggle over the Industrial Relations Act, the hostility of the courts to trade unions in the second half of the 1970s, and the catastrophic collapse of the Social Contract in the Winter of Discontent. Voluntarism continued to reflect the core belief, which had survived from the first decade of the twentieth century, that the labor movement needed protection from the state (understood primarily as the judiciary) rather than from employers. In other words, the expectation was that the labor market strength of unions could bring employers to the negotiating table so long as the capacity of unions to engage in industrial action was not limited by the courts. During the first and second systems of industrial relations, the largest and most influential unions came to believe that they could achieve their goals without a legislative framework of comprehensive rights at work. This did not mean that unions always opposed legislation—limits on working hours, and a range of other protective legislation were demanded and received by unions—but rather that the collective strength of unions was independent of resources acquired from the state. It meant that *collective* labor rights were not sought from the state.

This is not the place for a comprehensive survey of the strategic reorientation of the British labor movement,[146] and change has had numerous elements, including a wave of trade union mergers, a much greater emphasis on the recruitment and representation of women at work, and the search for some form of "social partnership" with employers (largely rebuffed). Two elements of the shift in ideology and in trade union practice should be emphasized here, however. First, British trade unions have effectively abandoned voluntarism. By the early 1990s, recognizing their vulnerability to both a hostile state and a hostile employer class, the trade union movement had adopted a position calling for extensive juridification of industrial relations, including a statutory union recognition procedure, rights to organize in the workplace, a statutory minimum wage, the rights embedded in the European Social Chapter, and collective representation for workers, *even* in the absence of a union (implying some kind of works councils).[147] As the next chapter will demonstrate, the bulk of this legislative agenda has been implemented, albeit minimally and grudgingly, by the current Labour government. This convergence between the strategies of the labor movement and the Labour Party around the greater juridification of labor law, and greater emphasis on individual rather than collective rights at work, is indicative of how far the trade union movement has moved from its voluntarist heyday.

Unions thus came to believe that they could not depend on their own industrial strength and the resources that they had traditionally relied on. Instead, all aspects of their activity—recruitment, collective bargaining, industrial action—required much stronger legal support. The labor movement now sees a wide range of legal rights, both for individual workers and for trade unions, as central to its basic function of protecting people at work. This strategic shift has entailed a series of other changes—in attitude toward the European Union, in recruitment activity, in collective bargaining, and so on. Of particular note is the shift on the EU. Hostility toward European integration had run deep in the British labor movement. After the 1975 referendum, during which the TUC campaigned for a "no" vote, the TUC supported integration; but support was only skin deep, and hostility resurfaced after Labour lost power in 1979. This view of Europe derived for the most part from a commitment to a national Keynesian model of economic management, and from a hostility to the language of free trade and free markets that underpins the Treaty of Rome.[148]

However, by the end of the 1980s, many unions felt that British capitalism was in such a state of crisis that there was much to learn from the rest of Europe, whether on issues of training policy, the coordination of wage bargaining, or even a more cooperative form of industrial relations. Comparisons with Europe became much more widespread in this period.[149] The main reason for the sudden enthusiasm in trade union circles for European integration was clearly political. Europe was "the only game in town" at a time when the Thatcher government was impermeable to union interests. Thus integration provided the potential to do an end run around the nation-state and win legislative protection that could not be won at the national level. The unions' main interest in European integration was to gain European legislation providing new forms of protection to British workers in the firm. Unions sought to win through the importation of EU directives, and action in the European Court of Justice what they could not win through bargaining. Unions had limited success protecting their members during privatization, or incorporating equality issues into collective bargaining; but their hope has been to use European legislation to achieve the same ends.

In part the new strategic orientation emphasizing statutory rights, whether derived from the British government or the EU, has been driven by external political events. Conservative hostility and Labour coolness have forced unions to recognize that they need a protective legal environment that is independent of whichever party is in power.[150] But there is more to this shift than simply a reaction to the end of corporatist bargaining and the deregulation of the labor market. It is also, and more importantly, the result of a strategic reevaluation of the sources of union strength in the workplace. The 1980s demonstrated the vulnerability of British unions to employer hostility. This vulnerability was not new, but in the 1970s it had been masked by government support and a reluctance on the part of employers to disrupt peaceful industrial relations. By the end of the 1980s, however, it was clear that unions simply could not force employers to recognize them, that recruitment policies were yielding limited new members, and that bargaining agendas were now dominated by the concerns of employers.

In this context a new strategy emerged in which industrial relations legislation came to play a role in redefining the role of trade unions, and in aiding in the recruitment of new members. The strategy involves using the establishment of new individual rights at work to undergird collective bargaining. As John Edmonds, then general secretary of GMB, put it:

> We must accept that within the next decade trade unions are not going to be in a position to force contract cleaners, for example, to pay reasonable pay and conditions through traditional trade union organization . . . That means you have got to rely on the law to create minimum rights for the people who work in those industries . . . and this will help us organizationally in these industries very substantially indeed. Because we can then go to the workers in a particular establishment and say, 'look, these are your legal rights. Are you getting them?' And if the answer is 'no,' we can say, 'join us, we can make bloody sure that your employer does what he has to.'[151]

Thus, unions will serve as enforcers of these new rights. This strategy recognizes that unions have been largely unsuccessful in organizing the low-paid and female workers, and that they therefore will have no protection unless it is provided by legislation. The provision of basic minimum rights enshrined in legislation then provides a wedge for unions to gain entry into firms.

A final factor in explaining this strategic shift lies in the changing balance of power within the TUC. It has traditionally been the industrial craft unions that have opposed the juridification of industrial relations, in the belief that minimum rights at work are of little interest to their members, while white-collar and public-sector unions, which organize a disproportionate number of the low-paid, women, and black workers, have wanted the establishment of legislative protection. In the 1960s the older industrial and craft unions were still able to maintain the voluntarist emphasis of the labor movement, against the challenge of service-sector unions. By the 1980s the weight of the trade union movement had shifted toward public-sector and white-collar unions. Furthermore, a 1982 reform of the manner in which the TUC General Council is chosen led to greater representation for white-collar and public-sector unions, and hence their greater influence in policymaking.[152]

This set of strategic developments suggests a partial shift in the focus of union activity away from collective bargaining toward a role as legal experts, enforcers of legal rights that represent their members in court rather than in collective bargaining. The priority unions have given to the use of EU directives demonstrates that unions are now seeking to win in the courts what they cannot win through bargaining. The TUC sees legislation as "supporting and underpinning, and not replacing and undermining, structured collective bargaining,"[153] but the obvious question is what role workers will see for trade unions once their rights are enshrined in legislation instead of resulting from the collective bargaining activities of their unions, particularly if legislation brings entirely new forms of worker representation.

The second major strategic shift within the labor movement has been a recognition of the dangers inherent in paying little attention to their recruitment function and relying instead on employers to recruit for them. Trade unions have paid much more attention to recruitment in recent years, especially recruitment of "new" workers, those traditionally underrepresented in unions, such as women, part-time workers, and those in private services (there is a great deal of overlap between these three categories).[154] Indeed this new emphasis on recruitment is linked to the legislative changes outlined above; recruitment in expanding areas of employment is precisely where minimum statutory rights are more likely to be valuable. As part of its "New Unionism" initiative, the TUC has borrowed many ideas for aggressive recruitment campaigns from the United States, including the creation of an "Organising Academy."

It is clear that the logic of these strategies has yet to be fully worked out. They are, instead, a series of strategic tendencies: some widely diffused within the union movement and some rarer and more isolated within a small number of unions. However, these are the dominant strategic tendencies; they have become much stronger and more entrenched in union thinking in the 1990s, and these are the strategies that the TUC and the larger, more influential trade unions are adopting. The last decade has seen a wide-ranging process of strategic reevaluation on the part of the labor movement. That trade union strategy had undergone a metamorphosis along almost every dimension by the end of the 1990s is one indication of the transformation of British industrial relations since 1979.

CHAPTER SIX

The Third Way and Beyond:
The Future of British Industrial Relations

Third Way Industrial Relations

One might anticipate that the end of the eighteen-year period of Conservative rule with the election of a Labour government in May 1997 would lead to some modification of the third system of industrial relations. In 1979 there was a sharp contrast between the reform efforts of the outgoing Labour government, which had legislated important aspects of the second system of industrial relations, and the promise of the incoming Conservative government to reverse much of that legislation, and indeed to modify the framework of labor law that had underpinned the industrial relations institutions constructed in the early twentieth century. By the time it won a general election in 1997, after four successive defeats, the Labour Party's conception of the appropriate institutions for the regulation of class relations had moved a very long way from that of the 1970s. An examination of New Labour's industrial relations project permits an evaluation of the extent to which it is compatible with the emerging architecture of a third system of industrial relations, and hence what prospect exists for some long-term political and social consensus over how class relations are regulated.

   The current leadership and intellectual direction of the British Labour Party emerged out of a long and bitter conflict within the party about how best to respond to both political defeat and the changed economic and social landscape of the British political economy at the end of the twentieth century.[1] No attempt to evaluate New Labour's industrial relations project is possible without recognizing the centrality of conflict over the party-union relationship for the broader project of "modernizing" the Labour Party itself in the period since 1983. The disastrous experience of the 1970s, specifically the electoral fallout from the Social Contract and the Winter of Discontent, was interpreted as a direct result of the close identification between the unions and the Labour Party. It is important to understand that ending the association, in the minds of voters and business, between the Labour Party and organized labor—entailing both the formal and informal ties between party and unions, and the role of labor law, labor market flexibility, and commitment to full employment of a Labour government—is *the* defining core of the modernization project for New Labour. It is seen as central to the ability to appeal to more affluent swing voters and to win the confidence of employers and financial interests. Thus institutional changes within the party, and changes in the policies to be followed by a Labour government, have been shaped with this in mind.

The party's leading expert on focus groups, Philip Gould, has argued that being "tough on the unions" is one of the three irreducible core elements of New Labour's identity (the other two being responsibility on the economy and strength in Europe).[2] John Monks, then general secretary of the TUC, complained early in the first term of the New Labour government about "the symbolic role that unions have been given by some in new Labour's Britain. For them our primary role is to be used to define what new Labour isn't."[3] And Bill Morris, then general secretary of the Transport and General Workers Union (TGWU), has referred to "a game of pro-business machismo, designed to prove how different this Labour government is from preceding ones."[4] Hostility to the trade unions has thus been an integral part of the modernization strategy.

Industrial relations policy was formulated with more than public opinion and business confidence in mind, though. As noted in the previous chapter, one distinction between New Labour's industrial relations project and that of Thatcherite Conservatism is New Labour's explicit linkage between post-Fordism, or contemporary economic conditions, and the framework of social regulation appropriate to it. Labour policy documents, and the speeches of party leaders, invariably emphasize the degree of change in the world economy and the implications that change has for established economic and social forms of regulation, from macroeconomic policy to welfare policy to industrial relations policy. While there is much debate over the extent to which contemporary economic restructuring, particularly that which is linked to globalization, does indeed require dramatic changes in regulatory institutions, as Hay and Watson have pointed out, "New Labour clearly acts *as if* the globalization hypothesis were an accurate description of reality."[5]

New Labour is also far more explicit than its Thatcherite predecessor in recognizing the importance of the state in the regulation of social relations, arguing that law can operate to deepen, widen, and embed cultural practices. As Tony Blair put it:

> My ambition . . . is nothing less than to change the culture of relations in and at work—and to reflect a new relationship between work and family life. It is often said that a change of culture cannot be brought about by a change in the framework of law. But a change in law can reflect a new culture, can enhance its understanding and support its development.[6]

For New Labour, the state cannot evacuate the terrain of work, leaving social regulation to employers and employees alone, because it is possible for employers to organize social relations within their firms in a manner that is not even in their own interests, let alone those of the economy as a whole. The attractions of "a low-skill, low-wage, low-quality, low-value economy" can lead to a kind of market failure, so it is appropriate for the state to encourage social relations likely to push employers toward "high quality, high performance, high skills, high productivity, high value."[7] The role of the state for the Labour government was thus to close off the "low road" available to firms while simultaneously seeking to coax better practices out of employers and trade unions.[8]

Brief comment on the broad contours of Labour economic policy is necessary because macro- and microeconomic policy help to structure social relations between unions and employers. In practice, the dominant motif of Labour macroeconomic policy has been convergent with Conservative policy. That is to say, it has emphasized the need for fiscal neutrality and the use of monetary policy to prevent inflation. Within less than a week of taking office in 1997, the chancellor of the exchequer, Gordon Brown, handed control over interest rates to the Bank of England monetary policy committee, essentially establishing the independence of the bank to set monetary policy. Once Labour endorsed the priority of fighting inflation over full employment in the late 1980s, it needed a way to make that commitment credible. Membership in the European Exchange Rate Mechanism (ERM) was the first such mechanism, but with the collapse of British membership in the ERM in 1992, and with Britain still ambivalent about embarking on Economic and Monetary Union (EMU), Bank of England independence was the chosen solution. All in all, it is hard to see New Labour macroeconomic policy as more than a more competent and consistent version of Conservative policy. At the microeconomic level New Labour has rejected any meaningful industrial policy, or indeed any policy to improve the level of productive investment, and has not developed the tools to intervene on the supply side.[9] Welfare reform has become the main tool for reforming the labor market. The result is that all that is left is anti-inflationary policy at the macroeconomic level and labor market flexibility at the microeconomic level. This severely constrains the space for a distinctive industrial relations policy.

That is probably a large part of the reason why, for all the centrality of the relationship between the Labour Party and the labor movement for internal party conflict after 1979, industrial relations reform has in fact been peripheral to the intellectual development of New Labour and the "Third Way." New Labour has defined what it is against in the area of industrial relations, but it is much more difficult to identify what it is for. Blair argued in the course of the election campaign that "the essential elements of the trade union legislation of the 1980s will remain. . . . The changes that we do propose would leave British law the most restrictive on trade unions in the Western world," but it was not until after he had become prime minister that one could begin to see the outlines of a distinct New Labour project of industrial relations.[10]

A certain poorly defined "Third Way" model of industrial relations has appeared in New Labour discourse. Prior to the 1997 election, and following several speeches by Blair in 1996, the notion of "stakeholding" was proffered, and this remains the closest thing to an articulated theory of industrial relations.[11] If firms have multiple stakeholders, of which shareholders are only one element—employees, consumers, lenders, and debtors being others—public policy should encourage the participation of all stakeholders. This might imply minimum rights, job security, and some voice for workers in the firm. All but the most minimal definition of stakeholding was disavowed by New Labour in advance of the election, but it remains as an alternative discourse, suggesting inclusiveness, social solidarity, and fairness, in contrast to the atomism, individualism, and exclusive concern with profitability allegedly characterizing Thatcherism.

More inchoate, but much more widespread in New Labour discourse, is the notion of "partnership." Firms are most successful, it is argued, when employers, managers, and employees work together, so the goal of public policy should be to encourage partnership. The Department of Trade and Industry (DTI) created a Partnership at Work Fund in 1999 designed to encourage concrete experiments in partnership, and the government warmly welcomed the TUC's creation of a Partnership Institute. A wide range of policies can be considered under the heading of "partnership," encompassing everything from suggestion boxes to codetermination, and one of the appeals of the term is precisely that it is such a broad tent.[12] Wood has argued that at the heart of the Third Way is a notion of partnership understood as "high-involvement HRM" with the emphasis on encouraging worker commitment to the firm with the goal of improving productivity and quality.[13] This certainly meshes with the public statements of ministers. Importantly, as Wood also notes, there is "nothing in the notion of partnership to link it exclusively with unions."[14]

New Labour's conception of industrial relations rests on a series of assumptions about the role of power in the workplace, and the relationship between employment rights and economic efficiency. Blair has argued that the interests of business and labor are not opposed: "My vision is where the boundaries between management and workforce erode";[15] "the government's programme [is] to replace the notion of conflict between employers and employees with the promotion of partnership."[16] The role of labor law is therefore to "put a very minimum infrastructure of decency and fairness around people in the workplace."[17] Fairness and competitiveness in the marketplace go hand in hand; there is no conflict between them, because "a competitive and growing economy itself requires a culture of fairness and opportunity at work so that Britain can harness the talents of our people."[18] But, fairness is in the service of competitiveness, not the other way round; it is the junior partner. Regulation of the labor market must always be undertaken with an eye to its effects on efficiency and competitiveness.

Thus the primary task of industrial relations institutions is not to correct an imbalance of power in the workplace but to create a context in which the productivity and creativity of workers is properly harnessed for the good of the firm:

> Let us build trades unions and businesses that are creative, not conservative, unions that show they can work with management to make better companies. Let us build unions that people join not just out of fear of change or exploitation but because they are committed to success, unions that look forwards not backwards and that support workers and foster the true adaptability they need to be secure in that competitive and fast changing world.[19]

Thus there has been no return to a public presumption in favor of the collective regulation of class relations. The government has repeatedly argued that trade unions need to demonstrate value to employers. Their role is to provide services to their members and help firms become more competitive, not to protect their members from employers; individual rights at work enshrined in legislation serve the protective function. This explains why state regulation under a Labour government remains highly restrictive of the ability to engage in industrial action but does encourage minimum rights and a *voice* for workers.

The relationship between organized labor and the New Labour government has been quite different from the labor movement's relationships both with previous Labour governments and with Conservative governments after 1979. On the one hand, unions have had very little formal, or institutional, access to this government.[20] The regular meetings under the auspices of the Trade Union Liaison Committee in the 1970s no longer take place, though there have been quarterly meetings between general secretaries, ministers, and civil servants since late 2000. While there has been a sizable influx of business people into the government, as ministers, advisers, and heads of various task forces, unionists have only rarely been tapped for office (Alan Johnson being the most prominent). Evidence from three hundred government task forces suggests that businesspeople vastly outnumber trade unionists, with only 2 percent from trade unions, compared with 36 percent from private business and trade associations.[21] Union influence has been more informal, dependent on personal relations between unions and individual ministers.

On the other hand, despite government disavowals of a return to corporatism, the Labour government has chosen to implement its commitments to the labor movement through quasi-corporatist institutions. In contrast to most other policy areas, where the government has simply legislated with only limited prior consultation, in the area of labor legislation there has been an effort to *depoliticize* government action, and disarm criticism that the government favors labor, by seeking prior agreement between employers and unions. This occurred most clearly in the area of union recognition, where the government urged the TUC and the CBI to negotiate an agreement, which would then be implemented by legislation—very much on the EU model of social policymaking. Similarly, in fulfilling Labour's longtime pledge of a statutory minimum wage, a Low Pay Commission was set up, representing employers and unions, to take evidence and make recommendations on the level of a minimum wage. A task force on family-friendly working (with a remit not to create onerous burdens on business) was created in 2001 with representatives of the CBI, TUC, and Equal Opportunity Commission. Similarly, after efforts to derail an EU directive on consultation and information failed, the Department of Trade and Industry sought talks with the TUC and CBI in the hopes of reaching an agreement that could become the basis for legislation. New Labour has sought political cover for labor legislation, either by these efforts to gain agreement ahead of legislation, or by permitting labor market regulation courtesy of the EU once Britain's opt-out from the Social Chapter was ended. Thus the government can claim to be acting, not at the behest of organized labor, but in response to broad-based agreements beyond its direct control. That said, the government has been willing to reject or modify aspects of proposed policy that emerge from these quasi-corporatist institutions, always, as it happens, in a direction more favorable to employers.

There were three main areas of industrial relations policy during Labour's first term in office: a statutory minimum wage; EU social directives; and individual and collective rights at work embodied primarily in the 1999 Employment Relations Act. The second term in office brought one further package of industrial relations legislation, this one primarily aimed at reducing recourse to industrial tribunals. Before examining these one by one, however, it is worth noting that the Labour government has made a number of more minor, though symbolically important, interventions in industrial relations. On coming to power, the New Labour government moved rapidly to fulfill a long-standing pledge to permit staff members at the Government Communications Headquarters (GCHQ) to have union representation. After the union was derecognized in 1984, those who refused to give up their union membership were fired. In 1997 some of those workers returned to GCHQ, after the union agreed to a no-strike agreement. Similarly, the government repealed the Conservative requirement that union dues checkoff arrangements be reauthorized in writing every three years.

On the other side of the ledger, the prison officers' union was infuriated by a Home Office ruling that upheld a 1994 measure outlawing industrial action by prison officers. In the public sector New Labour has proven less ideological than its predecessor. Privatization has not been the automatic response, though the major components of the public sector had already been privatized, so there were few obvious targets. Still, minor privatizations (of the Tote, the Royal Mint, and the air traffic control system) have been proposed, and there has been greater emphasis on public-private partnerships (for the London Underground and hospital building, most notably). As such, the boundaries of the relatively protected state sector continue to shrink. Since unions are much stronger and more secure in the public sector, privatization affects their ability to maintain recognition and full representational rights, and their capacity to engage in industrial action.

The Statutory Minimum Wage

Before turning to the creation of a statutory minimum wage, it is important to note that after 1979 incomes policies completely fell off Labour's policy agenda. There was strong union opposition to such policies, but there was also a recognition that the twin capacities of organized labor and the state to operate an incomes policy were much diminished. On the one hand, the collapse of collective bargaining coverage in the 1980s, allied with the continued decentralization of collective bargaining, made it extremely difficult for union leaders to make wage restraint work. On the other hand, governments were less able to impose an incomes policy, because such policies tend to be most effective in the public sector and the public sector is now much smaller as a result of privatization, to say nothing of the weaker capacity of governments to credibly promise full employment and a higher social wage—the essential quid for the quo of traditional incomes policies—in return for restraint.[22] Incomes policies are now structurally all but impossible, regardless of whether unions or a Labour government want them. The most that is possible is strict wage restraint in the public sector. In any case, neither unions nor the Labour Party have shown any inclination to return to incomes policies.

The creation of a national, statutory minimum wage was a long-term promise of the Labour Party, inherited by Blair. In advance of the 1997 election it was announced that no level for the minimum wage would be set; instead, a representative Low Pay Commission (LPC) would be set up to gather evidence and recommend a level. This structure guaranteed that the level would be set well below what trade unions were asking for. The eventual recommendations of the LPC, in May 1998, exempted workers under 18, suggested that 18-to-20-year-olds receive a lower "development rate," and those 21 and above would get £3.60, to be uprated with inflation. But even these recommendations were not accepted in their entirety by the government. Following disagreement between the chancellor and the president of the Board of Trade, the development rate was phased in and was to apply to 21- years-olds as well as those 18–20, and the rates were not to be automatically uprated in line with inflation but monitored over time.[23] The practical implementation of the new minimum wage also showed the close attention that the government was paying to the concerns of business.[24]

The national minimum wage is an important indicator of New Labour's conception of industrial relations, and it is a clear area of contrast with its Conservative predecessor. The new minimum wage brings Britain into line with most European countries and affects some two million people, the vast majority of them women and part-time workers. It indicates a commitment to certain basic minimum standards at work. That said, the impact will be relatively small, and it is worth noting the main distinction between the structure of this minimum wage and that of the old wages councils. The councils were designed to be industry-level collective bargaining institutions in embryo; the goal was always that the councils would evolve, over time, in the direction of collective bargaining and thus, in the long run, strengthen collective representation and bargaining. A statutory national minimum wage will not have this effect, and it may possibly weaken unions because workers can make gains through legislation rather than collective action. The form that the minimum wage took indicates a state preference for regulation of the labor market by legislation rather than collective bargaining.

The European Dimension

The second major plank of labor legislation promised by Labour while in opposition was an end to Britain's opt-out from the European Social Chapter. Trade unions came to see European social legislation as having the potential to counteract deregulation at home, and the Labour Party found it electorally popular to argue that British workers were being denied basic rights granted their European counterparts. Thus, within days of winning the election in 1997, the foreign secretary announced that Britain would sign on to the Social Chapter. The importance of this act was initially largely symbolic. There were only two European directives implemented under the Social Chapter, one on parental leave and the other creating European works councils in large firms employing significant numbers of workers in two or more EU countries.

Nonetheless, the importance of Britain's accepting European social legislation lay in the potential for the future. Some commentators have argued that Europe will become a steadily more important source of social/labor legislation as time goes on.[25] However, those who hoped prior to the election that New Labour would use European social legislation as political cover for regulating the labor market have been disappointed. Blair very early on made it clear that, while seeking minimum standards of fairness for workers, he placed a high priority on labor market flexibility. In June 1997 Blair lectured other EU leaders on New Labour's "third way, a way of marrying together an open, competitive and successful economy with a just, decent and humane society. . . . Our aim must be to tackle the obstacles to job creation and labour market flexibility . . . making sure the Social Chapter and Employment Chapter help job creation, not hinder it."[26]

A pattern of initial rejection of EU social legislation, followed by minimalist interpretation and implementation, has repeated itself since 1997. For example, in response to a European proposal to extend works councils to solely national firms, Britain made it known that it was unconvinced of the need for further EU legislation to enhance the rights of workers to consultation and information. Only after extracting concessions concerning the phasing in of consultation rights and the size of firms affected did Britain sign on to the directive.[27]

The working time directive (which did not originate from the Social Chapter and would have affected Britain even in the absence of signing on) was also implemented into British law in an extremely limited manner. In July 1999 government guidelines seemed to suggest that all salaried employees would be exempted from the directive. Negotiations with trade unions led to a partial retreat by the DTI, but it remained the case that employees were allowed to choose to work more than the maximum number of hours, opening the door to employer coercion.

A similar effort to minimize the impact of European directives appeared with the directive giving full employment rights to part-time workers: government guidelines for its implementation suggested that the directive would benefit less than 1 percent of part-time workers, because most do not qualify as "employees." The DTI subsequently broadened the legislation to cover temporary and casual workers under pressure from unions, all the while emphasizing its "light touch" approach, with minimal red tape.[28] The same tactic of narrowing the scope of applicability to employees with formal contracts has been used in the implementation of the fixed-term directive in 2002, and the British government has already expressed its displeasure with the draft EU directive guaranteeing equal treatment to temporary workers. Overall, then, EU legislation has contributed to the creation of new rights and protections at work. At the same time, New Labour's acceptance of European social legislation has been limited and grudging.

The Employment Rights Act

The central pillar of the New Labour industrial relations project was the 1999 Employment Relations Act (ERA).[29] The process by which this package of legislation made it onto the statute books, and the manner of its presentation, were interesting in their own right, but here I will simply examine the main components of the legislation.[30]

The ERA contained a number of new or enhanced individual and collective rights at work, including the third key preelection pledge of a statutory right to union recognition. The main changes for individual rights are to reduce the qualifying period before benefiting from claims for unfair dismissal from two years to one, to raise the limit on compensation claims for unfair dismissal, to give workers on fixed contracts the right to claim unfair dismissal, to extend maternity leave to eighteen weeks, and to give an enhanced right to parental leave. These individual rights were very limited. The change in the qualifying period for unfair dismissal does not even return the situation to the status quo in 1979, when six months was the qualifying period, and estimates suggest that a third of parents will be unable to take advantage of the parental leave provisions because leave is unpaid.[31]

Trade unions and their members made a number of gains under the heading of collective rights at work. The central new right was a statutory right to union recognition, but the legislation also permitted workers fired for engaging in lawful industrial action the right to use the unfair dismissal procedure,[32] made blacklisting of, or discrimination against, union members illegal, and created a new legal right for individuals to be accompanied by a fellow employee or union representative during grievance and disciplinary proceedings even if a union is not recognized at that workplace.

With regard to the statutory right to union recognition, the devil is in the details, and both business and unions had something to cheer about.[33] Perhaps the biggest surprise was that recognition would be automatic where a union can demonstrate that a majority of employees are members of the union, though the Central Arbitration Committee (CAC) can intervene to force a ballot where it suspects that worker support for the union is weak and recent. This form of "card-check" recognition exists in Canada and has long been a demand of U.S. unions. Additionally, the union(s) and not the employer will propose the scope of the bargaining unit.

On the other hand, employers won most of the battles for the application of the statutory right. The legislation does not apply to firms employing twenty or fewer workers, meaning that about 1 million firms and 5.2 million workers are excluded from the legislation,[34] and a threshold was created such that a union needs favorable votes from a majority of those voting and at least 40 percent of those eligible to vote in favor in order to gain recognition.

These collective rights at work are, again, fairly limited, particularly in the context of eighteen years of Conservative legislation restricting collective representation, collective bargaining, and collective action at work. Strike action remains as restrictive as before with the single exception of providing greater safeguards for those engaged in lawful industrial action. Indeed, on several occasions Labour ministers have gone beyond their Conservative predecessors, suggesting mandatory arbitration in the public-sector, and Blair has called public sector strikes "totally unacceptable."[35]

It is too early for a comprehensive evaluation of the effect of the statutory right to recognition. After two years of operation, 175 applications under Part 1 of Schedule 1 were made to the CAC, with recognition granted in 34 cases, 14 of which came without a ballot.[36] These cases covered about ten thousand workers, 40 percent of them from a single successful ballot at Honda. Trade unions have reason to be pleased with the procedural decisions made by the CAC on such issues as the composition of the bargaining unit and access to the workplace during a recognition campaign. On the other hand, the legislation mandated quite long periods between each step of the statutory process, and in practice the CAC exceeded even these, to the chagrin of trade unions. As Wood has pointed out, the legislation was drafted so as to create the maximum likelihood that voluntary agreement could be reached without requiring the imposition of a union on an employer.[37]

Recognition achieved through the statutory provisions has been dwarfed by voluntary recognition agreements, which rose rapidly between 1999 and 2001.[38] Cases of voluntary employer recognition of unions were climbing while cases of derecognition were declining prior to the implementation of the recognition legislation, suggesting that the "climate" of industrial relations has improved for unions, regardless of the impact of legislation. Since the rise in voluntary union recognition also appears to be accompanied by a rise in agreements sometimes characterized pejoratively as "sweetheart deals," including "no strike" elements, it may be that employers sought better agreements ahead of legislation.[39]

Overall, the ERA contained very little by way of direct rights or gains for unions themselves, beyond the statutory right to recognition. For example, the right to be accompanied by a union official is an individual right, as are rights against blacklisting and dismissal for strike action. The legislation did not seek to directly strengthen unions, and if they gain, it will be indirectly through additional rights for individual workers.

Trade union criticism of the limitations of the legislation remained, particularly of the small-firm exclusion and 40 percent threshold in the recognition machinery, and the one-year waiting period for unfair dismissal rights, and in the run-up to the 2001 election the government promised a "root and branch review of employment law."[40] This was not forthcoming, and unions were highly critical of the fact that the Employment Bill, introduced in 2001, did not revisit issues dealt with in the ERA.[41] It was not until July of 2002, in an effort to head off conflict with organized labour over the public sector, that a consultation process reviewing the ERA was promised for later that year. The unions were deeply disappointed by the results of that process as the government proposed no significant changes to the recognition legislation.[42]

The Employment Act

The centerpiece of industrial relations reform in Labour's second term was the 2002 Employment Act (EA).[43] While it covered a number of areas, the core of the legislation was aimed at a reform of the employment tribunals system, with the goal of reducing the number of cases handled by the tribunal system.

The backdrop to the legislation was the steady increase in the caseload, from under 36,000 in 1990 to almost 104,000 in 1999–2000,[44] and strong business pressure to reduce the costs—in time, expenses, and compensation—that were resulting from individual claims brought by workers against their employers. There are multiple causes of this increase, including the greater number of rights that workers have, and can therefore claim are being violated, and the increase in compensation provided by the ERA, but it is also likely that the collapse in union membership and collective bargaining coverage (including the narrower scope of bargaining) of the past two decades have forced the tribunal system to do some of the work previously handled by voluntary collective procedures.[45] That is certainly the TUC's position, as its response to the consultation document that preceded publication of the Employment Bill made clear.[46]

The EA contained a series of measures designed to reduce the numbers of cases brought forward to tribunals, though a plan to charge a fee to bring complaints was dropped.[47] The government argued that a significant source of tribunal complaints was the absence of proper dismissal and grievance procedures in many firms, especially small firms, itself in part a result of the shrinkage of union presence in the workplace. So the legislation created minimum statutory internal procedures covering dismissal and grievances and made them implied terms of contract. Once these statutory procedures are in place, certain complaints cannot go to a tribunal until the internal procedure has been completed, and failure to follow these procedures can lead to variations in the award made by a tribunal. It is worth noting that, again, one of the traditional benefits of trade unionism and collective bargaining is now provided in statutory form even where unions are not recognized.

The goal of reducing costs to business as a result of this legislation was made clear by the explanatory notes that accompanied the legislation. The government estimated that the reforms would reduce the number of tribunal cases by about a quarter, between 30,000 and 40,000 a year, with an estimated savings of £65–90 million for employers.[48] These reforms were heavily criticized, not only by trade unions, but by the judge heading the employment tribunal system, who argued that many workers will be denied proper compensation,[49] and by the all-party parliamentary committee on human rights, which suggested that the legislation violates the 1998 Human Rights Act.

While reform of the tribunal system is the central element of the EA, it also contains several other provisions. These include an extension of paid maternity leave, a new statutory right to paid paternity leave and adoption leave, a statutory right to time off for "Union Learning Representatives," and regulations incorporating the EU framework agreement on fixed-term work into British law. It should be noted that the Exchequer, not employers, will be responsible for most of the cost of the new family-friendly measures.

BRITISH INDUSTRIAL RELATIONS IN
COMPARATIVE PERSPECTIVE

How should New Labour's industrial relations project be evaluated, and how compatible is it with that of its Conservative predecessor? Note first that, with the passage of the Employment Relations Act, New Labour interest in the reform of industrial relations ended until after the 2001 election, and the only industrial relations legislation in the second term was primarily concerned with limiting access to employment tribunals, not adding new rights at work. In Blair's words, the ERA "seeks to draw a line under the issue of industrial relations law . . . here are our proposals for an industrial relations settlement for this parliament."[50] Thus after eighteen years in which Conservative governments practically rewrote British industrial relations law, and reconfigured the balance of power between workers, unions, and employers, only very limited industrial relations reform was proposed by this aggressively modernizing Labour government.

The central elements of the current industrial relations system then are as follows. The overwhelming bulk of Conservative industrial relations legislation remains in force, and has been endorsed by New Labour. This entails strict regulation of, and limits on, industrial action and accompanying picketing, such that strikes are possible only between workers and their direct employers, and then only after a postal ballot. While New Labour has been prepared to accept, and even offer cautious encouragement to, collective representation and bargaining, it is every bit as hostile to the exercise of the right to strike as previous Conservative governments. It also means state regulation of the internal affairs of unions, particularly elections of officers, and the abolition of the closed shop. To this basic framework of labor law has been added limited regulation of the labor market. This regulation has taken the form of a set of minimum rights at work, including a minimum wage, limits on working hours, expanded rights of unfair dismissal, expanded rights for working women and parents, and some regulation of precarious, "atypical" forms of labor contract.

Regulation of the labor market has taken the form of individual legal rights, enforceable through labor courts and state agencies (the CAC and ACAS), not, for the most part, collective rights designed to strengthen trade unions, which could then take on the role of regulating social relations through collective bargaining. With a few exceptions, any benefits likely to accrue to unions will come indirectly, by virtue of a more regulated labor market, or a new role as enforcers of legal rights.[51] Thus, of the two parallel tracks along which social relations have been regulated in Britain, as elsewhere in the advanced capitalist world—collective regulation by unions and legal regulation by the state—it is the latter that has become the focus of New Labour attention. This continues and accelerates the trend since the 1960s in Britain of a shift from voluntarism toward individual rights at work. But it is very important to recognize that even legal regulation of the labor market remains extremely limited because of a concern that employment rights encroach as little as possible on labor market flexibility.

In comparative perspective it has been argued that New Labour's industrial relations reforms are based on the conception of a "European model" of industrial relations,[52] though in practice this argument emphasizes elements of the German system of industrial relations: the greater role of law in regulating social relations; nonunion forms of collective representation in the workplace, such as works councils; joint union and employer commitment to high-skill, high-wage production, underpinned by a sophisticated training regime.

Despite the greater role of law in British industrial relations, this argument is not persuasive. The application of European works councils to British multinationals, the right of a worker to be accompanied by a union or nonunion supporter in grievance and disciplinary hearings, and the (thus far unspecified) right to consultation over layoffs and transfers of ownership do not come close to the rights that elected works councils have in Germany. This kind of collective representation requires strong legal underpinning, and while the Blair government appears willing to accept collective representation where it can be voluntarily negotiated between employer and employees, it is loath to impose it through legislation. In this, it mirrors the position of British employer organizations, which have consistently opposed statutory requirements that they create forms of collective representation.

More importantly, the German model of industrial relations (like that of similar social democratic and corporatist countries such as Sweden and Austria) remains organized around trade unionism and collective bargaining.[53] Strong unions and industry-level bargaining are a precondition for the successful operation of works councils and for managing the collective action problems that arise around training and wage issues. In the absence of a public policy commitment to strengthening and privileging collective bargaining, the trajectory of British industrial relations is away from the German model.

If one were seeking national models with which to compare the emerging system of industrial relations in Britain, the United States and France would offer a better fit. A framework of basic minimum rights at work, enforced by the state rather than unions, and a statutory union recognition procedure overseen by labor courts, is now common to both Britain and the United States.[54] Indeed, in an amusing exchange in the House of Commons during debate over the ERA, a Labour MP defended the government's proposed legislation, arguing that it is "nothing other than a version of what has existed in the United States since 1935, wholly supported and endorsed by Republican Congresses and Republican Presidents." To this, the Conservative employment spokesperson responded: "That is an interesting principle, which the honorable Gentleman might like to try out on the Prime Minister—that new

Labour should subcontract policy making to the Republican party in the American Congress."[55]

There are also important similarities between the British and the French industrial relations regimes. Following the gradual rejection of the statist planning model in France, a process that accelerated from 1983 onward,[56] the Auroux Laws provided a set of "citizenship rights" to workers inside the firm, designed to strengthen job security and voice, and to engage in partnership.[57] Trade unionism and collective bargaining were indirectly weakened through the development of new forms of consultation inside the firm that bypassed unions. Successive Socialist governments have used legislation on flexible working and the reduction of work time in order to both regulate the labor market and, through derogation, encourage partnership agreements in the workplace.[58]

There are, of course, significant differences between the industrial relations systems of the United States, France, and Britain. But one can detect the outlines of a distinct model of industrial relations centered on the enforcement of individual rights in the workplace by the state, with only a peripheral role for collective representation and collective bargaining. The United States, France, and Britain have seen declines in trade union membership that are among the greatest in the OECD since the mid-1970s, and in all three cases, efforts by center-left governments to regulate the labor market through the provision of individual rights have been eroded by the absence of countervailing collective power in the workplace.[59] Those rights are always subject to appropriation or reinterpretation by employers where organized labor is weak.

A greater state role in the provision and enforcement of labor rights is a feature of industrial relations systems where the weakness of employer and labor organizations forces the state to substitute for the absence of social bargaining as a mechanism for regulating class relations. For center-left governments in countries without strong nonmarket coordinating mechanisms, conflict over the appropriate degree of state regulation has become the central battleground of industrial relations reform. In such political economies center-left governments cannot rely on bargaining and nonmarket coordination to regulate the labor market; the choices instead are deregulation or regulation by the state.

The industrial relations project of the New Labour government in Britain has modified the institutions and practices of industrial relations bequeathed it in a manner that is both distinctive and innovative in comparison to its Labour and Conservative predecessors. "Third Way" industrial relations in the British context mean a repudiation of the first and second systems of industrial relations when collective bargaining was the primary mechanism for the regulation of the labor market and class relations, with statutory individual labor rights playing a limited and supporting role. It is now individual legal rights at work, provided and enforced by the state, that are the primary motor of industrial relations, with collective bargaining relegated to the public sector and declining areas of the private sector. Both collective bargaining and statutory rights at work are now justified by their contribution to the construction of partnership in the workplace in the quest for global competitiveness. Even the TUC has acknowledged the "absolute imperative" of competitiveness in legitimizing employment regulation.[60]

It is too soon to evaluate the impact of New Labour industrial relations reforms: the central elements of those reforms have been in effect for only three years as this concluding chapter is being written. But it is in any case not clear how one would be able to evaluate the reforms, what measures one would look for to identify success. It is certainly not the case that these reforms can be expected to lead to anything more than a limited resurgence of trade union strength and collective regulation of industrial relations. That was not their intent, and the evidence thus far is that the replacement of a Conservative with a Labour government brought only a brief period of stabilization of union membership.[61] Rather, measures of success will be more intangible and will be found in the practices of firms, in the forms of firm-level partnership that appear, and in the role and caseload of specialized state agencies and labor courts, as they come to substitute for regulation by collective bargaining. The institutions for the collective regulation of industrial relations, which were central to both public policy and industrial relations practice in Britain for a century after 1890, are now almost certainly in terminal decline.

In terms of industrial relations, the current Labour government is best understood as a consolidation of, rather than a radical departure from, Thatcherism. They share a broad acceptance of the current balance of social power in the workplace, a largely unitarist view of industrial relations, and, most fundamentally, an emphasis on individual rather than collective regulation of social relations. It is hard to disagree with Crouch's assessment that "in the industrial relations field New Labour represents a continuation of the neoliberalism of the Conservative government, but one required to make more concessions than its predecessor with trade unions and social-democratic policy preferences."[62]

Conservative governments of the 1980s and 1990s began the task of reconstructing the industrial relations system with their assault on the collective power of trade unions. The Labour Party modernizers might not admit this publicly, but they broadly believe that this assault was necessary. But it was only part of necessary reform; it was the destructive phase, which cleared away the obstacles to the creation of new, more appropriate social relations in the firm. The task of New Labour has been to cautiously coax these social relations out of the debris of Britain's postwar system of industrial relations.

As such, it is now reasonable to assume that a new consensus has been reached (recalling that the earlier postwar consensus was consistent with partisan political skirmishes at its boundaries) between the main political parties around an industrial relations settlement. The Labour Party's election to a second term of government maintained Conservative industrial relations institutions, while a future Conservative victory is likely to bring about only minor changes to New Labour's reforms. The current Conservative leadership has endorsed the statutory minimum wage, though it still claims that it will abolish the statutory recognition procedure. Whether it does or not will probably depend on how effective the legislation has been in increasing recognition; as I have argued above, the procedure is unlikely to have a sufficiently dramatic effect to make abolition an important goal of a future Conservative government. Similarly, both the labor movement and the main employers' organizations seem broadly content with this industrial relations settlement. After the traumatic experience of Thatcherism, the trade unions above all seek a settlement that all political parties agree on,[63] and the CBI, while anxious about the financial burden of new regulations on small business, appears to have come to terms with New Labour's industrial relations innovations.

CONCLUSION

Three distinct systems of industrial relations have been constructed in Britain in the past century. Each one emerged out of a crisis of the last as changing economic conditions rendered existing industrial relations institutions incapable of containing industrial conflict and permitting economic restructuring. In each case heightened levels of strikes triggered a public debate about the source of conflict and the shape of future institutions better suited to emerging patterns of economic growth. And in each case it was the British state that played a central role in the construction, embedding, and legitimization of new industrial relations institutions. This despite the longtime characterization of the British state as abstentionist and industrial relations as voluntarist, a characterization that has never been adequately reconceptualized even as evidence of state activism mounted from the late 1960s onward; accounts of state intervention in British industrial relations have tended to emphasize ad hoc, incoherent, or narrowly political explanations of state action, and they have rarely pushed the analysis back in time to challenge the voluntarist account of the first half of the twentieth century. The result has been both a failure to identify the *systemic* qualities of British industrial relations institutions (the extent to which sets of institutions formed distinct interlocking systems of industrial relations) and a tendency to overestimate the autonomous strength of British trade unionism. To the extent that trade unions shared that interpretation of British industrial relations they were woefully unprepared for the radical reforms of the Thatcherite period, with the result that they lost close to half of their members and a good deal more of their political influence.

The first system of industrial relations emerged in the early decades of the twentieth century as a response to the first major crisis of Britain's staple industries, those same industries which had powered the second industrial revolution, and it sought to use industry-level collective bargaining as a mechanism both for limiting industrial conflict between trade unions and employers and for limiting market competition between firms in highly competitive industries where the industrial structure made self-regulation by employers extremely difficult.

The second system of industrial relations developed in the early postwar decades when the center of economic gravity had shifted from the industrial staples to newer industries for whom the central problem was how to reorganize work so as to improve the productivity of more capital-intensive technology and skilled labor. Industry bargaining had sought to regulate wages and hours across each industry while largely leaving firms without well-developed mechanisms for regulating conflict and managing change. The first system of industrial relations lasted as long as it did in part because, while it responded to the needs of one set of industries, it did not act as an obstacle to the development of industrial relations in other industries. But by the 1960s there was a widespread perception that the lack of firm-level industrial relations institutions was both generating industrial conflict and contributing to poor productivity performance. The next two decades saw the spread of a panoply of firm-level institutions for the collective regulation of industrial relations, which had the effect of broadening the coverage of collective bargaining across the economy, decentralizing its locus to the firm, and expanding the scope of bargaining within the firm to include an ever wider range of work issues under the ambit of collective regulation.

The third system of industrial relations to some extent responded to a similar set of concerns, namely how to improve productivity. But by the 1980s, under conditions of heightened international competition, and as the weight of manufacturing employment shrunk to around a fifth of the total, employers came to place much greater emphasis on *flexibility* in all its myriad forms, and on increasingly individualized relationships between employers and employees, as the manner in which productivity gains could be made; just as different national variants of Fordism appeared in the thirty years after the Second World War, so a particular "hyperflexibility" came to mark British post-Fordism in the absence of many of the political-economic institutions characteristic of coordinated market economies, and with the arrival in power of a government that aggressively sought to dismantle those coordinating institutions which did exist. Moreover, employers had become disillusioned with joint regulation of economic change and were more prepared to take unilateral action in the firm. The result was the wholesale collapse of institutions of collective regulation at both the industry and the firm level, and the emergence of institutions suited to ensuring employers the maximum flexibility in the deployment of labor.

In the construction phase of each system of industrial relations, while employers and trade unions were often able to create an industry bargaining forum, or set of workplace institutions, the state nonetheless played a central role in diffusing industrial relations developments, providing forms of support that reduced the costs to industrial actors of adopting new institutions, overcoming collective action problems, and creating a climate in which certain institutions and practices were considered more legitimate than others. At certain points, legislation was of particular importance—for example, in the implantation of institutions for the collective regulation of the workplace in the 1970s, and in constraining the collective power of trade unions in the 1980s—while at other points the role of administrative action through state agencies played a significant role in translating industrial conflict into institutions of collective regulation. The public sector was used both as a model of industrial relations to be adopted elsewhere and later as a demonstration of the legitimacy of withstanding bitter strikes and weakening or breaking trade unions. On three occasions, the 1894 and 1968 royal commissions and the 1917 Whitley Committee Report, quasi-state institutions shaped the discourse of industrial relations reform, selecting one set of institutions for public favor and limiting the range of discursively viable policy alternatives.

The British state was not monolithic, nor did it act alone, independently of class forces. Tension between the judiciary's attachment to common law notions of the limitations on collective economic action, for example, and the preference of specialized labor departments of the state for collective solutions to industrial conflict, has been a persistent theme of industrial relations reform over the past century. At no point did British governments seek to impose industrial relations institutions on both business and labor. Even in the 1980s, the point in the past century in which the state has acted most decisively to reshape industrial relations, Conservative governments correctly anticipated employer acquiescence to reforms and permitted employers to opt out of them if they wished. For the most part, the importance of state action has been, not that it single-handedly engaged in institution-building, but rather that the British state had capacities that industrial actors did not. The role of the British state was itself conditioned by the particular organizational and ideological structures of business and labor, inherited from the process of industrialization. Britain lacked the kinds of highly organized and centralized class associations and corporatist traditions that might have permitted institution-building with a less obtrusive role for the state. In the British context, only the state had the capacity to create a *system* out of scattered industrial relations experiments.

By the end of the 1970s, a clear partisan divide had opened up between the two major political parties over the future shape of the industrial relations system. Employers and trade unions were also sharply divided. Industrial relations reform lacked the degree of political and social consensus that had been a feature of the first system, and even of the central goal (if not the details) of the second system. The second system of industrial relations became associated with the Labour Party and the trade union movement, with the result that was challenged almost as soon as it came into being.

What of the third system of industrial relations, the central elements of which were put in place by Conservative governments between 1979 and 1997? If it too failed to develop some degree of political and social consensus, one would anticipate that it would be short-lived, better understood as a purely political project than an enduring system of industrial relations. This final chapter has examined the New Labour industrial relations project in some detail in order to reach some conclusion about its relationship with the institutions of the third system, put in place in the previous two decades. I have argued that while the industrial relations institutions currently being constructed by New Labour differ in some respects from those of the government's Conservative predecessor, they are fundamentally convergent with the decollectivist thrust of the third system of industrial relations. New Labour legislation has grafted a framework of greater legal regulation of social relations onto Conservative reforms, while not challenging the decollectivist architecture of the third system of industrial relations. The distinction between the two approaches lies in the degree of labor market regulation undertaken by the state, not the agent of that regulation. Both largely reject collective regulation.

It is now reasonable to assume that a new consensus has been reached between the main political parties around an industrial relations settlement embodying a new class compromise, resting on a particular interpretation of the imperatives of British post-Fordism. As such, the third system of industrial relations has achieved the kind of political consensus enjoyed by the first system but which eluded the second, and there is a strong case for seeing this as a long-lasting, stable set of industrial relations institutions.

Notes

1. From "Part of the Union," performed by the Strawbs. The lyrics of the song and details of its commercial success can be found at the official Web site for the band: http://www.strawbpage.ndirect.co.uk/. Lyrics by Richard Hudson and John Ford. Copyright Fazz Music Ltd.

2. For an important contribution, both to theorizing the role of the state in the evolution of labor movements and to explaining divergent patterns of union development in France and the United States, see Friedman, *State-Making and Labor Movements*.

3. Richard Hyman, in *Understanding European Trade Unionism*, has recently theorized trade union identities in terms of a triangle of positions, in which European unions are located between the three poles of market, class, and society. This does not explicitly theorize the role of the state, though the "society" pole implies a greater trade union interest in using collective power to influence public policy in order to reshape society through the state.

4. It was Ernest Bevin who used this phrase in the annual conference report of the Labour Party in 1935. It is cited in the definitive work on the relationship between the Labour Party and the trade unions: Minkin, *The Contentious Alliance*, p. 3.

5. To cite just three among many, Aldcroft and Oliver, *Trade Unions and the Economy*; Coates, *The Question of UK Decline*; and Coates and Hillard, eds., *UK Economic Decline*.

6. For details of the film and its awards see the Internet Movie Database Web site: http://us.imdb.com/Title?0052911.

7. Hanson, *Taming the Trade Unions*. See also Margaret Thatcher's memoir of her time as prime minister, *The Downing Street Years*, especially chapters 4 and 13.

8. Goldthorpe, "Industrial Relations in Great Britain."

9. Ibid., p. 452.

10. For accounts of the pervasiveness of these elements of "New Right" thinking see Dennis Kavanagh, *Thatcherism and British Politics*, chapter 3, and Gamble, *The Free Economy and the Strong State*, chapter 2.

11. Howell, *Regulating Labor*.

12. Martin, et al., *The Brave New World of European Labor*.

13. *Royal Commission on Trade Unions and Employer Associations, 1965–1968: Report*.

14. For a thoughtful account of the relationship between pluralism and Marxism in industrial relations see Hyman, *The Political Economy of Industrial Relations*, especially part 1. See also Hyman, *Industrial Relations*.

15. For surveys of British industrial relations research, see Bain and Clegg, "A Strategy for Industrial Relations Research in Great Britain"; Winchester, "Industrial Rela-

tions Research in Britain"; and Brown and Wright, "The Empirical Tradition in Workplace Bargaining Research."

16. Winchester, "Industrial Relations Research in Britain," p. 101.

17. The best recent examples are Kelly, *Rethinking Industrial Relations*, and Hyman, *Understanding European Trade Unionism*.

18. Cited in McCarthy, "The Rise and Fall of Collective Laissez-Faire."

19. Ibid., pp. 6–7.

20. For an analysis and survey of Kahn-Freund's life and work see Lewis, "Kahn-Freund and Labour Law.

21. Cited in McCarthy, "The Rise and Fall of Collective Laissez-Faire." p.1.

22. Flanders, *Management and Unions*, p. 94.

23. Ibid., p. 97. There was a third core principle, which was a preference for procedural over substantive rules.

24. For a fine summary of developments in postwar British labor law see Davies and Freedland, *Labour Legislation and Public Policy*, especially chapter 1.

25. Steinmetz, "Introduction."

26. Flanders, "The Tradition of Voluntarism," p. 355.

27. Cited in McCarthy, "The Rise and Fall of Collective Laissez-Faire," p. 6.

28. Hyman, *Understanding European Trade Unionism*, p. 66.

29. Ibid., p. 2.

30. See Clegg, *The System of Industrial Relations in Great Britain*, and also his *Changing System of Industrial Relations in Great Britain*.

31. Clegg, *The Changing System of Industrial Relations in Great Britain*, p. 7.

32. Wright, "Working-Class Power, Capitalist-Class Interests, and Class Compromise."

33. Ibid., pp. 30–32.

34. Clegg, *The System of Industrial Relations in Great Britain*, p. 39.

35. For Alan Fox's critique see his *Beyond Contract*. The Marxist position is best articulated in various works by Richard Hyman. See his seminal critique of pluralism, "Pluralism, Procedural Consensus, and Collective Bargaining," in his *Political Economy of Industrial Relations*. See also his *Industrial Relations*.

36. Zeitlin, "From Labour History to the History of Industrial Relations," p. 165.

37. Clegg, *The Changing System of Industrial Relations in Great Britain*, p. 452.

38. See the concluding chapter of McKibbin, *Classes and Cultures*.

39. The sociologists were Shils and Young, quoted in McKibbin, *Classes and Cultures*, p. 535.

40. Davies and Freedland, *Labour Legislation and Public Policy*.

41. The past decade has seen the growth of academic studies, particularly historical accounts, that have examined the role of the state in British industrial relations. The best statement of the renewed emphasis on the role of the state can be found in Zeitlin, "Shopfloor Bargaining and the State."

42. See, for example, industrial relations textbooks by Kessler and Bayliss, *Contemporary British Industrial Relations*, and Edwards, *Industrial Relations*.

43. See the contributions to the *Industrial Law Journal* and Ewing, "The State and Industrial Relations."

44. Zeitlin, "Shopfloor Bargaining and the State."

45. Ewing, "The State and Industrial Relations."

46. The diaries of Barbara Castle, secretary of state for employment (effectively minister of labour) from 1968 to 1970, show detailed micromanagement of industrial disputes on the part of the state. Castle, *The Castle Diaries*.

47. Fulcher, *Labour Movements, Employers, and the State*.

48. Lindblom, "The Market as Prison."

49. David Coates used this term in a personal communication with the author.

50. See, for example, Hall, *Governing the Economy*, chapters 2 and 3.

CHAPTER TWO
CONSTRUCTING INDUSTRIAL RELATIONS INSTITUTIONS

1. The full quotation is: "The crisis exists precisely in the fact that the old is dying and the new cannot be born; in this interregnum a great variety of morbid symptoms appear." Antonio Gramsci, *Selections from the Prison Notebooks*, p. 276.

2. Jane Jenson made these comments in the course of discussion at the workshop "Transforming the Democratic Balance among State, Market and Society: Comparative Perspectives on France and the Developed Democracies," Minza de Gunzburg Center for European Studies, Harvard University, May 17–18, 2002.

3. Another approach to this question is Peter Hall's notion of "policy paradigms." For Hall, first- and second-order changes—essentially evolutionary change—occur frequently, and can result from change within the state, but third-order policy change (a shift in the policy paradigm) involves changes in the hierarchy of goals (in response to new patterns and processes of economic growth). Thus epochal change would be roughly equivalent to moments of third-order change, of a shift in the policy paradigm. Hall, "Policy Paradigms, Social Learning and the State."

4. For a survey of industrial relations developments across Europe see Crouch, *Industrial Relations and European State Traditions*.

5. This point is made well by Torben Iversen and Jonas Pontusson, "Comparative Political Economy."

6. For an exception see the forthcoming volume, edited by David Coates, *Varieties of Capitalism*. Exceptionally, it brings together neoclassical, institutional, and Marxist accounts of political economy in one place.

7. Lieberman, "Ideas, Institutions, and Political Order," p. 698.

8. For some general accounts of the character of industrial relations in capitalist societies see Poole, *Theories of Trade Unionism*; Roberts, *Industrial Relations*; and Hyman, *Industrial Relations*.

9. Zeitlin, "From Labour History to the History of Industrial Relations."

10. Douglas Hay, "Property, Authority and the Criminal Law."

11. Hyman, "Strategy or Structure?" p. 27.

12. Pontusson, "From Comparative Public Policy to Political Economy."

13. Crouch, *Industrial Relations and European State Traditions*.

14. Ibid., p. 337.

15. Dobbin, *Forging Industrial Policy*.

16. Howell, "The State and the Reconstruction of Industrial Relations Institutions after Fordism."

17. The state of the art of this approach can be found in three collections of edited essays: Kitschelt, et al., *Continuity and Change in Contemporary Capitalism*; Iversen, Pontusson, and Soskice, *Unions, Employers, and Central Banks*; and Hall and Soskice, *Varieties of Capitalism*. For an extended review and critique of the VoC approach see my review essay, "Varieties of Capitalism."

18. For a taste of theoretical differences within the VoC approach see Iversen and Pontusson, "Comparative Political Economy."

19. Culpepper, "Employers, Public Policy, and the Politics of Decentralized Cooperation in Germany and France."

20. Peter A. Hall and David Soskice, in "An Introduction to Varieties of Capitalism," p. 21, suggest the possibility of a Mediterranean form of capitalism, encompassing Spain, Italy, France, and others.

21. Ibid., p. 6.

22. Ibid., p. 45.

23. Stewart Wood, "Business, Government, and Patterns of Labor Market Policy in Britain and the Federal Republic of Germany," p. 247.

24. The contributors who most emphasize the political dimension are Thelen, "Varieties of Labor Politics in the Developed Democracies"; Culpepper, "Employers, Public Policy, and the Politics of Decentralized Cooperation"; and Stewart Wood, "Business, Government, and Patterns of Labor Market Policy in Britain and the Federal Republic of Germany."

25. See also Thelen, "The Political Economy of Business and Labor in the Developed Democracies."

26. The term "powering" comes from Hall, "Policy Paradigms, Social Learning and the State."

27. This "dual convergence" argument is made by Iversen and Pontusson, "Comparative Political Economy," p. 7.

28. Silver, *Forces of Labor*.

29. Cronin, *Industrial Conflict in Modern Britain*, p. 17.

30. Ibid., p. 38.

31. Ibid., p. 187.

32. Ibid., p. 179.

33. Waddington, *The Politics of Bargaining*, p. xi.

34. The first merger wave was characterized by the creation of national unions out of regional unions and federations of unions, in order to better participate in industry-level bargaining, while the second wave was characterized by the horizontal expansion of unions into new recruitment areas in response to decentralized bargaining.

35. Silver, *Forces of Labor*, draws on the World Labor Group Database for cross-national data on labor unrest. See appendix A of her book.

36. See the evidence cited in Kelly, *Rethinking Industrial Relations*, chapter 6. This whole section on long waves and industrial relations is heavily indebted to Kelly's discussion.

37. Ibid., pp. 96–97.

38. Ibid., chapter 6, has a good survey of the literature on Kondratieff long waves.

39. Katznelson, "Structure and Configuration in Comparative Politics," p. 83.

40. For a good summary of the Regulationist approach see Boyer, *La Théorie de la Régulation*.

41. I am heavily indebted, for the account of the development of Regulation Theory that follows, to Bob Jessop's paper "Twenty Years of the Regulation Approach."

42. Robert Boyer's work within the Regulation approach comes closest to the VoC approach.

43. Jessop, "Twenty Years of the Regulation Approach," n.p.

44. Jessop, "What Follows Fordism?"

45. Ibid.

46. I am grateful to Colin Hay for this formulation of one of the weaknesses of the Regulation approach in a personal communication to the author.

47. Bob Jessop has been toiling almost alone in this area for more than a decade. His *Future of the Capitalist State* is a major theoretical advance, and though it appeared late in the writing of this current work, it and Jessop's papers and articles have been an important and continuing influence on my work.

48. See Swenson, *Capitalists Against Markets*, chapter 2.

49. For a good account of the main features of Fordist production see Harvey, *The Condition of Postmodernity*, chapter 8, and Sabel, *Work and Politics*, chapter 2.

50. Jessop, "Fordism and Post-Fordism."

51. The argument made here is similar to that made by Perry Anderson in *Lineages of the Absolutist State*, where he argues that the European absolutist state acted as a transitional state during the transition from feudalism to capitalism.

52. Jessop, "Twenty Years of the Regulation Approach," n.p.

53. Jessop, *The Future of the Capitalist State*, chapter 1, especially pp. 36–48, offers a useful discussion of the role of the state.

54. Jane Jenson's early work pointed in the direction of incorporating a discursive element into the Regulation approach, but scholars have largely ignored that promising direction of research. See Jenson, "Representations in Crisis."

55. For a useful application of the notion of class compromises see the account of the rise and fall of class compromise in Sweden in Stephens, *The Transition from Capitalism and Socialism*.

56. For a somewhat different role for the state, one emphasizing political institutions and the degree of state repression of union movements, see the important contribution of Friedman, *State-Making and Labor Movements*.

57. That may explain why the survey of evidence of state intervention in industrial relations provided by Crouch (*Industrial Relations and European State Traditions*) demonstrates a bunching of state reform projects, in response to synchronous strike waves in the decade before World War I, in the late 1960s/early 1970s and again in the early 1980s.

58. Swenson, "Arranged Alliance."

59. Wright, "Working-Class Power, Capitalist-Class Interests, and Class Compromise." Wright builds on the argument of Rogers and Streeck, "Productive Solidarities."

60. This may be one reason why the one example Swenson gives of a failure on the part of state actors to reduce business opposition during the New Deal was not in the realm of social policy but rather the Wagner Act, which forced business to share power with unions in the workplace. He argues that better drafting of the legislation might have limited business opposition. "Arranged Alliance," pp. 84–85.

61. While disagreeing with Peter Swenson's preference for using the notion of cross-class alliance in place of class compromise, I am indebted to Swenson for pushing my thinking on this issue in a series of personal communications.

62. Jessop, *The Future of the Capitalist State*, p. 92.

63. Colin Hay, "Rethinking Crisis," and Colin Hay, *Re-stating Social and Political Change*.

64. Gerhard Lehmbruch, "The Institutional Embedding of Market Economies," p. 41. Italics in the original.

65. Streeck, "Introduction," p. 9.

66. Dobbin, *Forging Industrial Policy*.

67. This formulation of the role of ideas is borrowed from Colin Hay, *Political Analysis*, chapter 6.

68. Colin Hay, "The Invocation of External Economic Constraint."

69. Blyth, *Great Transformations*, chapter 2.

70. Colin Hay, *Political Analysis*, pp. 170–71.

71. Hall, "Policy Paradigms, Social Learning and the State."

72. Fuchs, "Institutions, Values, and Leadership in the Creation of Welfare States," p. 474. In thinking about the legitimacy of institutions, I am indebted to Frieda Fuchs, both for the arguments she makes in her dissertation and for several conversations.

73. This term comes from David Coates, personal communication.

74. For this argument and examples from French industrial relations, see Howell, *Regulating Labor*.

75. Coates, *Models of Capitalism*, p. 225.

76. Esping-Andersen, *Politics Against Markets*.

77. For a good survey of the role of institutions see Steinmo, Thelen, and Longstreth, *Structuring Politics*, especially the first chapter by Thelen and Steinmo.

78. Paul Pierson has brought some much-needed rigor to the concept of path dependence and the issue of historical sequencing more generally. See Pierson, "Not Just What, but *When*."

79. Fox and Flanders, "Collective Bargaining." In a similar vein Simon Deakin, "Labour Law and the Developing Employment Relationship in the UK," has explored the normative and discursive effects of particular forms of labor contract.

80. Pierson, "Not Just What, but *When*," pp. 82–84.

CHAPTER THREE
THE CONSTRUCTION OF THE COLLECTIVE LAISSEZ-FAIRE SYSTEM, 1890–1940

1. Royal Commission on Labour, *Fifth and Final Report*. The 1890s were important also because that decade saw the creation of a set of national agreements and procedures in several industries. In all cases, the agreements followed lockouts by employers and were imposed on unions. The Brooklands Agreement was reached in 1893 in the cotton-spinning industry, a national procedure agreement followed in footwear in 1895, and the 1897–98 engineering lockout also led to a national disputes procedure. In all cases, the national agreement included a statement of management rights. See Gospel, *Markets, Firms, and the Management of Labour in Modern Britain*, p. 34, and Clegg, Fox, and Thompson, *A History of British Trade Unions since 1889: Volume 1*, chapter 3.

2. Silver and Arrighi, "Polanyi's 'Double Movement,' " p. 336.

3. For good general economic accounts see Aldcroft, *The Inter-War Economy*, and Pollard, *The Development of the British Economy*.

4. For citations to sources for the debate over British economic decline see chapter 1, note 3.

5. Examples include Gospel, *Markets, Firms, and the Management of Labour in Modern Britain* (see especially chapter 1 for a summary of the argument), and several works by Steven Tolliday and Jonathan Zeitlin, including Tolliday and Zeitlin, *Between Fordism and Flexibility*.

6. Clearly this grouping is a little crude. There were important examples of paternalism among large textile mills, and the rail companies tended to have more developed and bureaucratic forms of industrial relations. Thus the age of the industry and form of industrial structure do not correlate perfectly. Nevertheless, it remains a fair generalization, as practically every account acknowledges. See both Pollard, *The Development of the British Economy*, chapter 3, and Gospel, *Markets, Firms, and the Management of Labour in Modern Britain*, chapter 3.

7. Gospel, *Markets, Firms, and the Management of Labour in Modern Britain*, p. 57.

8. Tolliday, "The Failure of Mass Production in the Motor Industry."

9. Gospel, *Markets, Firms, and the Management of Labour in Modern Britain*, p. 8. There were, of course, exceptions, particularly in the new industries. Examples include ICI in chemicals and Pilkingtons in the glass industry.

10. Ibid., pp. 55 and 71-72.

11. This argument, and the account that follows, lean heavily on the pathbreaking work of Richard Price, particularly his *Labour in British Society*.

12. Hobsbawm, "The 'New Unionism' Reconsidered."

13. Price, *Labour in British Society*, p. 180.

14. Wrigley, "The Government and Industrial Relations," p.145.

15. Ibid., p. 143.

16. Milner and Metcalf, "A Century of UK Strike Activity." See figure 1 and table 1.

17. Bowman, *Capitalist Collective Action*, chapter 1.

18. Dobbin, *Forging Industrial Policy*. Dobbin also argues that national cultural traditions have a tendency to reproduce themselves over time, so that similar solutions are adopted in response to new challenges.

19. Gospel, *Markets, Firms, and the Management of Labour in Modern Britain*, confirms this practice by noting the rise of cartels during this period. Cartelization and new forms of industrial relations went hand in hand as mechanisms for limiting market competition.

20. Dobbin, *Forging Industrial Policy*, p. 25.

21. This section owes a great deal to Gospel's account, *Markets, Firms, and the Management of Labour in Modern Britain*, chapter 5.

22. See the debate here between Gospel and Tony Adams. First, Adams, "Market and Institutional Forces in Industrial Relations." Then the response of Gospel, "Markets, Institutions, and the Development of National Collective Bargaining in Britain." Finally, Adams's reply, "Employers, Labour, and the State in Industrial Relations History." Clearly, there was a great deal of class conflict and worker resistance, but the key point to make is that the trigger for the restructuring of industrial relations was less important than the particular forms of industrial relations that emerged. Industry bar-

gaining with managerial prerogative in the firm was the preferred response of employers, and, with the exception of 1910–20, it is very hard to argue that unions or groups of workers were strong enough to impose specific forms of industrial relations on employers.

23. The classic works on this early period are Clegg, Fox, and Thompson, *A History of British Trade Unions since 1889*; Fox, *History and Heritage*; and Phelps-Brown, *The Growth of British Industrial Relations*.

24. Simon Milner, "The Coverage of Collective Pay-Setting Institutions in Britain," p. 82.

25. Tarling and Wilkinson, "The Movement of Real Wages and the Development of Collective Bargaining in the U.K."

26. Porter, "Wage Bargaining under Conciliation Agreements."

27. Phelps Brown, *The Growth of British Industrial Relations*, chapter 3.

28. *Report on Collective Agreements between Employers and Workpeople*, pp. xi–xii.

29. Ibid.

30. Burgess, "New Unionism for Old?"

31. Richard Price, "The New Unionism and the Labour Process," p.145.

32. Hyman, "Mass Organization and Militancy in Britain," p. 258.

33. Zeitlin, "Industrial Structure, Employer Strategy and the Diffusion of Job Control in Britain."

34. Ingham, *Strikes and Industrial Conflict*.

35. For discussions of judicial decisions and developments see Klarman, "The Judges versus the Unions," and Kenneth Brown, "Trade Unions and the Law."

36. Alastair J. Reid, "Old Unionism Reconsidered," p. 229.

37. Davidson, *Whitehall and the Labour Problem in Late-Victorian and Edwardian Britain*, chapter 2.

38. Ibid., p. 64.

39. The *Times* of London ran a series of articles on industrial relations in November 1901. One of them in the *Times*, November 18, 1901 usefully defined ca'canny as "a new instrument or policy which may be used by the workers in place of a strike."

40. Davidson, "The Board of Trade and Industrial Relations," p. 590.

41. Klarman, "The Judges versus the Unions," part 2.

42. Ibid., p. 1559.

43. Saville, "The Trade Disputes Act of 1906," p. 13.

44. See Wedderburn, *Labour Law and Freedom*, chapter 1, p. 31, for the argument that, with regard to relations between employers and workers, common law is inherently subject to a class bias.

45. Blakeman, "Injunctive Relief and Appellate Courts," p. 96.

46. Ibid., p. 106.

47. Royal Commission on Trade Disputes and Trade Combinations, *Report*.

48. Ibid., p. 16.

49. Pelling, "Trade Unions, Workers and the Law," pp. 73–74.

50. W. Mosses, quoted in ibid., p. 75.

51. Klarman, "The Judges versus the Unions," p. 1602.

52. Royal Commission on Labour, *Fifth and Final Report*, para. 90.

53. Ibid., para. 86, my emphasis.

54. Ibid.

55. Ibid., para. 91.

56. Ibid., para. 363.

57. Quoted in Davidson, "The Board of Trade and Industrial Relations," p. 580.

58. Saville, "The Trade Disputes Act of 1906," p. 30.

59. Davidson, *Whitehall and the Labour Problem in Late-Victorian and Edwardian Britain*, p. 79.

60. Phelps Brown, *The Growth of British Industrial Relations*, p 314.

61. Askwith, *Industrial Problems and Disputes* (1920).

62. Ibid., p. 97.

63. Ibid., p. 100.

64. Ibid., p. 177.

65. Ibid., p. 142.

66. Ibid., p. 129.

67. Davidson, "Government Administration."

68. Fox, *History and Heritage*, p. 250.

69. Roger Davidson, introduction to Askwith, *Industrial Problems and Disputes* (1974), p. x.

70. Fulcher, *Labour Movements, Employers, and the State*, p. 102.

71. Davidson, "Government Administration," p. 168.

72. Davidson, "The Board of Trade and Industrial Relations," p. 576.

73. Quoted in Kitson and Wilkinson, "How Paying the Minimum Raises the Stakes."

74. Clegg, Fox, and Thompson, *A History of British Trade Unions since 1889: Volume I*, p. 471.

75. Clegg, *A History of British Trade Unions since 1889: Volume III*, pp. 413–414.

76. Gospel, *Markets, Firms, and the Management of Labour in Modern Britain*, p. 81.

77. Clegg, *A History of British Trade Unions since 1889: Volume II*, p. 168.

78. Fulcher, *Labour Movements, Employers, and the State*, chapter 5.

79. Waddington, *The Politics of Bargaining*. See p. 59 for the positive impact of legislation on trade union merger activity.

80. Charles, *The Development of Industrial Relations in Britain*, p. 97.

81. Ibid., p. 99.

82. Ibid., p. 106.

83. Ibid., p. 100.

84. From the second report of the Whitley Committee, quoted in Ewing, "The State and Industrial Relations," p. 19.

85. The next section relies heavily on the account of Charles, *The Development of Industrial Relations in Britain*.

86. Lowe, "The Failure of Consensus in Britain," p. 672.

87. Henry Clay quoted in Bain, *Royal Commission on Trade Unions and Employers' Associations Research Papers 6*, p. 33.

88. Charles, *The Development of Industrial Relations in Britain*, p. 125.

89. Ewing, "The State and Industrial Relations," p. 21.

90. See the next chapter for more discussion of this process, and also Carter and Fairbrother, "The Transformation of British Public-Sector Industrial Relations."

91. Gospel, *Markets, Firms, and the Management of Labour in Modern Britain*, p. 84.

92. Milner, "The Coverage of Collective Pay-Setting Institutions in Britain," p. 82.

93. Bain and Price, "Union Growth," p. 7.

94. Milner, "The Coverage of Collective Pay-Setting Institutions in Britain," p. 82.

95. In his exchange with Adams (see note 20), Gospel has pointed out that, while worker and trade union pressure can account for some part of the spread of collective bargaining between 1910 and 1920, pressure from the labor side was simply too weak to explain the persistence of national bargaining after 1920.

96. Gospel, Markets, Firms, and the Management of Labour in Modern Britain, p. 87.

97. Clegg, The Changing System of Industrial Relations in Great Britain, p. 70.

98. Lowe, "The Failure of Consensus in Britain."

99. Ibid., and Charles, The Development of Industrial Relations in Britain, parts 3 and 4.

100. Fulcher, Labour Movements, Employers, and the State.

101. Lowe, "The Failure of Consensus in Britain," pp. 672–73.

102. Lowe, Adjusting to Democracy, p. 67.

103. Ibid., p. 77.

104. Ministry of Labour Report for 1934, quoted in Ewing, "The State and Industrial Relations," p. 27.

105. Clegg, A History of British Trade Unions since 1889: Volume III, pp. 32–33.

106. Ibid., p. 92.

107. Ibid., p. 91.

108. Ibid., p. 92.

109. Milner, "The Coverage of Collective Pay-Setting Institutions in Britain," p. 82.

110. The term is from Wright, "Working-Class Power, Capitalist-Class Interests, and Class Compromise."

111. The terms "managerial control" and "market control" come from Allan Flanders, cited in Gospel, Markets, Firms, and the Management of Labour in Modern Britain, p. 90.

112. Zeitlin, "From Labour History to the History of Industrial Relations."

113. Royal Commission on Trade Disputes and Trade Combinations, Report especially paras. 63–65.

114. Price and Bain, "Union Growth Revisited," p. 340.

115. Clegg, A History of British Trade Unions since 1889: Volume II, chapter 14.

116. See Waddington, The Politics of Bargaining, for a discussion of this process.

117. Heery and Kelly, "Professional, Participative and Managerial Unionism."

118. Ibid., p. 3.

119. Ibid., p. 4.

120. Bain, The Growth of White-Collar Unionism, p. 140.

121. This phenomenon is discussed in Flanders, "The Tradition of Voluntarism."

122. The emphasis on immunities rather than positive rights also had ideological effects because immunities could be more easily portrayed as creating "trade union privileges," making them more vulnerable to political challenge in the future. When concern about the economic impact of industrial relations institutions reemerged in the 1960s, the manner in which the reform debate took place was heavily influenced by the ideological context inherited from this earlier period.

123. This argument is made powerfully by Summers, "Lord Wedderburn's New Labour Law.

124. This term comes from Dobbin, Forging Industrial Policy, p. 12.

CHAPTER FOUR
DONOVAN, DISSENSION, AND THE DECENTRALIZATION
OF INDUSTRIAL RELATIONS, 1940–1979

1. Wedderburn, *Labour Law and Freedom*, chapter 1.
2. Gospel, *Markets, Firms, and the Management of Labour in Modern Britain*, chapter 1.
3. Ibid.
4. Ibid., p. 127.
5. Milner, "The Coverage of Collective Pay-Setting Institutions in Britain," pp. 82–83.
6. Pendleton, "The Evolution of Industrial Relations in UK Nationalized Industries," p.149.
7. The official history of NALGO (Spoor, *White-Collar Union*) describes how the extension of public ownership to gas and electricity led to employees in these industries "clamouring to join" the union, and union branches being set up even before NALGO's leadership authorized them (p. 312).
8. Carter and Fairbrother, "The Transformation of British Public-Sector Industrial Relations," p. 123.
9. Quoted Clegg, *A History of British Trade Unions since 1889: Volume III*, p.166.
10. Ibid., p. 222.
11. The best source on these developments and their impact is Latta, "The Legal Extension of Collective Bargaining." Note that the same broad points can be made about the 1946 Fair Wages Resolution, the latest in a line of such resolutions dating back to 1891, which required that government contractors observe collectively agreed standards.
12. Ibid., pp. 218–19.
13. Nina Fishman, " 'A Vital Element in British Industrial Relations.' "
14. Ibid., p. 50.
15. Ibid. See also Smith, *The Attlee and Churchill Administrations and Industrial Unrest*, which makes a similar argument, that the use of this legislation had the effect of protecting union leaders from rank-and-file opposition within their own unions.
16. This is from the Wage Councils Act, quoted by Clegg, *A History of British Trade Unions Since 1889: Volume III*, pp. 327–28.
17. Unemployment averaged 1.5 percent for the twenty years after 1945. Gospel, *Markets, Firms, and the Management of Labour in Modern Britain*, p. 108.
18. Very few cases were brought under Order 1376 and Section 8 of the Terms and Conditions of Employment Act (Latta, "The Legal Extension of Collective Bargaining"), and, as we shall see, the numbers and coverage of wages councils declined from the 1960s onward.
19. Smith, *The Attlee and Churchill Administrations*, p. 145. The word "Butskellism" derived from putting together the names of the Conservative chancellor R. A. Butler and the Labour shadow chancellor Hugh Gaitskell.
20. The *Industrial Charter* was published in 1947. For a discussion of its contents see Dorey, *Wage Politics in Britain*, chapter 3.
21. Quoted in ibid., p.38.
22. Pollard, *The Development of the British Economy*, p. 275.

23. Purcell and Sisson, "Strategies and Practices in the Management of Industrial Relations," p. 96.

24. For an account of these developments see Coates, *The Crisis of Labour*, p. 21.

25. See the accounts in Gospel, *Markets, Firms, and the Management of Labour in Modern Britain*, chapter 6, and in Pollard, *The Development of the British Economy*, chapter 7.

26. Pollard, *The Development of the British Economy*, p. 304.

27. Ibid., pp. 301–2.

28. Gospel, *Markets, Firms, and the Management of Labour in Modern Britain*, p.109.

29. Latta, "The Legal Extension of Collective Bargaining," pp. 226–27.

30. This quotation comes from Courtauld's book *Ideal and Industry* and is cited in Gospel, *Markets, Firms, and the Management of Labour in Modern Britain*, p.137.

31. Gospel, *Markets, Firms, and the Management of Labour in Modern Britian*, p. 141.

32. The definitive study of productivity bargaining is McKersie and Hunter, *Pay, Productivity and Collective Bargaining*.

33. The best account of the Fawley agreement comes from Allan Flanders, "The Fawley Experiment" in his *Management and Unions*.

34. Topham, "New Types of Bargaining."

35. Sisson, "Employers and the Structure of Collective Bargaining, p. 260.

36. Ibid.

37. Coates, *The Crisis of Labour*, p. 25.

38. This line comes from Turner, cited in ibid., p. 26.

39. Bélanger, "Job Control under Different Labor Relations Regimes."

40. The term "flawed Fordism" is Bob Jessop's; see his "Regulation Theories in Retrospect and Prospect," p. 189.

41. For a summary of these studies see Terry, "Shop Steward Development and Managerial Strategies." For a case study of this issue in the engineering industry see Terry and Edwards, *Shopfloor Politics and Job Controls*.

42. Wells, "Uneven Development and De-industrialization in the UK since 1979," pp. 32–33.

43. Allen, "Towards a Post-Industrial Economy?" See the useful table of employment changes in different service industries, p. 99.

44. Wells, "Uneven Development and De-industrialization," p. 32.

45. Allen, "Towards a Post-Industrial Economy?" p. 97.

46. Bain, *Research Papers 6, Royal Commision on Trade Unions and Employers' Associations Research Papers 6*, p.73.

47. See the autobiography of Clive Jenkins, *All Against the Collar*, chapters 7 and 8. See also Jenkins and Sherman, *White-Collar Unionism*.

48. Blackburn, *Union Character and Social Class* is a study of trade unionism and collective bargaining in the banking industry. Similar arguments were made to the author in an interview with Lief Mills, November 14, 1995, in London. Mills was then general secretary of the Banking Insurance and Finance Union (BIFU), the successor to NUBE.

49. Blackburn, *Union Character and Social Class*, chapter 3.

50. Coates, *The Crisis of Labour*, p. 19.

51. Blank, "Britain."

52. The seminal account of British incomes policies is Panitch, *Social Democracy and Industrial Militancy*. For an updating to the present see Dorey, *Wage Politics in Britain*.

53. Gospel, *Markets, Firms, and the Management of Labour in Modern Britain*, p. 139.

54. Spoor, *White-Collar Union*, chapter 33. This is the official history of the first sixty years of NALGO.

55. Davies and Freedland, *Labour Legislation and Public Policy*, chapter 4.

56. Hall, *Governing the Economy*, chapter 4.

57. Milner and Metcalf, "A Century of UK Strike Activity," table A1.

58. Cronin, *Industrial Conflict in Modern Britain*, p. 138.

59. This point was suggested by John Kelly in a personal communication with the author.

60. For a good analysis of media representations of strikes see Claydon, "Tales of Disorder."

61. Inns of Court Conservative and Unionist Society, *A Giant's Strength*.

62. This argument has been forcefully made by Wedderburn, *Employment Rights in Britain and Europe*, chapter 1.

63. *Royal Commission on Trade Unions and Employers' Associations, 1965–1968: Report.*

64. For examples, see the editorial in the *Times* of London, "A Sorry Story," February 1, 1957, p. 9; Shanks, *The Stagnant Society*; and the film *I'm All Right Jack*, released in 1959, and starring Peter Sellers.

65. Davies and Freedland, *Labour Legislation and Public Policy*, p. 246.

66. A somewhat partisan story of internal conflicts and compromises within the royal commission was told in "How the 'Doves' Won," an article in the *Sunday Times* (London), June 16, 1968, pp. 13–14. No author was listed.

67. *Royal Commission on Trade Unions and Employers' Associations, 1965–1968: Report*, para. 46.

68. Ibid., para. 65.

69. Ibid., para. 130.

70. Ibid., para. 149.

71. Ibid., para. 154. This paragraph echoes the line from Gramsci cited in chapter 2 of this book: "The crisis exists precisely in the fact that the old is dying and the new cannot yet be born; in this interregnum a great variety of morbid symptoms appear." Gramsci, *Selections from the Prison Notebooks*, p. 276.

72. *Royal Commission on Trade Unions and Employers' Associations, 1965–1968: Report*, para. 155.

73. This comes from Flanders's essay presented to the royal commission, "Collective Bargaining: A Prescription for Change," reprinted in his *Management and Unions*. The phrase is quoted in Kessler and Bayliss, *Contemporary British Industrial Relations*, p. 36.

74. *Royal Commission on Trade Unions and Employers' Associations, 1965–1968: Report*, para. 196.

75. For details of new individual labor law see later sections of this chapter.

76. This argument is developed in Davies and Freedland, *Labour Legislation and Public Policy*, chapter 5, and Collins, "Capitalist Discipline and Corporatist Law—Part I," pp. 87–88.

77. *Royal Commission on Trade Unions and Employers' Associations, 1965–1968: Report*, pp. 288–302.

78. Andrew Shonfield, "Why I Think We Didn't Go Far Enough," *Sunday Times*, June 16, 1968.

79. Wedderburn, *Employment Rights in Britain and Europe*, p. 32.

80. See, in particular, chapter 14 of the *Royal Commission on Trade Unions and Employers' Associations, 1965–1968: Report*.

81. Ibid., para. 203.

82. Davies and Freedland, *Labour Legislation and Public Policy*, section 6.2.

83. Turner, "The Donovan Report," p. 5.

84. Trade Union Congress, *Trade Unionism*.

85. The debate took place on July 16, 1968. *Hansard*, vol. 768, no. 156, col. 1260. One interesting point from that debate is that Nicholas Ridley, Conservative MP, argued that plant-level bargaining should not simply augment but rather supplant industry bargaining. When he became a cabinet minister in the Thatcher government after 1979, this argument was revived, as chapter 5 indicates.

86. See Castle, *The Castle Diaries*, entries for 1969, and E. P. Thompson, "Yesterday's Manikin," in Thompson, *Writing by Candlelight*.

87. Davies and Freedland, *Labour Legislation and Public Policy*, chapter 6.

88. The joint statement was published by the TUC and titled *Action on Donovan* (London: TUC, 1968), pp. 47–48.

89. Purcell and Sisson, "Strategies and Practice in the Management of Industrial Relations," p. 103.

90. Wedderburn, *Employment Rights in Britain and Europe*, p. 39.

91. One should also mention the 1964 Trade Union Amalgamation Act, which made it easier for larger unions to take over small ones, essentially deregulating one aspect of the internal affairs of trade unions. This act played an important part in the acceleration in trade union mergers, which can be dated from 1966. Waddington, *The Politics of Bargaining*, p. 191.

92. The year 1965 alone saw three major government inquiries, into the printing, railway, and shipping industries. The mid-1960's also saw inquiries into the banking, steel, and automobile industries.

93. Castle, *The Castle Diaries*. This position was essentially minister of labour, but the title was newly created for Barbara Castle in order to make it a senior enough ministerial job that she would agree to take it.

94. For an explicit statement of this argument, see the speech in the House of Commons by a government minister, Ray Gunter, April 26, 1965. Quoted in Davies and Freedland, *Labour Legislation and Public Policy*, p. 156.

95. OECD, *Manpower Policy in the UK*, para. 13.8. Cited in Davies and Freedland, *Labour Legislation and Public Policy*, p. 158.

96. Castle, *The Castle Diaries*, p. 281.

97. For an exhaustive and partisan account of the struggle over *In Place of Strife* see the account of Peter Jenkins, *The Battle of Downing Street*.

98. For a comprehensive description of the Conservative industrial relations legislation see Davies and Freedland, *Labour Legislation and Public Policy*, chapter 7.

99. For a discussion of this tension see Kahn-Freund, "The Industrial Relations Act 1971— Some Retrospective Reflections."

100. It is worth noting that registration was tempting for some unions, particularly white-collar unions, both because of a fear that rival staff associations would use the legislation to gain official recognition and because of the opportunity to gain recognition themselves where they had been too weak to impose it on employers. NUBE, for example, registered under the act in order to win recognition at foreign-owned banks

in Britain, and was briefly expelled from the TUC as a result. This point was made by Lief Mills in an interview with the author, November 14, 1995.

101. Davies and Freedland, *Labour Legislation and Public Policy*, p. 386.

102. Wedderburn, *Employment Rights in Britain and Europe*, p. 54. Here Wedderburn cites himself from a 1975 article.

103. For details see Benedictus, "Employment Protection."

104. Quoted in Michael Jones, "C.A.C. and Schedule 11," p. 29.

105. For details of how the legislation was used see Beaumont, "Trade Union Recognition"; Kessler, "Trade Union Recognition"; and Stephen Wood, "Learning through ACAS." The acronym AUEW-TASS refers to Amalgamated Union of Engineering Workers—Technical, Administrative, and Supervisory Section; APEX is the Association of Professional, Executive, Clerical and Computer Staff.

106. Chris Pond, "Wages Councils, the Unorganised, and the Low Paid," p. 198.

107. The term is used by Wood, "Learning Through ACAS," p. 124.

108. For a detailed account of the dispute see Rogaly, *Grunwick*.

109. About one-fifth of outstanding cases fell into this category. Stephen Wood, "Learning through ACAS,." p. 131.

110. The ACAS Council wrote to the secretary of state for employment to this effect in June 1979. Kessler, "Trade Union Recognition," p. 65.

111. See Jack Jones's autobiography, *Union Man*, p. 285.

112. Kahn-Freund, "Industrial Democracy."

113. Davies and Freedland, *Labour Legislation and Public Policy*, p. 400.

114. Clegg, *The Changing System of Industrial Relations in Great Britain*, chapter 2.

115. The reports of the sectoral conferences were published by the TUC as *Collective Bargaining and Trade Union Development*.

116. Heery and Kelly, "Professional, Participative and Managerial Unionism."

117. Gospel, *Markets, Firms, and the Management of Labour in Modern Britain*, p. 146.

118. For a discussion of the formalization and extension of bargaining scope to cover more issues during this period see Brown, Deakin, Nash, and Oxenbridge, "The Employment Contract."

119. The benchmark for evidence of these developments comes from the 1980 and 1984 Workplace Industrial Relations Survey: Millward and Stevens, *British Workplace Industrial Relations, 1980–1984*.

120. William Brown, *The Changing Contours of British Industrial Relations*, based on a survey of manufacturing firms conducted in 1978, showed major changes in these directions over the previous decade.

121. Millward and Stevens, *British Workplace Industrial Relations, 1980–1984*, p. 232.

122. Winchester, "Industrial Relations in the Public Sector," p. 163.

123. Clegg, *The Changing System of Industrial Relations in Great Britain*, p. 36.

124. Bain and Price, "Union Growth," p. 5.

125. Evaluating the impact of the new statutory procedures on union membership is difficult because separating out the direct and indirect effects of the legislation cannot easily be done. There is also evidence that the existence of the statutory mechanism pushed employers to use the voluntary procedure more to avoid having recognition imposed on them; in this regard, it is worth noting that recognition through the

voluntary procedure collapsed after the statutory procedure was abolished in 1980. Beaumont, "Trade Union Recognition and the Recession in the UK," estimates that the combined impact of ACAS's role was to account for about 20 percent of new union members between 1976 and 1980.

126. See Terry, "Shop Steward Development and Managerial Strategies," p. 67, for the 1961 estimate, and Millward and Stevens, *British Workplace Industrial Relations, 1980–1984*, p. 85, for the 1980 estimate. The latter also estimate a small rise to 335,000 by 1984.

127. Terry, "Shop Steward Development and Managerial Strategies."

128. Gennard, Dunn, and Wright, "The Content of British Closed Shop Agreements."

129. Millward and Stevens, *British Workplace Industrial Relations, 1980–1984*, p. 92.

130. Paradoxically, this period coincided with a second wave of trade union mergers (the earlier one being immediately after the First World War). But as Waddington, *The Politics of Bargaining*, chapter 6, argues, the form of mergers was quite different after 1967, permitting considerable bargaining autonomy for local and occupational sections within unions, and facilitating the diversification of trade union recruitment in the context of rising white-collar and service-sector unionization.

131. Undy, Ellis, McCarthy, and Halmos, *Change in Trade Unions*.

132. Undy, "The Devolution of Bargaining Levels."

133. Heery and Kelly, "Professional, Participative and Managerial Unionism," p. 4.

134. Note that Heery and Kelly see the source of these change as internal and mimetic as well as external.

135. Quoted in Wedderburn, *Employment Rights in Britain and Europe*, p. 44.

136. See the discussion in Blakeman, "Injunctive Relief and Appellate Courts," chapter 4.

137. Ewing, "The Golden Formula," p. 135.

138. Simpson, "Judicial Control of A.C.A.S.

139. See, for example, Batstone, *The Reform of Workplace Industrial Relations*, chapter 3, and William Brown, *The Changing Contours of British Industrial Relations*, also chapter 3.

140. Batstone, *The Reform of Workplace Industrial Relations*, p. 97.

141. Terry, "Shop Steward Development and Managerial Strategies," p. 80.

142. Hugh Clegg, quoted in McCarthy, "The Rise and Fall of Collective Laissez-Faire," p. 36.

143. See Dorey, *Wage Politics in Britain*, chapters 5 and 7, for an account of the shift within the Conservative Party. Within the Labour Party, the Social Democratic Party defection took members of the Labour Party who saw union power as too great. But even the Labour Party never seriously considered wage restraint again. See the next chapter for debate within the Labour Party after 1979 about the future of trade unionism.

144. Bain, *Royal Commision on Trade Unions and Employers' Associations Research Papers 6*, chapter 4.

145. This information comes from Lief Mills, in an interview with the author, November 14, 1995.

146. See the *Annual Reports* of the TUC throughout the 1960s for debates on a variety of motions concerning the problems of obtaining recognition in private ser-

vices. For a particularly interesting debate on the subject, see the debate reported in the 1965 TUC *Annual Report* (London: TUC, 1965), pp. 396–399.

147. Trade union evidence is collected in *Royal Commission on Trade Unions and Employers' Associations: Selected Written Evidence.*

148. *Trades Union Congress, Report of the Proceedings at the 92nd Annual Trades Union Congress*, p.328.

149. See the TUC's evidence, published as Trades Union Congress, *Trade Unionism*, p. 31.

150. Ibid., p. 113.

151. This argument was made by David Lea, then assistant general secretary of the TUC, in an interview with the author, July 9, 1996, London.

152. However, many white-collar unions remained favorable to some kind of recognition legislation. In the heat of the battle over *In Place of Strife*, Gerald Kaufman, MP, transmitted to Prime Minister Harold Wilson a memorandum listing trade unions and how they were expected to vote on the legislation. It was primarily white-collar unions, NALGO and USDAW, that presumably believed the quid was worth the quo. The memorandum, dated January 14, 1969, is reproduced at www.pro.gov.uk/releases/nyo2000/prem13–2724–1000p1.jpg.

153. Summers, "Lord Wedderburn's New Labour Law." This argument was made in the previous chapter.

154. William Brown, "The Changed Political Role of Unions under a Hostile Government," p. 281.

CHAPTER FIVE
THE DECOLLECTIVIZATION OF INDUSTRIAL RELATIONS, 1979–1997

1. See chapter 4 for a discussion of the high point of trade union strength and for sources on collective bargaining coverage and union membership.

2. Brook, "Trade Union Membership," p. 343. Union density was 29.1 percent.

3. Milner, "The Coverage of Collective Pay-Setting Institutions in Britain, p. 87.

4. Cully et al., *Britain at Work*, p. 109.

5. Davies, "Labour Disputes in 1999,"p. 259.

6. Millward, Bryson, and Forth, *All Change at Work?*, p. 234.

7. Millward, Stevens, Smart and Hawes, *Workplace Industrial Relations in Transition*, p. 350.

8. For Conservative views of trade unionism see Thatcher, *The Downing Street Years*, and Tebbit, "Industrial Relations in the Next Two Decades." For a survey of New Right thinking see Kavanagh, *Thatcherism and British Politics*, especially chapters 4 and 7.

9. Gamble, *The Free Economy and the Strong State*, p. 32.

10. The classic version of this argument is Piore and Sabel, *The Second Industrial Divide*. See also Harvey, *The Condition of Postmodernity*.

11. Again, there is a very large literature on this subject. See in particular the contributions to the edited volumes by Berger and Dore, *National Diversity and Global Capitalism*, and Hollingsworth and Boyer, *Contemporary Capitalism*. For both theoretical discussion of post-Fordism and national case studies see Boyer and Saillard, *Regulation Theory*, especially part 5.

12. See the argument in Stewart Wood, "Business, Government, and Patterns of Labor Market Policy in Britain and the Federal Republic of Germany."

13. The term is used by Amoore, *Globalisation Contested*, chapter 3.

14. Tony Blair, speech at the TUC annual congress, September 1997.

15. Ibid.

16. Coates, *Models of Capitalism*; Hall, *Governing the Economy*, chapter 2; and Blank, "Britain."

17. Labour Research Department, "Globalisation of UK Manufacturing," p. 158.

18. Marginson, "Multinational Britain,"pp. 64–65.

19. Labour Research Department, "Foreign Ownership of UK Manufacturing Industry," p. 5.

20. Millward, Bryson, and Forth, *All Change at Work?* p. 32.

21. "A Rentier Economy in Reverse," *Economist*, September 22, 1990.

22. Labour Research Department, "Foreign Investment in the UK by Country," p. 191.

23. "A Rentier Economy in Reverse," *Economist*.

24. Labour Research Department, "Employment Changes, 1979–96," p. 54.

25. Labour Research Department, "Size of UK Firms," p. 81.

26. Labour Research Department, "Share of Small and Medium-Sized Plants Grows." Look also at the Trades Union Congress's *Economic Report: Small Firms—Myths and Realities*, published on the TUC Web site in 2002: http://www.tuc.org.uk/em_research/tuc-6012-f0.pdf. It has various time series for firm size and argues that most of the growth in the number of small firms was in one-to-two employee firms. It contains data by industry.

27. Labour Research Department, "Employment Changes, 1979–96," p. 54.

28. Watson, "The Flexible Workforce and Patterns of Working Hours in the UK," p. 241.

29. See McKersie and Hunter, *Pay, Productivity and Collective Bargaining*.

30. Peter Ingram, "Changes in Working Practices in British Manufacturing Industry in the 1980s." Similarly, Marsden and Thompson, "Flexibility Agreements and Their Significance in the Increase in Productivity in British Manufacturing since 1980," found a large increase in flexibility agreements signed in the 1980s compared with the 1970s, and progressively more such agreements as the 1980s went on.

31. Beatson, *Labour Market Flexibility*, chapter 13.

32. Heery, "Partnership versus Organising."

33. See Boswell and Peters, *Capitalism in Contention*, chapters 7–9.

34. Millward, Stevens, Smart, and Hawes, *Workplace Industrial Relations in Transition*, p. 350; Millward, Bryson, and Forth, *All Change at Work?* pp. 233–34.

35. Machin, "Union Decline in Britain."

36. Poole and Mansfield, "Patterns of Continuity and Change in Managerial Attitudes and Behaviour in Industrial Relations."

37. Cully et al., *Britain at Work*, p. 88.

38. Millward, Bryson, and Forth, *All Change at Work?* p. 146.

39. House of Commons Employment Committee, *The Future of Trade Unions*, vols. I—III.

40. Ibid., vol. III. See in particular the evidence given by representatives on the Institute of Directors and the Confederation of British Industry.

41. Ibid., para. 2, p. 279.

42. Ibid., para. 66, p. 323.

43. See Stewart Wood, "Business, Government, and Patterns of Labor Market Policy in Britain and the Federal Republic of Germany."

44. This can be thought of as an example of Swenson's suggestion that states can anticipate alliances before class actors have articulated a demand for change: Swenson, "Arranged Alliance."

45. This term was used by Robbie Gilbert, research director at the CBI, in an interview with the author, September 1992.

46. Dunn and Metcalf, "Trade Union Law since 1979," p. 22.

47. Millward, Bryson, and Forth, *All Change at Work?* pp. 234–35.

48. Colin Hay, "Narrating Crisis," p. 254.

49. Ibid.

50. For example, a Lexis-Nexis search, conducted in mid-December 2002, in the course of an industrial dispute in the fire service in Britain, found seventy-four newspaper references to the term "winter of discontent."

51. Thompson, *Writing by Candlelight.*

52. Cited in Colin Hay, "Narrating Crisis," p. 274.

53. Cited in Labour Research Department, *Fact Service* 54:16 (April 16, 1992), p. 63.

54. *Economist,* July 24, 1993.

55. There is a large literature on the coal strike. See Adeney and Lloyd, *The Miners' Strike;* Saville, "An Open Conspiracy" ; and Kahn, "Union Politics and the Restructuring of the British Coal Industry."

56. Undy, Fosh, Morris, Smith, and Martin, *Managing the Unions,* p. 29.

57. Ibid., p. 74.

58. Quoted in McIlroy, "Ten Years for the Locust," p. 163.

59. See the Conservative government white paper, *People, Jobs, Opportunity,* p.15.

60. See the discussion by Lord Wedderburn in his "Freedom of Association and Philosophies of Labour Law."

61. Dunn and Metcalf, "Trade Union Law since 1979," p. 8.

62. The following books contain extensive surveys of Conservative industrial relations legislation, and I have relied on them for the summary that follows: Davies and Freedland, *Labour Legislation and Public Policy,* chapter 9; McIlroy, *The Permanent Revolution?* Marsh, *The New Politics of British Trade Unionism,* chapter 3; and Kessler and Bayliss, *Contemporary British Industrial Relations,* chapter 5.

63. Undy, Fosh, Morris, Smith, and Martin, *Managing the Unions,* p. 137.

64. Ewing, "Swimming with the Tide."

65. Carter and Fairbrother, "The Transformation of British Public-Sector Industrial Relations."

66. Ibid., and also Beaumont, *Public Sector Industrial Relations;* Kessler and Bayliss, *Contemporary British Industrial Relations,* chapter 7; and Seifert, *Industrial Relations in the NHS.*

67. On several occasions in the public sector, management has used the threat of ending the mechanism of the dues checkoff (which saves unions tremendous resources

in collecting dues) during industrial disputes. The Conservative London borough of Wandsworth ended checkoff arrangements in 1991, as did British Coal in 1993. British Rail demonstrated the explicitly punitive goal of ending checkoff arrangements when it did so only for the RMT union, with which it was in dispute, in 1993.

68. See note 55 for sources on the 1984–85 miners' strike.

69. Milne, *The Enemy Within*.

70. Wainwright and Nelsson, "Long Decline of a Once Mighty Union."

71. Labour Research Department, "Public Sector Workforce," p. 97.

72. Bird and Corcoran, "Trade Union Membership and Density," p. 196.

73. Labour Research Department, "Pay in the Privatized Utilities."

74. Pendleton, "The Evolution of Industrial Relations in UK Nationalized Industries," p. 165.

75. Labour Research Department, "Pay Review Bodies Examined," pp. 12–14. See also Bailey, "Annual Review Article 1993."

76. McIlroy, "Ten Years for the Locust."

77. Mitchell, "Changing Pressure-Group Politics," p. 517.

78. For the importance of interlocutory injunctions in the sphere of industrial relations see Blakeman, "Injunctive Relief and Appellate Courts."

79. McKay, "The Law on Industrial Action under the Conservatives," p. 16.

80. Blakeman, "Injunctive Relief and Appellate Courts, " pp. 117–18.

81. Quoted in Mike Grindley, "The GCHQ Union Ban," p. 15.

82. Kessler and Bayliss, *Contemporary British Industrial Relations*, p. 60.

83. Purcell, "The End of Institutional Industrial Relations."

84. Offe and Wiesenthal, "Two Logics of Collective Action."

85. The argument rests here on a multiplicity of, and contradictions among, worker interests, in contrast to the manner in which the market enforces a single interest on employers, and differential feedback from society of the legitimacy of competing class interests. For Offe and Wiesenthal, the "insuperable individuality" (ibid., p. 178) of labor puts a special premium on collective organization.

86. Flanders, "The Tradition of Voluntarism," p. 365.

87. See Elgar and Simpson for a good survey of the debate on the impact of the Conservative industrial relations legislation: "The Impact of the Law on Industrial Disputes in the 1980s." Also Labour Research Department, "Are the Anti-strike Laws Working?" and Ingram, Metcalf, and Wadsworth, "Strike Incidence and Duration in British Manufacturing Industry in the 1980s." On union recognition see Disney, Machin, and Gosling, "What Has Happened to Union Recognition in Britain?" For the impact of legislation on union organization see Undy, Fosh, Morris, Smith, and Martin, *Managing the Unions*.

88. The debate about how to explain changes in union density can be found in various articles in the *British Journal of Industrial Relations*. Disney, "Explanations of the Decline in Trade Union Density in Britain," argues that macroeconomic conditions are the main explanation for declining union density. Green, "Recent Trends in British Trade Union Density," argues that only about a third of the decline in union density can be explained by compositional factors. Freeman and Pelletier, "The Impact of Industrial Relations Legislation on British Union Density," argue that almost the entire decline can be explained by legal changes. Andrews and Naylor, "Declining Union

Density in the 1980s," see a limited role played by business cycle and compositional effects. Machin, "Union Decline in Britain," sees the absence of union organization in new firms as the major reason for declining union density.

89. Millward, Bryson, and Forth, *All Change at Work?* p. 234.

90. House of Commons Employment Committee, *The Future of Trade Unions*, vol. III, para. 63, p. xvi.

91. Ibid., para. 11, p. 280.

92. Brook, "Trade Union Membership," p. 343.

93. Ibid., p. 345.

94. The Workplace Industrial Relations Surveys (now renamed "Workplace Employment Relations Surveys," to capture the decline in collective forms of labor regulation), which have already been referred to several times in this chapter, are particularly good for capturing the extent of institutional change in industrial relations. There have been four thus far, the first in 1980, before the impact of Conservative industrial relations legislation had made itself felt, and the most recent in 1998, just before the impact of New Labour's Employment Relations Act became law. Hence the surveys provide a series of snapshots that help to show the impact of the Conservative reform program. It is important to note, though, that only firms employing twenty-five or more people are covered by the surveys, which tends to overstate the strength of trade unions and collective bargaining because the institutions of collective regulation are much weaker in small firms.

95. Millward, Bryson, and Forth, *All Change at Work?* p. 89.

96. Ibid., p. 98.

97. Gall and McKay, "Trade Union Derecognition in Britain."

98. Dunn and Metcalf, "Trade Union Law since 1979," p. 24.

99. Millward, Bryson, and Forth, *All Change at Work?* p. 140.

100. Ibid., p. 147.

101. William Brown, Deakin, and Ryan, "The Effects of British Industrial Relations Legislation, p. 75.

102. Dunn and Metcalf, "Trade Union Law since 1979," p. 20.

103. Millward, Bryson, and Forth, *All Change at Work?* p. 221.

104. Ibid., p. 188.

105. Ibid., p. 191.

106. Ibid., p. 160.

107. Brown and Walsh, "Pay Determination in Britain in the 1980s," p. 49.

108. Millward, Bryson, and Forth, *All Change at Work?* p. 186.

109. Ibid.; see tables on pp. 188, 191, and 194.

110. Brown, Deakin, Nash, and Oxenbridge, "The Employment Contract," p. 617.

111. Undy, Fosh, Morris, Smith, and Martin, *Managing the Unions*, p.164.

112. Ibid., p. 174.

113. Ibid., p. 260.

114. Heery and Kelly, "Professional, Participative and Managerial Unionism," p. 7.

115. Davies, "Labour Disputes in 1998," p. 299.

116. Davies, "International Comparisons of Labour Disputes in 1999," p. 195.

117. Millward, Bryson, and Forth, *All Change at Work?* p. 178.

118. McKay, *The Law on Industrial Action under the Conservatives*, p.15.

119. Ibid., p. 27.

120. Dunn and Metcalf, "Trade Union Law since 1979," p. 16.

121. Undy, "Annual Review Article," p. 322.

122. Kelly and Heery, *Rethinking Industrial Relations*, p. 45.

123. For example, see Taylor, "New Labour, the Unions and the Government."

124. Bacon and John Storey, "New Employee Relations Strategies in Britain."

125. This distinction is made and elaborated by Brown, Deakin, Hudson, Pratten and Ryan, "The Individualisation of Employment Contracts in Britain."

126. The evidence offered by employers to the House of Commons Employment Select Committee inquiry into the future of trade unions is a good source in this regard: House of Commons Employment Committee, *The Future of Trade Unions*, vol. III.

127. "CBI Rejects 'Back-Door' Worker Participation," *CBI News* 18 (November 4–17, 1988), p. 12.

128. Millward, *The New Industrial Relations?* chapter 4.

129. Cully, et al., *Britain at Work*, chapter 5.

130. See, for example, "The Employment Policies of Inward Investors: The Scottish Dimension," *IRS Employment Trends* 480 (January 1991); and Peck and Stone, "New Inward Investment and the Northern Region Labour Market."

131. Millward, *The New Industrial Relations?* p. 81.

132. Ibid., p.133.

133. This section is drawn from Millward, Bryson, and Forth, *All Change at Work?* chapter 4. My conclusions, even based on the evidence of the survey itself, are less sanguine than those of the authors.

134. See the study by Michael Terry, "Systems of Collective Employee Representation in Non-union Firms in the UK."

135. Brown, Deakin, Hudson, Pratten, and Ryan, "The Individualisation of Employment Contracts in Britain."

136. Millward, Bryson, and Forth, *All Change at Work?* p. 214.

137. Brown, Deakin, and Ryan, "The Effects of British Industrial Relations Legislation," p. 75.

138. Millward, Bryson, and Forth, *All Change at Work?* p. 167.

139. Brown, Deakin, Hudson, Pratten, and Ryan, "The Individualisation of Employment Contracts in Britain," p. iii.

140. Ibid., p. 69.

141. Ibid., p. 75.

142. Wolfgang Streeck, "Neo-corporatist Industrial Relations and the Economic Crisis in West Germany."

143. Kelly and Heery, *Working for the Union*, p. 172.

144. Disney, Gosling, Machin, and McCrae, "The Dynamics of Union Membership in Britain."

145. Purcell, "The End of Institutional Industrial Relations," p. 23.

146. For an extended survey and discussion of British union strategic reorientation see my "Unforgiven."

147. The key document here is the Trades Union Congress *Your Voice at Work*.

148. Teague, "The British TUC and the European Community."

149. Of particular importance was a speech by Jacques Delors, then president of the European Commission, to the 1988 annual congress of the TUC. His plea for British

unions to turn toward Europe for a renewal of trade unionism was influential among unions.

150. See John Monks's speech, "Renewing the Unions," delivered at the "Unions 95" conference, November 18, 1995.

151. Campbell, "New Wave Unions."

152. Labour Research Department, "TUC 1983," p. 257.

153. Trades Union Congress, Collective Bargaining Strategy for the 1990s, p. 16.

154. Howell, "Women as the Paradigmatic Trade Unionists?" pp. 513–15.

CHAPTER SIX
THE THIRD WAY AND BEYOND: THE FUTURE OF BRITISH INDUSTRIAL RELATIONS

1. There are numerous accounts of conflict and modernization within the Labour Party after 1979. See Shaw, The Labour Party since 1979; Colin Hay, The Political Economy of New Labour; Panitch and Leys, The End of Parliamentary Socialism; and Minkin, The Contentious Alliance.

2. Draper, Blair's Hundred Days, p. 72. See also Philip Gould's memoir, The Unfinished Revolution, especially pp. 352–54.

3. Quoted in Riddell, "Trade Unions Stuck with New Symbolic Role."

4. Morris, "A Defining Moment for Our 'One Nation.' "

5. Hay and Watson, "The Discourse of Globalization and the Logic of No Alternative," p. 15.

6. Tony Blair wrote the foreword to the government white paper Fairness at Work, which laid out proposals for what became the 1999 Employment Relations Act. Department of Trade and Industry (DTI), Fairness at Work. It can be found at http://www.dti.gov.uk/er/fairness/index.htm.

7. DTI, Fairness at Work, para. 1.3.

8. The argument that the Employment Relations Act sought to encourage partnership arrangements between employers and employees rather than impose trade union recognition is made by Stephen Wood, "From Voluntarism to Partnership."

9. King and Wickham-Jones, "Training without the State?"

10. Blair, "We Won't Look Back to the 1970s." It could be argued, in fact, that New Labour has no distinctive project in this area and that its interventions are little more than a payoff to old Labour. See Undy, "Annual Review Article." But even if not fully articulated, I think that we can identify such a project, as the remainder of this chapter will suggest.

11. Blair, New Britain, part 6.

12. For a survey of different conceptions of partnership see Heery, "Partnership versus Organising."

13. Stephen Wood, "From Voluntarism to Partnership," p. 131. HRM means Human Resource Management.

14. Ibid., p.134.

15. Tony Blair, speech at the TUC annual congress, September 1997.

16. From Blair's foreword to DTI, Fairness at Work.

17. Ibid.

18. Ibid.

19. Blair, speech at the TUC annual congress, September 1997.

20. Taylor, "New Labour, the Unions and the Government."

21. Foot, "Trade Union Castaways."

22. Cameron, "Social Democracy, Corporatism, Labour Quiescence, and the Representation of Economic Interest in Advanced Capitalist Society."

23. Department of Trade and Industry, "Two Million to Benefit from National Minimum Wage."

24. Regulations were introduced to prevent the need for employers to keep special records or to provide details of the minimum wage on employee pay slips, making it less likely that employees would be aware of their rights. Fines for noncompliance were set at a low level, and only one hundred new inspectors were provided to enforce the law. Workers in their first year of an apprenticeship, au pairs and the self-employed were excluded from the law.

25. Taylor, "New Labour, the Unions and the Government."

26. Tony Blair, "Speech by the Prime Minister, the Rt. Hon. Tony Blair MP, to the Party of European Socialists' Congress," Malmö, June 6, 1997.

27. Black and Wintour, "UK Caves in on Work Directive."

28. Toynbee, "Stabbed in the Back."

29. The Employment Relations Act, 1999, can be found at http://www.hmso.gov.uk/acts/acts1999/19990026.htm.

30. For a more detailed discussion of New Labour industrial relations legislation see Howell, "Is There a Third Way for Industrial Relations?"

31. The estimate is based on TUC research, reported in Ward, "New Parents Fear Cost of Taking Family Leave."

32. Between the publication of *Fairness at Work* and the Employment Relations Bill being drafted, this was changed to provide this protection only for the first eight weeks of employment. This raises the possibility that employers will have an incentive to drag out conflicts.

33. For analyses of the union recognition provisions see Wood and Godard, "The Statutory Recognition Procedure in the Employment Relations Bill," and Smith and Morton, "New Labour's Reform of Britain's Employment Law."

34. Oldfield and Higgins, "Union Law 'Will Cripple Growth Firms.' "

35. Groom and Adams, "Blair Calls for Arbitration over Rail Strikes."

36. Central Arbitration Committee, *Annual Report 2001/02*, p. 20. Available at http://www.cac.gov.uk/.

37. Stephen Wood, "From Voluntarism to Partnership."

38. Trades Union Congress, *New Record High for Employers Recognising Unions.*

39. Gall and McKay, "Developments in Union Recognition and Derecognition in Britain."

40. Baldwin, "Unions Win Policy Review."

41. Trades Union Congress, *TUC Submission to the Government: Review of the 1999 Employment Relations Act.*

42. Department of Trade and Industry, "Review of the Employment Relations Act 1999."

43. The Employment Act, 2002, is available at http://www.legislation.hmso.gov.uk/acts/acts2002/20020022.htm.

44. "Tribunal Figures Show Union Success," *Labour Research* 5 (2001), p.14.

45. McKay, "Annual Review Article 2000," p. 298.

46. Trades Union Congress, *TUC Response to Government Consultation*.

47. For example, a deposit can be charged as a condition for a full hearing of cases deemed weak, costs can be awarded against a side if it engages in time-wasting behavior, and there is provision for determination without a hearing.

48. The Employment Act, 2002, para. 197.

49. Maguire, "Judge Warns of Disaster for Sacked Workers."

50. From Blair's foreword to DTI, *Fairness at Work*.

51. Tony Blair's Fabian pamphlet, *The Third Way*, does not appear to mention trade unions, instead reserving for the state the role of protecting the weak through minimum standards at work (p. 11).

52. Taylor, "New Labour, the Unions and the Government."

53. Thelen, "Varieties of Labor Politics"; Thelen, "Why German Employers Cannot Bring Themselves to Dismantle the German Model"; Thelen and Kume, "The Future of Nationally Embedded Capitalism."

54. MacShane, "New Labour and New Unionism."

55. *Hansard*, April 6, 1998, cols. 23–24.

56. This process is traced in Hall, *Governing the Economy*, chapter 7.

57. Howell, *Regulating Labor*, chapter 7.

58. Howell, "The State and the Reconstruction of Industrial Relations Institutions after Fordism."

59. Howell, "Marktversagen oder Politisches Versagen?"

60. Trades Union Congress, *TUC Submission to the Government: Review of the Employment Relations Act 1999*, p. 2.

61. Brook, "Trade Union Membership," p. 344.

62. Crouch, "A Third Way in Industrial Relations?" p. 104.

63. John Edmonds, then general secretary of the GMB union, made this argument to the TUC. Cited in Undy, "Annual Review Article," p. 315.

References

Adams, Tony. "Market and institutional Forces in Industrial Relations: The Development of National Collective Bargaining, 1910–1920." *Economic History Review* 50:3 (1997).

———. "Employers, Labour, and the State in Industrial Relations History: A Reply to Gospel." *Economic History Review* 51:3 (1998).

Adeney, Martin, and John Lloyd. *The Miners' Strike, 1984–5: Loss without Limit.* London: Routledge and Kegan Paul, 1986.

Aldcroft, Derek. *The Inter-War Economy: Britain, 1919–1939.* New York: Columbia University Press, 1970.

Aldcroft, Derek H., and Michael J. Oliver. *Trade Unions and the Economy, 1870–2000.* Aldershot, UK: Ashgate Publishing, 2000.

Allen, John. "Towards a Post-Industrial Economy?" In John Allen and Doreen Massey, eds., *The Economy in Question.* London: SAGE Publications, 1988.

Amoore, Louise. *Globalisation Contested: An International Political Economy of Work.* New York: Manchester University Press, 2002.

Anderson, Perry. *Lineages of the Absolutist State.* London: Verso, 1974.

Andrews, Martyn, and Robin Naylor. "Declining Union Density in the 1980s: What Do Panel Data Tell Us?" *British Journal of Industrial Relations* 32:3 (September 1994).

Askwith, Lord. *Industrial Problems and Disputes.* London: John Murray, 1920. Reprint, Brighton, UK: The Harvester Press, 1974.

Bacon, Nicholas, and John Storey. "New Employee Relations Strategies in Britain: Towards Individualism or Partnership?" *British Journal of Industrial Relations* 38:3 (September 2000).

Bailey, Rachel. "Annual Review Article 1993: British Public Sector Industrial Relations." *British Journal of Industrial Relations* 32:1 (March 1994).

Bain, George Sayers. *Royal Commission on Trade Unions and Employers' Associations Research Papers 6: Trade Union Growth and Recognition.* London: HMSO, 1967.

———. *The Growth of White-Collar Unionism.* Oxford: Clarendon Press, 1970.

Bain, G. S., and H. A. Clegg. "A Strategy for Industrial Relations Research in Great Britain." *British Journal of Industrial Relations* 12:1 (1974).

Bain, George Sayers, and Robert Price. "Union Growth: Dimensions, Determinants, and Density." In George Sayers Bain, ed., *Industrial Relations in Britain.* Oxford: Basil Blackwell, 1983.

Baldwin, Tom. "Unions Win Policy Review." *Times,* July 10, 2000.

Batstone, Eric. *The Reform of Workplace Industrial Relations.* Oxford: Clarendon Press, 1988.

Beatson, Mark. *Labour Market Flexibility.* Employment Department Research Series No. 48, April 1995.

Beaumont, Phil B. "Trade Union Recognition: The British Experience, 1976–80." *Employee Relations* 3:6 (1981).

Beaumont, Phil B. "Trade Union Recognition and the Recession in the UK." *Industrial Relations Journal* 16:2 (1985).

———. *Public Sector Industrial Relations*. New York: Routledge, 1992.

Bélanger, Jacques. "Job Control under Different Labor Relations Regimes: A Comparison of Canada and Great Britain." In Jacques Bélanger, P. K. Edwards, and Larry Haiven, eds., *Workplace Industrial Relations and the Global Challenge*. Ithaca, NY: ILR Press, 1994.

Benedictus, Roger. "Employment Protection: New Institutions and Trade Union Rights." *Industrial Law Journal* 5:1 (March 1976).

Berger, Suzanne, and Ronald Dore, eds. *National Diversity and Global Capitalism*. Ithaca, NY: Cornell University Press, 1996.

Bird, Derek, and Louise Corcoran. "Trade Union Membership and Density, 1992–93." *Employment Gazette* 102:6 (June 1994).

Black, Ian, and Patrick Wintour. "UK Caves in on Work Directive." *Guardian*, June 12, 2001.

Blackburn, R. M. *Union Character and Social Class: A Study of White-Collar Unionism*. London: Batsford, 1967.

Blair, Tony. *New Britain: My Vision of a Young Country*. London: Fourth Estate, 1996.

———. "We Won't Look Back to the 1970s." *Times*, March 31, 1997.

———. *The Third Way: New Politics for a New Century*. Fabian Pamphlet 588, September 1998.

Blakeman, John. "Injunctive Relief and Appellate Courts: The United States Supreme Court, the British House of Lords, and Appellate Court Policymaking in Comparative Perspective." PhD dissertation, University of Virginia, 1996.

Blank, Stephen. "Britain: The Politics of Foreign Economic Policy, the Domestic Economy, and the Problem of Pluralistic Stagnation." In Peter Katzenstein, ed., *Between Power and Plenty*. Madison: University of Wisconsin Press, 1978.

Blyth, Mark. *Great Transformations: Economic Ideas and Institutional Change in the Twentieth Century*. New York: Cambridge University Press, 2002.

Boswell, Jonathan, and James Peters. *Capitalism in Contention: Business Leaders and Political Economy in Modern Britain*. New York: Cambridge University Press, 1997.

Bowman, John. *Capitalist Collective Action: Competition, Cooperation, and Conflict in the Coal Industry*. New York: Cambridge University Press, 1989.

Boyer, Robert. *La Théorie de la Régulation: Une Analyse Critique*. Paris: Editions La Découverte, 1986.

Boyer, Robert, and Yves Saillard, eds. *Regulation Theory: The State of the Art*. New York: Routledge, 2002.

Brook, Keith. "Trade Union Membership: An Analysis of Data from the Autumn 2001 LFS." *Labour Market Trends*, July 2002.

Brown, Kenneth D. "Trade Unions and the Law." In Chris Wrigley, ed., *A History of British Industrial Relations 1875–1914*. Amherst, MA: University of Massachusetts Press, 1982.

Brown, William, ed. *The Changing Contours of British Industrial Relations*. Oxford: Blackwell, 1981.

———. "The Changed Political Role of Unions under a Hostile Government." In Ben Pimlott and Chris Cook, eds., *Trade Unions in British Politics: The First 250 Years*. New York: Longman, 1991.

Brown, William, Simon Deakin, Maria Hudson, Cliff Pratten, and Paul Ryan. "The Individualisation of Employment Contracts in Britain." Department of Trade and Industry Employment Relations Research Series Working Paper No. 4, 1999.

Brown, William, Simon Deakin, David Nash, and Sarah Oxenbridge. "The Employment Contract: From Collective Procedures to Individual Rights." *British Journal of Industrial Relations* 38:4 (December 2000).

Brown, William, Simon Deakin, and Paul Ryan. "The Effects of British Industrial Relations Legislation, 1979–97." *National Institute Economic Review* 161 (July 1997).

Brown, William, and Janet Walsh. "Pay Determination in Britain in the 1980s: The Anatomy of Decentralisation." *Oxford Review of Economic Policy* 7:1 (Spring 1991).

Brown, William, and Martyn Wright. "The Empirical Tradition in Workplace Bargaining Research." *British Journal of Industrial Relations* 32 (June 1994).

Burgess, Keith. "New Unionism for Old? The Amalgamated Society of Engineers in Britain." In Wolfgang Mommsen and Hans-Gerhard Husung, eds., *The Development of Trade Unionism in Great Britain and Germany, 1880–1914.* London: George Allen & Unwin, 1985.

Cameron, David. "Social Democracy, Corporatism, Labour Quiescence, and the Representation of Economic Interest in Advanced Capitalist Society." In John H. Goldthorpe, ed., *Order and Conflict in Contemporary Capitalism: Studies in the Political Economy of Western European Nations.* Oxford: Clarendon Press, 1984.

Campbell, Beatrix. "New Wave Unions." Interview of John Edmonds. *Marxism Today* 30:9 (September 1986).

Carter, Bob, and Peter Fairbrother. "The Transformation of British Public-Sector Industrial Relations: From 'Model Employer' to Marketized Relations." *Historical Studies in Industrial Relations* 7 (Spring 1999).

Castle, Barbara. *The Castle Diaries, 1964–1976.* London: Macmillan, 1990.

Central Arbitration Committee. *Annual Report 2001/02.* Available at: http://www.cac .gov.uk/cac_2_annual_report/Reports/CACReport200102.pdf.

Charles, Roger. *The Development of Industrial Relations in Britain, 1911–1939.* London: Hutchinson, 1973.

Claydon, Tim. "Tales of Disorder: The Press and the Narrative Construction of Industrial Relations in the British Motor Industry, 1950–79." *Historical Studies in Industrial Relations* 9 (Spring 2000).

Clegg, Hugh Armstrong. *The System of Industrial Relations in Great Britain.* Oxford: Basil Blackwell, 1972.

———. *The Changing System of Industrial Relations in Great Britain.* Oxford: Basil Blackwell, 1979.

———. *A History of British Trade Unions since 1889: Volume II, 1911–1933.* Oxford: Clarendon Press, 1985.

———. *A History of British Trade Unions since 1889: Volume III, 1934–1951.* Oxford: Clarendon Press, 1994.

Clegg, H. A., Alan Fox, and A. F. Thompson. *A History of British Trade Unions since 1889: Volume I, 1889–1910.* Oxford: Clarendon Press, 1964.

Coates, David. *The Crisis of Labour: Industrial Relations and the State in Contemporary Britain.* Oxford: Philip Allan, 1989.

———. *The Question of UK Decline.* Hemel Hempstead, UK: Harvester Wheatsheaf, 1994.

Coates, David. *Models of Capitalism: Growth and Stagnation in the Modern Era*. Malden, MA: Polity Press, 2000.

———, ed. *Varieties of Capitalism; Varieties of Approaches*. New York: Palgrave, forthcoming 2005.

Coates, David, and John Hillard, eds. *UK Economic Decline: Key Texts*. Hemel Hempstead, UK: Prentice Hall/Harvester Wheatsheaf, 1995.

Collins, Hugh. "Capitalist Discipline and Corporatist Law—Part I." *Industrial Law Journal* 11:2 (June 1982).

Confederation of British Industry. "CBI Rejects 'Back-Door' Worker Participation." *CBI News* 18 (November 4–17, 1988).

Cronin, James. *Industrial Conflict in Modern Britain*. London: Croom Helm, 1979.

Crouch, Colin. *Industrial Relations and European State Traditions*. Oxford: Oxford University Press, 1993.

———. "A Third Way in Industrial Relations?" In Stuart White, ed., *New Labour: The Progressive Future?* New York: Palgrave, 2001.

Cully, Mark, Stephen Woodland, Andrew O'Reilly, and Gill Dix. *Britain at Work: As Depicted by the 1998 Workplace Employee Relations Survey*. New York: Routledge, 1999.

Culpepper, Pepper D. "Employers, Public Policy, and the Politics of Decentralized Cooperation in Germany and France." In Peter Hall and David Soskice, eds., *Varieties of Capitalism*. New York: Oxford University Press, 2001.

Davidson, Roger. "The Board of Trade and Industrial Relations, 1896–1914." *The Historical Journal* 21:3 (1978).

———. "Government Administration." In Chris Wrigley, ed., *A History of British Industrial Relations, 1875–1914*. Amherst, MA: University of Massachusetts Press, 1982.

———. *Whitehall and the Labour Problem in Late-Victorian and Edwardian Britain*. London: Croom Helm, 1985.

Davies, Jackie. "Labour Disputes in 1998." *Labour Market Trends* 107:6 (June 1999).

———. "Labour Disputes in 1999." *Labour Market Trends* 108:6 (June 2000).

———. "International Comparisons of Labour Disputes in 1999." *Labour Market Trends* 109:4 (April 2001).

Davies, Paul, and Mark Freedland. *Labour Legislation and Public Policy*. New York: Oxford University Press, 1993.

Deakin, Simon. "Labour Law and the Developing Employment Relationship in the UK." *Cambridge Journal of Economics* 10 (1986).

Department of Trade and Industry. *Fairness at Work*. Cm 3968. London: HMSO, 1998.

———. "Two Million to Benefit from National Minimum Wage: Beckett Announces Government Response to LPC Report." Press Release, Department of Trade and Industry, June 18, 1998.

———. "Review of the Employment Relations Act 1999." (2003). Available at: http://www.dti.gov.uk/er/erareview.htm.

Disney, Richard. "Explanations of the Decline in Trade Union Density in Britain: An Appraisal." *British Journal of Industrial Relations* 28:2 (July 1990).

Disney, Richard, Amanda Gosling, Stephen Machin, and Julian McCrae. "The Dynamics of Union Membership in Britain: A Study Using the Family and Working Lives Survey." Department of Trade and Industry Employment Relations Research Series No. 3, 1999.

Disney, Richard, Stephen Machin, and Amanda Gosling. "What Has Happened to Union Recognition in Britain?" Centre for Economic Performance Discussion Paper, 1993.

Dobbin, Frank. *Forging Industrial Policy.* New York: Cambridge University Press, 1994.

Dorey, Peter. *Wage Politics in Britain: The Rise and Fall of Incomes Policies since 1945.* Portland: Sussex Academic Press, 2001.

Draper, Derek. *Blair's Hundred Days.* London: Faber and Faber, 1997.

Dunn, Stephen, and David Metcalf. "Trade Union Law since 1979: Ideology, Intent, Impact." Centre for Economic Performance Working Paper, October 1994.

Edwards, Paul, ed. *Industrial Relations: Theory and Practice in Britain.* Oxford: Blackwell Publishers, 1995.

Elgar, J., and R. Simpson. "The Impact of the Law on Industrial Disputes in the 1980s." Centre for Economic Performance Discussion Paper No. 104, September 1992.

Esping-Andersen, Gosta. *Politics Against Markets.* Princeton, NJ: Princeton University Press, 1985.

Ewing, Keith. "The Golden Formula: Some Recent Developments." *Industrial Law Journal* 8:3 (September 1979).

———. "Swimming with the Tide: Employment Protection and the Implementation of European Labour Law." *Industrial Law Journal* 22:3 (September 1993).

———. "The State and Industrial Relations: 'Collective Laissez-Faire' Revisited." *Historical Studies in Industrial Relations* 5 (Spring 1998).

Fishman, Nina. "'A Vital Element in British Industrial Relations': A Reassessment of Order 1305, 1940–51." *Historical Studies in Industrial Relations* 8 (Autumn 1999).

Flanders, Allan D. "The Tradition of Voluntarism." *British Journal of Industrial Relations* 12 (November 1974).

———. *Management and Unions: The Theory and Reform of Industrial Relations.* London: Faber and Faber, 1975.

Foot, Paul. "Trade Union Castaways." *Guardian,* November 30, 1999.

Fox, Alan. *Beyond Contract.* London: Faber and Faber, 1974.

———. *History and Heritage.* London: Allen & Unwin, 1985.

Fox, Alan, and Allan Flanders. "Collective Bargaining: From Donovan to Durkheim." In Allan Fox, *Management and Unions: The Theory and Reform of Industrial Relations.* London: Faber and Faber, 1975.

Freeman, Richard, and Jeffrey Pelletier. "The Impact of Industrial Relations Legislation on British Union Density." *British Journal of Industrial Relations* 28:2 (July 1990).

Friedman, Gerald. *State-Making and Labor Movements: France and the United States, 1876–1914.* Ithaca, NY: Cornell University Press, 1998.

Fuchs, Frieda. "Institutions, Values, and Leadership in the Creation of Welfare States: A Comparison of Protective Labor Legislation in Britain and France, 1833–1914." PhD dissertation, Department of Government, Harvard University, May 2001.

Fulcher, James. *Labour Movements, Employers, and the State: Conflict and Co-operation in Britain and Sweden.* Oxford: Clarendon Press, 1991.

Gall, Gregor, and Sonia McKay. "Trade Union Derecognition in Britain, 1988–1994." *British Journal of Industrial Relations* 32:3 (1994).

———. "Developments in Union Recognition and Derecognition in Britain, 1994–98." *British Journal of Industrial Relations* 37:4 (1999).

Gamble, Andrew. *The Free Economy and the Strong State: The Politics of Thatcherism.* Basingstoke, UK: Macmillan, 1988.

Gennard, John, Stephen Dunn, and Michael Wright. "The Content of British Closed Shop Agreements." *Department of Employment Gazette*, November 1979.

Goldthorpe, John H. "Industrial Relations in Great Britain: A Critique of Reformism." *Politics and Society* 4:4 (1974).

Gospel, Howard F. *Markets, Firms, and the Management of Labour in Modern Britain.* New York: Cambridge University Press, 1992.

———. "Markets, Institutions, and the Development of National Collective Bargaining in Britain: A Comment on Adams." *Economic History Review* 51:3 (1998).

Gould, Philip. *The Unfinished Revolution: How the Modernisers Saved the Labour Party.* London: Abacus, 1998.

Gramsci, Antonio. *Selections from the Prison Notebooks.* New York: International Publishers, 1971.

Green, Francis. "Recent Trends in British Trade Union Density: How Much of a Compositional Effect?" *British Journal of Industrial Relations* 30:3 (September 1992).

Grindley, Mike. "The GCHQ Union Ban." *International Union Rights* 1:5 (1993).

Groom, Brian, and Christopher Adams. "Blair Calls for Arbitration over Rail Strikes." *Financial Times*, January 10, 2002.

Hall, Peter. *Governing the Economy: The Politics of State Intervention in Britain and France.* New York: Oxford University Press, 1986.

———. "Policy Paradigms, Social Learning and the State." *Comparative Politics* 25:3 (April 1993).

Hall, Peter A., and David Soskice. "An Introduction to Varieties of Capitalism." In Peter Hall and David Soskice, eds., *Varieties of Capitalism.* New York: Oxford University Press, 2001.

———, eds. *Varieties of Capitalism.* New York: Oxford University Press, 2001.

Hanson, Charles G. *Taming the Trade Unions: A Guide to the Thatcher Government's Employment Reforms, 1980–90.* Basingstoke, UK: Macmillan, 1991.

Harvey, David. *The Condition of Postmodernity.* Oxford: Oxford University Press, 1989.

Hay, Colin. "Rethinking Crisis: Narratives of the New Right and Constructions of Crisis." *Rethinking Marxism* 8:2 (Summer 1995).

———. "Narrating Crisis: The Discursive Construction of the 'Winter of Discontent.'" *Sociology* 30:2 (May 1996).

———. *Re-stating Social and Political Change.* Philadelphia: Open University Press, 1996.

———. *The Political Economy of New Labour: Labouring under False Pretences?* Manchester, UK: Manchester University Press, 1999.

———. "The Invocation of External Economic Constraint: A Genealogy of the Concept of Globalization in the Political Economy of the British Labour Party, 1973–2000." *European Legacy* 6:2 (2001).

———. *Political Analysis.* New York: Palgrave, 2002.

Hay, Colin, and Matthew Watson. "The Discourse of Globalization and the Logic of No Alternative: Rendering the Contingent Necessary in the Downsizing of New Labour's Aspirations for Government." Paper presented at the Annual Conference of the Political Studies Association, University of Keele, April 1998.

Hay, Douglas. "Property, Authority and the Criminal Law." In Douglas Hay, Peter Linebaugh, John Rule, E. P. Thompson, and Cal Winslow, *Albion's Fatal Tree*. New York: Pantheon Books, 1975.

Heery, Edmund. "Partnership versus Organising: Alternative Futures for British Trade Unionism." *Industrial Relations Journal* 33:1 (2002).

Heery, Edmund, and John Kelly. "Professional, Participative and Managerial Unionism: An Interpretation of Change in Trade Unions." *Work, Employment and Society* 8:1 (March 1994).

Hobsbawm, Eric. "The 'New Unionism' Reconsidered." In Wolfgang Mommsen and Hans-Gerhard Husung, eds., *The Development of Trade Unionism in Great Britain and Germany, 1880–1914*. London: George Allen & Unwin, 1985.

Hollingsworth, J. Rogers, and Robert Boyer, eds. *Contemporary Capitalism: The Embeddedness of Institutions*. Cambridge: Cambridge University Press, 1997.

House of Commons Employment Committee. *The Future of Trade Unions*, vols. I—III. Third Report. London: HMSO, 1994.

Howell, Chris. *Regulating Labor: The State and Industrial Relations Reform in Postwar France*. Princeton, NJ: Princeton University Press, 1992.

———. "Women as the Paradigmatic Trade Unionists? New Work, New Workers and New Trade Union Strategies in Conservative Britain." *Economic and Industrial Democracy* 17:4 (November 1996).

———. "Unforgiven: British Trade Unionism in Crisis." In Andrew Martin and George Ross, eds., *The Brave New World of European Labor: European Trade Unions at the Millennium*. New York: Berghahn Books, 1999.

———. "Marktversagen oder Politisches Versagen? Das Schicksal der Gewerkschaften in Grossbritannien, Frankreich und den USA." In Klaus Armingeon and Simon Geissbühler, eds., *Gewerkschaften in der Schweiz: Herausforderungen und Optionen*. Zurich: Seismo-Verl., 2000.

———. "Varieties of Capitalism: And Then There Was One?" *Comparative Politics* 36:1 (October 2003).

———. "Is There a Third Way for Industrial Relations?" *British Journal of Industrial Relations* 42:1 (March 2004).

———. "The State and the Reconstruction of Industrial Relations Institutions after Fordism: Britain and France Compared." In Jonah Levy, ed., *The State after Statism: New State Activities in the Age of Globalization and Liberalization*. Work in progress.

Hyman, Richard. *Industrial Relations: A Marxist Introduction*. Basingstoke, UK: Macmillan, 1975.

———. "Mass Organization and Militancy in Britain: Contrasts and Continuities." In Wolfgang Mommsen and Hans-Gerhard Husung, eds., *The Development of Trade Unionism in Great Britain and Germany, 1880–1914*. London: George Allen & Unwin, 1985.

———. "Strategy or Structure? Capital, Labour and Control." *Work, Employment and Society*, March 1987.

———. *The Political Economy of Industrial Relations: Theory and Practice in a Cold Climate*. Basingstoke, UK: Macmillan, 1989.

———. *Understanding European Trade Unionism: Between Market, Class and Society*. London: SAGE Publications, 2001.

Ingham, Geoffrey K. *Strikes and Industrial Conflict: Britain and Scandinavia.* London: Macmillan, 1974.

Ingram, Peter. "Changes in Working Practices in British Manufacturing Industry in the 1980s." *British Journal of Industrial Relations* 29:1 (March 1991).

Ingram, Peter, David Metcalf, and Jonathan Wadsworth. "Strike Incidence and Duration in British Manufacturing Industry in the 1980s." Centre for Economic Performance Discussion Paper No. 48, August 1991.

Inns of Court Conservative and Unionist Society. *A Giant's Strength.* London, 1958.

Iversen, Torben, and Jonas Pontusson. "Comparative Political Economy: A Northern European Perspective." In Torben Iversen, Jonas Pontusson, and David Soskice, eds., *Unions, Employers, and Central Banks: Macroeconomic Coordination and Institutional Change in Social Market Economies.* New York: Cambridge University Press, 2000.

Iversen, Torben, Jonas Pontusson, and David Soskice, eds. *Unions, Employers, and Central Banks: Macroeconomic Coordination and Institutional Change in Social Market Economies.* New York: Cambridge University Press, 2000.

Jenkins, Clive. *All Against the Collar.* London: Methuen, 1990.

Jenkins, Clive, and Barrie Sherman. *White-Collar Unionism: The Rebellious Salariat.* London: Routledge and Kegan Paul, 1979.

Jenkins, Peter. *The Battle of Downing Street.* London: Charles Knight & Co., 1970.

Jenson, Jane. "Representations in Crisis: The Roots of Canada's Permeable Fordism." *Canadian Journal of Political Science* 24:3 (1990).

Jessop, Bob. "Regulation Theories in Retrospect and Prospect." *Economy and Society* 19:2 (May 1990).

———. "Fordism and Post-Fordism: A Critical Reformulation." Lancaster Regionalism Group Working Paper No. 4, March 1991.

———. "Twenty Years of the Regulation Approach: Has It Been Worth It?" Paper presented at the Twelfth Conference of Europeanists, Chicago, March 2000.

———. *The Future of the Capitalist State.* Cambridge: Polity Press, 2002.

———. "What Follows Fordism? On the Periodisation of Capitalism and Its Regulation." Unpublished, undated paper, University of Lancaster, UK.

Jones, Jack. *Union Man: The Autobiography of Jack Jones.* London: Collins, 1986.

Jones, Michael. "C.A.C. and Schedule 11: The Experience of Two Years." *Industrial Law Journal* 9:1 (March 1980).

Kahn, Peggy. "Union Politics and the Restructuring of the British Coal Industry." In Miriam Golden and Jonas Pontusson, eds., *Bargaining for Change: Union Politics in North America and Europe.* Ithaca, NY: Cornell University Press, 1992.

Kahn-Freund, Otto. "The Industrial Relations Act 1971—Some Retrospective Reflections." *Industrial Law Journal* 3:4 (1974).

———. "Industrial Democracy." *Industrial Law Journal* 6:2 (1977).

Katznelson, Ira. "Structure and Configuration in Comparative Politics." In Mark Lichbach and Alan Zuckerman, eds., *Comparative Politics.* New York: Cambridge University Press, 1997.

Kavanagh, Dennis. *Thatcherism and British Politics: The End of Consensus?* New York: Oxford University Press, 1990.

Kelly, John, and Edmund Heery. *Working for the Union: British Trade Union Officers.* New York: Cambridge University Press, 1994.

———. *Rethinking Industrial Relations: Mobilization, Collectivism and Long Waves.* New York: Routledge, 1998.

Kessler, Sid. "Trade Union Recognition: CIR and ACAS Experience." *Employee Relations* 17:6 (1995).

Kessler, Sid, and Fred Bayliss. *Contemporary British Industrial Relations.* Third edition. Basingstoke, UK: Macmillan, 1998.

King, Desmond, and Mark Wickham-Jones. "Training without the State? New Labour and Labour Markets." *Policy and Politics* 26:4 (October 1998).

Kitschelt, Herbert, Peter Lange, Gary Marks, and John D. Stephens, eds. *Continuity and Change in Contemporary Capitalism.* New York: Cambridge University Press, 1999.

Kitson, Mike, and Frank Wilkinson. "How Paying the Minimum Raises the Stakes." *Guardian,* September 25, 2000.

Klarman, Michael. "The Judges versus the Unions: The Development of British Labor Law, 1867–1913." *Virginia Law Review* 75:8 (September 1989).

Labour Research Department. "TUC 1983: Decisions and the New General Council." *Labour Research* 72:10 (October 1983).

———. "Size of UK Firms." *Fact Service* 52:21 (May 24, 1990).

———. "Are the Anti-strike Laws Working?" *Labour Research* 79:9 (September 1990).

———. "Foreign Investment in the UK by Country." *Fact Service* 53:48 (November 28, 1991).

———. "Pay Review Bodies Examined." *Bargaining Report* 115 (March 1992), pp. 12–14.

———. "Pay in the Privatized Utilities." *Bargaining Report* 136 (February 1994).

———. "Share of Small and Medium-Sized Plants Grows." *Fact Service* 57:31 (August 3, 1995).

———. "Employment Changes, 1979–96." *Fact Service* 59:14 (April 10, 1997).

———. "Foreign Ownership of UK Manufacturing Industry." *Fact Service* 60:2 (January 15, 1998).

———. "Public Sector Workforce." *Fact Service* 61:25 (June 24, 1999).

———. "Globalisation of UK Manufacturing." *Fact Service* 61:40 (October 7, 1999).

———. "Tribunal Figures Show Union Success." *Labour Research* 90:5 (2001).

Latta, Geoff. "The Legal Extension of Collective Bargaining: A Study of Section 8 of the Terms and Conditions of Employment Act 1959." *Industrial Law Journal* 3:4 (December 1974).

Lehmbruch, Gerhard. "The Institutional Embedding of Market Economies: The German 'Model' and Its Impact on Japan." In Wolfgang Streeck and Kozo Yamamura, eds., *The Origins of Nonliberal Capitalism: Germany and Japan in Comparison.* Ithaca, NY: Cornell University Press, 2001.

Lewis, Roy. "Kahn-Freund and Labour Law: An Outline Critique." *Industrial Law Journal* 8:4 (December 1979).

Lichbach, Mark Irving, and Alan Zuckerman, eds. *Comparative Politics.* New York: Cambridge University Press, 1997.

Lieberman, Robert C. "Ideas, Institutions, and Political Order: Explaining Political Change." *American Political Science Review* 96:4 (December 2002).

Lindblom, Charles. "The Market as Prison." *Journal of Politics* 44:2 (May 1982).

Lowe, Rodney. "The Failure of Consensus in Britain: The National Industrial Conference, 1919–1921." *The Historical Journal* 21:3 (1978).

Lowe, Rodney. *Adjusting to Democracy: The Role of the Ministry of Labour in British Politics, 1916–1939*. Oxford: Clarendon Press, 1986.

Machin, Stephen. "Union Decline in Britain." *British Journal of Industrial Relations* 38:4 (December 2000).

MacShane, Denis. "New Labour and New Unionism." Paper presented at the New Labour and the Labour Movement Conference, June 19–20, 1998, University of Sheffield.

Maguire, K. "Judge Warns of Disaster for Sacked Workers." *Guardian*, January 18, 2002.

Marginson, Peter. "Multinational Britain: Employment and Work in an International-ised Economy." *Human Resource Management Journal* 4:4 (Summer 1994).

Marsden, David, and Marc Thompson. "Flexibility Agreements and Their Significance in the Increase in Productivity in British Manufacturing since 1980." *Work, Employment and Society* 4:1 (March 1990).

Marsh, David. *The New Politics of British Trade Unionism: Union Power and the Thatcher Legacy*. Ithaca, NY: ILR Press, 1992.

Martin, Andrew, and George Ross, eds. *The Brave New World of European Labor: European Trade Unions at the Millennium*. New York: Berghahn Books, 1999.

McCarthy, William. "The Rise and Fall of Collective Laissez-Faire." In William Mc-Carthy, ed., *Legal Intervention in Industrial Relations: Gains and Losses*. Oxford: Basil Blackwell, 1992.

McIlroy, John. *The Permanent Revolution? Conservative Law and the Trade Unions*. Nottingham, UK: Spokesman, 1991.

———. "Ten Years for the Locust: The TUC in the 1980s." In Derek Cox, ed., *Facing the Future*. Department of Adult Education, University of Nottingham, 1992.

McKay, Sonia "The Law on Industrial Action under the Conservatives." The Institute of Employment Rights (February 1996).

———. "Annual Review Article 2000. Between Flexibility and Regulation: Rights, Equality and Protection at Work." *British Journal of Industrial Relations* 39:2 (June 2001).

McKersie, Robert B., and Laurence C. Hunter. *Pay, Productivity and Collective Bargaining*. London: Macmillan, 1973.

McKibbin, Ross. *Classes and Cultures: England 1918–1951*. New York: Oxford University Press, 1998.

Millward, Neil. *The New Industrial Relations?* London: PSI, 1994.

Millward, Neil, Alex Bryson, and John Forth. *All Change at Work? British Employment Relations, 1980–1998, as Portrayed by the Workplace Industrial Relations Survey Series*. New York: Routledge, 2000.

Millward, Neil, and Mark Stevens. *British Workplace Industrial Relations, 1980–1984: The DE/ESRC/PSI/ACAS Surveys*. Aldershot, UK: Gower, 1986.

Millward, Neil, Mark Stevens, David Smart, and W. R. Hawes. *Workplace Industrial Relations in Transition: The ED/ESRC/PSI/ACAS Surveys*. Aldershot, UK: Dartmouth, 1992.

Milne, Seumas. *The Enemy Within*. London: Verso, 1994.

Milner, Simon. "The Coverage of Collective Pay-Setting Institutions in Britain, 1895–1990." *British Journal of Industrial Relations* 33:1 (March 1995).

Milner, Simon, and David Metcalf. "A Century of UK Strike Activity: An Alternative Perspective." CEP Paper, February 1991.

Minkin, Lewis. *The Contentious Alliance: Trade Unions and the Labour Party*. Edinburgh: Edinburgh University Press, 1991.

Mitchell, Neil J. "Changing Pressure-Group Politics: The Case of the Trades Union Congress, 1976–84." *British Journal of Political Science* 17:4 (October 1987).

Morris, Bill. "A Defining Moment for Our 'One Nation.'" *Times*, May 5, 1998.

OECD. *Manpower Policy in the UK*. Paris: OECD, 1970.

Offe, Claus, and Helmut Wiesenthal. "Two Logics of Collective Action." In Claus Offe, *Disorganized Capitalism*. Cambridge, MA: MIT Press, 1985.

Oldfield, C., and S. Higgins. "Union Law 'Will Cripple Growth Firms.'" *Times*, May 24, 1998.

Panitch, Leo. *Social Democracy and Industrial Militancy: The Labour Party, the Trade Unions and Incomes Policy, 1945–1974*. New York: Cambridge University Press, 1976.

Panitch, Leo, and Colin Leys. *The End of Parliamentary Socialism: From New Left to New Labour*. New York: Verso, 1997.

Peck, Frank, and Ian Stone. "New Inward Investment and the Northern Region Labour Market: A Final Report." Employment Department Research Series No. 6, October 1992.

Pelling, Henry. "Trade Unions, Workers and the Law." In Henry Pelling, *Popular Politics and Society in Late Victorian Britain*. London: Macmillan, 1979.

Pendleton, Andrew. "The Evolution of Industrial Relations in UK Nationalized Industries." *British Journal of Industrial Relations* 35:2 (June 1997).

People, Jobs, Opportunity. London: HMSO, 1992.

Phelps Brown, E. H. *The Growth of British Industrial Relations*. London: Macmillan & Co., 1959.

Pierson, Paul. "Not Just What, but When: Timing and Sequence in Political Processes." *Studies in American Political Development* 14 (Spring 2001).

Piore, Michael J., and Charles F. Sabel. *The Second Industrial Divide: Possibilities for Prosperity*. New York: Basic, 1984.

Pollard, Sidney. *The Development of the British Economy, 1914–1980*. Third edition. London: Edward Arnold, 1983.

Pond, Chris. "Wages Councils, the Unorganised, and the Low Paid." In George Sayers Bain, ed., *Industrial Relations in Britain*. Oxford: Basil Blackwell, 1983.

Pontusson, Jonas. "From Comparative Public Policy to Political Economy." *Comparative Political Studies* 28:1 (1995).

Poole, Michael. *Theories of Trade Unionism: A Sociology of Industrial Relations*. Boston: Routledge and Kegan Paul, 1981.

Poole, Michael, and Roger Mansfield. "Patterns of Continuity and Change in Managerial Attitudes and Behaviour in Industrial Relations, 1980–1990." *British Journal of Industrial Relations* 31:1 (March 1993).

Porter, J. H. "Wage Bargaining under Conciliation Agreements, 1860–1914." *Economic History Review* 23:3 (1970).

Price, Richard. "The New Unionism and the Labour Process." In Wolfgang Mommsen and Hans-Gerhard Husung, eds., *The Development of Trade Unionism in Great Britain and Germany, 1880–1914*. London: George Allen & Unwin, 1985.

———. *Labour in British Society: An Interpretive History*. New York: Routledge, 1986.

Price, Robert, and George Sayers Bain. "Union Growth Revisited." *British Journal of Industrial Relations* 14:3 (November 1976).

Purcell, John. "The End of Institutional Industrial Relations." *Political Quarterly* 64:1 (January—March 1993).

Purcell, John, and Keith Sisson. "Strategies and Practices in the Management of Industrial Relations." In George Sayers Bain, ed., *Industrial Relations in Britain*. Cambridge, MA: Basil Blackwell, 1983.

Reid, Alastair J. "Old Unionism Reconsidered: The Radicalism of Robert Knight, 1870–1900." In Eugenio F. Biagini and Alastair J. Reid, eds., *Currents of Radicalism: Popular Radicalism, Organised Labour and Party Politics in Britain, 1850–1914*. New York: Cambridge University Press, 1991.

Report on Collective Agreements between Employers and Workpeople. London: HMSO, 1910.

Riddell, Peter. "Trade Unions Stuck with New Symbolic Role." *Times*, April 30, 1998.

Roberts, B. C., ed. *Industrial Relations: Contemporary Problems and Perspectives*. London: Methuen & Co., 1962.

Rogaly, Joe. *Grunwick*. New York: Penguin, 1977.

Rogers, Joel, and Wolfgang Streeck. "Productive Solidarities: Economic Strategy and Left Politics." In David Miliband, ed., *Reinventing the Left*. Cambridge: Polity Press, 1994.

Royal Commission on Labour. *Fifth and Final Report of the Royal Commission on Labour: The Report*. London: HMSO, 1894.

Royal Commission on Trade Disputes and Trade Combinations. *Report of the Royal Commission on Trade Disputes and Trade Combinations*. London: HMSO, 1906.

Royal Commission on Trade Unions and Employers' Associations, 1965–1968: Report. London: HMSO, 1968.

Royal Commission on Trade Unions and Employers' Associations: Selected Written Evidence Submitted to the Royal Commission. London: HMSO, 1968.

Sabel, Charles F. *Work and Politics: The Division of Labor in Industry*. New York: Cambridge University Press, 1982.

Saville, John. "An Open Conspiracy: Conservative Politics and the Miners' Strike, 1984–5." In Ralph Miliband, John Saville, Marcel Liebman, and Leo Panitch, eds., *Socialist Register 1985/86*. London: Merlin Press, 1986.

———. "The Trade Disputes Act of 1906." *Historical Studies in Industrial Relations* 1 (March 1996).

Seifert, Roger. *Industrial Relations in the NHS*. London: Chapman and Hall, 1992.

Shanks, Michael. *The Stagnant Society*. London: Harmondsworth, 1963.

Shaw, Eric. *The Labour Party since 1979: Crisis and Transformation*. New York: Routledge, 1994.

Silver, Beverly J. *Forces of Labor: Workers' Movements and Globalization since 1870*. New York: Cambridge University Press, 2003.

Silver, Beverly J., and Giovanni Arrighi. "Polanyi's 'Double Movement': The *Belle Époques* of British and U.S. Hegemony Compared." *Politics and Society* 31:2 (June 2003).

Simpson, R. C. "Judicial Control of A.C.A.S." *Industrial Law Journal* 8:2 (June 1979).

Sisson, Keith. "Employers and the Structure of Collective Bargaining: Distinguishing Cause and Effect." In Steven Tolliday and Jonathan Zeiltin, eds., *The Power to Manage? Employers and Industrial Relations in Comparative-Historical Perspective*. New York: Routledge, 1991.

Smith, Justin Davis. *The Attlee and Churchill Administrations and Industrial Unrest, 1945–1955*. London: Pinter Publishers, 1990.

Smith, Paul, and Gary Morton. "New Labour's Reform of Britain's Employment Law: The Devil Is Not Only in the Detail but in the Values and Policy Too." *British Journal of Industrial Relations* 39:1 (March 2001).

Spoor, Alec. *White-Collar Union: Sixty Years of NALGO*. London: Heinemann, 1967.

Steinmetz, Willibald. "Introduction: Towards a Comparative History of Legal Cultures, 1750–1950." In Willibald Steinmetz, ed., *Private Law and Social Inequality in the Industrial Age: Comparing Legal Cultures in Britain, France, Germany, and the United States*. New York: Oxford University Press, 2000.

Steinmo, Sven, Kathleen Thelen, and Frank Longstreth, eds. *Structuring Politics: Historical Institutionalism in Comparative Analysis*. New York: Cambridge University Press, 1994.

Stephens, John. *The Transition from Capitalism and Socialism*. Urbana: University of Illinois Press, 1986.

Streeck, Wolfgang. "Neo-corporatist Industrial Relations and the Economic Crisis in West Germany." In John H. Goldthorpe, ed., *Order and Conflict in Contemporary Capitalism*. Oxford: Clarendon Press, 1984.

———. "Introduction: Explorations into the Origins of Nonliberal Capitalism in Germany and Japan." In Wolfgang Streeck and Kozo Yamamura, eds., *The Origins of Nonliberal Capitalism: Germany and Japan in Comparison*. Ithaca, NY: Cornell University Press, 2001.

Summers, Clyde. "Lord Wedderburn's New Labour Law: An American Perspective." *Industrial Law Journal* 21:3 (September 1992).

Swenson, Peter. "Arranged Alliance: Business Interests in the New Deal." *Politics and Society* 25:1 (March 1997).

———. *Capitalists Against Markets: The Making of Labor Markets and Welfare States in the United States and Sweden*. New York: Oxford University Press, 2002.

Tarling, Roger, and Frank Wilkinson. "The Movement of Real Wages and the Development of Collective Bargaining in the U.K., 1855–1920." *Contributions to Political Economy* 1 (1982).

Taylor, Robert. "New Labour, the Unions and the Government." Paper presented at the New Labour and the Labour Movement Conference, June 19–20, 1998, University of Sheffield.

Teague, Paul. "The British TUC and the European Community." *Millennium: Journal of International Studies* 18:1 (1989).

Tebbit, Norman. "Industrial Relations in the Next Two Decades: Government Objectives." *Employee Relations* 5:1 (1983).

Terry, Michael. "Shop Steward Development and Managerial Strategies." In George Sayers Bain, ed., *Industrial Relations in Britain*. Oxford: Basil Blackwell, 1983.

———. "Systems of Collective Employee Representation in Non-union Firms in the UK." *Industrial Relations Journal* 30:1 (March 1999).

Terry, Michael, and P. K. Edwards, eds. *Shopfloor Politics and Job Controls: The Post-war Engineering Industry*. New York: Blackwell Press, 1988.

Thatcher, Margaret. *The Downing Street Years*. New York: HarperCollins, 1993.

Thelen, Kathleen. "Why German Employers Cannot Bring Themselves to Dismantle the German Model." In Torben Iversen, Jonas Pontusson, and David Soskice, eds.,

Unions, Employers, and Central Banks: Macroeconomic Coordination and Institutional Change in Social Market Economies. New York: Cambridge University Press, 2000.

———. "Varieties of Labor Politics in the Developed Democracies." In Peter Hall and David Soskice, eds., *Varieties of Capitalism.* New York: Oxford University Press, 2001.

———. "The Political Economy of Business and Labor in the Developed Democracies." In Ira Katznelson and Helen V. Milner, eds., *Political Science: The State of the Discipline.* New York: Norton, 2002.

Thelen, Kathleen, and Ikuo Kume. "The Future of Nationally Embedded Capitalism: Industrial Relations in Germany and Japan." In Kozo Yamamura and Wolfgang Streeck, eds., *The End of Diversity? Prospects for German and Japanese Capitalism.* Ithaca, NY: Cornell University Press, 2003.

Thompson, E. P. *Writing by Candlelight.* London: Merlin Press, 1980.

Tolliday, Steven. "The Failure of Mass Production in the Motor Industry, 1914–39." In Chris Wrigley, ed., *A History of British Industrial Relations, Volume II, 1914–1939.* Brighton, UK: Harvester Press, 1987.

Tolliday, Steven, and Jonathan Zeitlin, eds. *Between Fordism and Flexibility: The Automobile Industry and Its Workers.* New York: St. Martin's Press, 1992.

Topham, Tony. "New Types of Bargaining." In Robin Blackburn and Alexander Cockburn, eds., *The Incompatibles: Trade Union Militancy and the Consensus.* London: Penguin, 1967.

Toynbee, Polly. "Stabbed in the Back." *Guardian,* February 25, 2000.

Trades Union Congress. *Report of the Proceedings at the 92nd Annual Trades Union Congress.* London: TUC, 1961.

———. *Trade Unionism.* London: TUC, 1967.

———. *Collective Bargaining and Trade Union Development.* London: TUC, 1969.

———. *Collective Bargaining Strategy for the 1990s.* London: TUC, 1991.

———. *Your Voice at Work: TUC Proposals for Rights to Representation at Work.* London: TUC, 1995.

———. *TUC Submission to the Government: Review of the Employment Relations Act 1999.* London: TUC, October 1, 2000.

———. *TUC Submission to the Government: Review of the 1999 Employment Relations Act.* October 2, 2001.

———. *TUC Response to Government Consultation: Routes to Resolution: Improving Dispute Resolution in Britain.* October 3, 2001.

———. *New Record High for Employers Recognising Unions.* TUC press release, January 21, 2002.

Turner, H. A. "The Donovan Report." *Economic Journal* 79:313 (March 1969).

Undy, Roger. "The Devolution of Bargaining Levels and Responsibilities in the Transport and General Workers Union, 1965–75." *Industrial Relations Journal* 9:3 (1978).

———. "Annual Review Article: New Labour's 'Industrial Relations Settlement': The Third Way?" *British Journal of Industrial Relations* 37:2 (June 1999).

Undy, R., V. Ellis, W. E. J. McCarthy, and A. M. Halmos, eds. *Change in Trade Unions.* London: Hutchinson, 1981.

Undy, Roger, Patricia Fosh, Huw Morris, Paul Smith, and Roderick Martin. *Managing the Unions: The Impact of Legislation on Trade Union Behaviour.* Oxford: Clarendon Press, 1996.

Waddington, Jeremy. *The Politics of Bargaining.* London: Mansell Publishing, 1995.

Wainwright, Martin, and Richard Nelsson. "Long Decline of a Once Mighty Union." *Guardian*, January 15, 2002.

Ward, Lucy. "New Parents Fear Cost of Taking Family Leave." *Guardian*, March 11, 1999.

Watson, Gary. "The Flexible Workforce and Patterns of Working Hours in the UK." *Employment Gazette* 102:7 (July 1994).

Wedderburn, Lord. *Employment Rights in Britain and Europe: Selected Papers in Labour Law*. London: Lawrence and Wishart, 1991.

―――."Freedom of Association and Philosophies of Labour Law: The Thatcher Ideology." In Lord Wedderburn, *Employment Rights in Britain and Europe: Selected Papers in Labour Law*. London: Lawrence and Wishart, 1991.

―――. *Labour Law and Freedom: Further Essays in Labour Law*. London: Lawrence and Wishart, 1995.

Wells, John. "Uneven Development and De-industrialization in the UK since 1979." In Francis Green, ed., *The Restructuring of the UK Economy*. London: Harvester Wheatsheaf, 1989.

Winchester, David. "Industrial Relations in the Public Sector." In George Sayers Bain, ed., *Industrial Relations in Britain*. Oxford: Basil Blackwell, 1983.

―――. "Industrial Relations Research in Britain." *British Journal of Industrial Relations* 21 (March 1983).

Wood, Stephen. "From Voluntarism to Partnership: A Third Way Overview of the Public Policy Debate in British Industrial Relations." In H. Collins, P. Davies, and R. Rideout, eds., *Legal Regulation of the Employment Relation*. Dordrecht, Netherlands: Kluwer Law International, 2000.

―――. "Learning through ACAS: The Case of Union Recognition." In Brian Towers and William Brown, eds., *Employment Relations in Britain: 25 Years of the Advisory, Conciliation and Arbitration Service*. Oxford: Blackwell, 2000.

Wood, Stephen, and John Godard. "The Statutory Recognition Procedure in the Employment Relations Bill: A Comparative Analysis." *British Journal of Industrial Relations* 37:2 (1999).

Wood, Stewart. "Business, Government, and Patterns of Labor Market Policy in Britain and the Federal Republic of Germany." In Peter Hall and David Soskice, eds., *Varieties of Capitalism*. New York: Oxford University Press, 2001.

Wright, Erik Olin. "Working-Class Power, Capitalist-Class Interests, and Class Compromise." *American Journal of Sociology* 105:4 (January 2000).

Wrigley, Chris. "The Government and Industrial Relations," in Chris Wrigley, ed., *A History of British Industrial Relations, 1875–1914*. Amherst, MA: University of Massachusetts Press, 1982.

Zeitlin, Jonathan. "Industrial Structure, Employer Strategy and the Diffusion of Job Control in Britain, 1880–1920." In Wolfgang Mommsen and Hans-Gerhard Husung, eds., *The Development of Trade Unionism in Great Britain and Germany, 1880–1914*. London: George Allen & Unwin, 1985.

―――. "Shopfloor Bargaining and the State." In Steven Tolliday and Jonathan Zeitlin, eds., *Shopfloor Bargaining and the State*. New York: Cambridge University Press, 1985.

―――. "From Labour History to the History of Industrial Relations." *Economic History Review*, 2nd series, 40:2 (1987).

Index

Adams, Tony, 201–2n.22
Advisory, Conciliation and Arbitration Service (ACAS), 115–18, 124–25, 126, 152, 164; and Codes of Practice, 116
alliances, 56–57
Amalgamated Engineering Union (AEU), 114
Amalgamated Society of Engineers, 57
American Cyanamid v. Ethicon, 124
Anderson, Perry, 199n. 51
Annual Conference of Unions Catering for Non-Manual Workers, 128
Arbitration (Masters and Workmen) Act (1872), 66
Askwith, George, 57, 66–68, 76
Association of Scientific, Technical and Managerial Staffs (ASTMS), 97
Association of Supervisory Staffs, Executives and Technicians (ASSET), 97
Australia, and compulsory arbitration, 82

Bacon, Nicholas, 165
Bain, George Sayers, 84, 97, 102
Bank of England, 176
Barclays Bank, 127
bargaining. *See* collective bargaining
Batstone, Eric, 125
Bedaux System, 52
Bevin, Ernest, 90, 92, 195n. 4
Birmingham Alliance, 56
Blair, Tony, 3, 177, 181
Blyth, Mark, 40
Board of Trade, 65, 66–69, 73, 75–76, 81, 92; Labour Department in, 66; Labour Statistical Bureau in, 66; statistics on state intervention, 68
Bowman, John, 54
Britain, 4–5, 35, 123–24, 157; class relations in, 12–13, 31, 36–37, 49–54, 59–60; coal mining in, 50–51; and currency crisis, 97–98; decline of staple industries in, 86–87; economic development features, 51–52; labor force in, 138, 166–67; as "ungovernable," 6. *See also* capitalism, in Britain; economic restructuring; industrial relations; post-Fordism
British Leyland, 95, 154
British Rail, 154
British Steel, 154
British Telecom, 149, 155
Brooklands Agreement, 200n. 1
Brown, Gordon, 176
Brown, William, 168
Bullock Commission, 118, 119, 126
Burgess, Keith, 57
Burnham Committee, 156
"Butskellism," 93

Callaghan, James: Labour government of, 4
Cameron inquiry (1963), 97
Campbell-Bannerman, Prime Minister, 65
Canada, and compulsory arbitration, 82
capitalism, 17, 51, 199n. 51; and the labor force, 52–53; national modes of, 24–29; pre-Fordist competitive capitalism, 56; and Regulation Theory, 32. *See also* capitalism, in Britain
capitalism, in Britain, 136, 137, 171; institutional features of, 139
"card-check" recognition, 183
Carmichael, Ian, 4
cartelism, 34, 55, 201n. 19
Castle, Barbara, 110, 113, 208n. 93
Cave Committee, 76
Central Arbitration Council (CAC), 115, 183–85
Charles, Roger, 73
Churchill, Winston, 65, 69
Citizens Advice Bureaux, 164
"class drivers," 18
class relations. *See* Britain, class relations in
class structure, 42, 75
Clegg, Hugh, 8, 10, 11, 12, 13, 74, 78, 83, 102
Clerical and Administrative Workers Union, 127
Coal Board, 146
Coates, David, 18, 42, 98

collective bargaining, 43, 56, 80–81, 87, 90, 104, 110, 115, 132, 140, 146–47, 151–52, 161–63, 172–73, 180; bargaining-based institutions, 15–16; benefits of industry-level for employers, 54–56, 81; "common law" framework of, 96; decentralization of, 88, 103–4, 120–21; emergence of industry-level, 56–59, 86–87, 91–92, 198n. 34; expansion of in the 1930s, 78–79; industry-level, 42, 55–56, 69, 71, 81–82, 86, 88, 120–22, 162; productivity, 95, 104; and shop stewards, 104–5; "single-table," 155; voluntary, 92–93, 104. *See also* collective *laissez-faire* system; industrial relations, de-collectivization of; shop stewards, and collective bargaining; Whitley Committee
collective *laissez-faire* system (first system of industrial relations / 1890–1940), 8, 13, 26, 35, 57–58, 65, 79, 86–87, 133, 137, 191, 201n. 6; and the benefits of industry-level bargaining for employers, 54–56; consequences of, 82–86; decline and consolidation of, 74–75; economic decline and the restructuring of class relations, 49–54, 201–2n. 22; elements of, 46–47; emergence of industry bargaining, 56–59; emphasis on immunities, 9, 84, 100–101, 204n. 122; goals of, 47–48; high degree of political consensus in, 79–80; high point of, 89–93; impact of the First World War on, 70–71; judicial response to industrial conflict, 61–64; and recognition of trade unions, 84; reemergence of "the labour problem," 59–61; and reinforcement of the ideology of voluntarism, 84; role of state intervention in, 80–82; the state and institutional construction, 79–82; the Treasury versus the Ministry of Labour, 75–79. *See also* Board of Trade; Royal Commission on Labour; Whitley Committee
collective regulation, 16–17, 67, 117, 140, 142, 160; of class relations, 178
commissioner for protection against unlawful industrial action (CPUIA), 150
commissioner for the rights of trade union members (CROTUM), 150
Commission on Industrial Relations (CIR), 111–12
Commission on Industrial Unrest (1917), 71
competition, 54–55
compulsory arbitration, 82, 91, 95
Conciliation Act (1867), 66

Conciliation (Trades Dispute) Act (1896), 66, 92
Confederation of British Industry (CBI), 109, 179, 190
Conservative Party, 1, 88, 93, 119; and dissent over the class compromise, 100; election of in 1979, 125. *See also* Conservative Party industrial relations policy
Conservative Party industrial relations policy, 112–13, 131–34, 145–49, 189–90; and the activist state, 141–45; on employment rights and the labor market, 152–53; external support for trade unions and collective bargaining, 151–52; on industrial action, 149–50, 158, 164; legislation concerning, 147–48, 149; in the public sector, 153–56; on trade union governance, 150–51
Conspiracy and Protection of Property Act (1875), 46, 60, 61, 77
Contracts of Employment Act (1963), 111
corporatism, 82, 125, 178–79; collapse of, 156–57, 158
Cotton Manufacturing Industry (Temporary Provisions) Act (1934), 78
Courtauld, Samuel, 95
Criminal Law Amendment Act (1871), 60–61
crisis, and the activist state, 39–41, 141–45
Cronin, James, 29–30, 99
Crouch, Colin, 25, 39, 189, 199n. 57

Davidson, Roger, 66
Davies, Paul, 98, 107
Deakin, Simon, 168
deindustrialization, 96, 135, 137, 138, 139
Delors, Jacques, 216n. 149
Denning, Lord, 124
Department of Trade and Industry (DTI), 145, 177, 179, 182
Dobbin, Frank, 26, 40, 55
Donovan Commission, 9, 100, 101–6, 114, 118, 120–21, 128, 140; conclusions of, 10; and the "Note of Reservation," 105–6; reaction to its report, 106–9; remit of, 101. *See also* industrial relations reform, following the Donovan Commission's report
Dunn, Stephen, 142–43, 148–49

Economic and Monetary Union (EMU), 176
economic restructuring, 21–22, 48, 94–95; and economic decline, 49–54
Economist, 54, 145

Edmonds, John, 172
Edwards, Michael, 154
Employees and Workmen Act (1875), 61
"employee voice," 167
employers associations, 84, 104
Employment Act (EA, 1980), 148
Employment Act (EA, 1982), 148
Employment Act (EA, 1988), 148
Employment Act (EA, 1990), 148, 149
Employment Act (EA, 2002), 184–85; and reform of the tribunal system, 185, 219n. 47
Employment Protection Act (EPA, 1975), 114, 116–18, 129, 151; focus of, 115–16
employment relations, 158–64
Employment Relations Act (ERA, 1999), 179, 182–84, 186, 217n. 8
Equal Employment Commission, 179
Esping-Anderson, Gosta, 43
Essential Work Orders, 90
Esso, 95, 103
European Exchange Rate Mechanism (ERM), 176
European Social Chapter, 170, 181–82
European Union (EU), 145, 152–53, 165, 171–72, 179, 181–82; and trade unions, 173

Fair Wages Resolution, 129
Fawley oil refinery, 103–4
First World War, 70–71, 79
Flanders, Allan, 8, 9, 10, 102, 104, 159
flexibility. See labor flexibility
Ford, Henry, 51
Fordism, 51, 52, 104; and growth regimes, 33–35; and "job control," 96. See also post-Fordism
Fox, Alan, 8, 102
France: industrial relations in, 3, 26, 133, 187–88; unions in, 42
Freedland, Mark, 98, 107
Fuchs, Freida, 40
Fulcher, James, 75
Future of the Capitalist State (Jessop), 199n. 47
Future of Trade Unions, The, 141

Gamble, Andrew, 135
Geddes Committee (1922), 77
General Strike (1926), 74, 75, 77
George, Lloyd, 54
Germany: industrial relations in, 187; and technology, 50, 51
Giant's Strength, A, 100

globalization, 40, 137, 175
Goldthorpe, John, 5–6, 7, 11
Gospel, Howard F., 50, 51, 74, 87, 89, 201–2n. 22, 204n. 95
Gould, Philip, 175
Government Communications Headquarters (GCHQ), 158, 179
Gramsci, Antonio, 20
Great Depression (1873–96), 49, 56
Great Depression (1920s), 74, 77
Grocery Trade Board, 77
Grunwick Film Processing Laboratories, 117–18, 126

Hall, Peter, 40, 197n. 3
Hall, Stuart, 144
Hay, Colin, 143
Hay, Douglas, 24, 40
Hayek, Friedrich, 148
Heath, Edward: Conservative government of, 4, 113, 131
Heery, Edmund, 83, 123, 139, 163
Home Office, 66
House of Commons Employment Committee, 141, 142
Hyman, Richard, 10, 24, 58, 195n. 3
hyperflexibility, 136

ILO conventions, 128
I'm All Right Jack (1959), 4
incomes policies, 43, 98, 129
industrial action legislation, 149–50
Industrial Charter, 93
Industrial Conciliation and Arbitration Act (New Zealand, 1894), 62–63
Industrial Courts Act (1919), 72
industrial culture, 26, 40, 55
industrial democracy, 118–19
industrial relations, 3–5, 14–15, 26, 99–100, 196n. 41, 199n. 57; and the abstentionist state, 8–10, 13; academic, 7–8; and collective workplace institutions, 16; in comparative perspective, 186–90; contemporary sectors of, 169; cross-national, 30; debate of rights-based industrial relations, 127–30; empirical research on, 8; in France, 3, 26, 133, 187–88; in Germany, 187; individualization of, 165, 167–69; and industry bargaining-based institutions, 15–16; interpreting, 7–14; in Japan, 166; "step-by-step," 146; three major systems of in Britain, 15–17, 19, 190–93; in the United States, 3,

industrial relations (*cont'd*)
133, 187–88. *See also* collective *laissez-faire*
system; Conservative Party industrialrela-
tions policy; Donovan Commission; industrial relations, decentralization of; industrial relations, decollectivization of;
industrial relations and institutional development; industrial relations reform; Labour
Party industrial relations policy
Industrial Relations Act (IRA, 1971), 4,
109, 112, 113, 115, 129, 132, 146–47;
repeal of, 114
Industrial Relations Commission (IRC),
105, 107
industrial relations, decentralization of (second system of industrial relations / 1940–
79), 88–90, 103, 124, 127–30; as industrial
relations policy (1974–79), 113–19; and
the pressure on industrial relations institutions, 93–101; reform of the industrial relations system, 103–4, 109–13, 119–27. *See
also* Donovan Commission
industrial relations, decollectivization of
(third system of industrial relations / 1979–
97), 35, 132–34, 137, 146, 174–80, 191–
93; and the collapse of corporatism, 156–
57; and Conservative industrial relations
policy, 145–53; and construction of a British post-Fordism, 134–41; and the emergence of new industrial relations institutions, 164–70; and employment relations,
158–64; and Europe, 181–82; evaluation
of, 186–90; importance of the state in,
141–45; and judicial activism, 157–58; public-sector industrial relations reform, 153–
56; and the statutory minimum wage, 180–
81; and trade union ideology and strategy,
170–73. *See also* Thatcherism
*Industrial Relations and European State Tradi-
tions* (Crouch), 25
industrial relations and institutional development, 18–22, 31, 50, 58, 133; and class conflict, 31, 36, 47–48; and crisis narration,
39–41, 144; discontinuous and synchronous, 29–31; duality of industrial relations
institutions, 23–24; emergence of new institutions, 164–69; from the mid-1950s
through the 1970s, 93–101; and industrial
conflict, 36–37, natural traditions of, 25–
26, 67; in the public sector, 43; specificity
of institutions, 22–24; and the state, 13–
14, 37–39, 79–82, 134, 199n. 57. *See also*

path dependence, and structuring of class
relations
industrial relations reform, 93, 96–97, 118,
135, 176; and economic growth, 20–22;
evaluation of industrial relations of the
1970s, 119–27; following the Donovan
Commission's report, 109–13; in the 1960s,
110–11; in the public sector, 153–56
Industrial Training Act (1964), 111
Ingram, Peter, 139
In Place of Strife (Labour Party white paper),
108, 109, 111–13, 115, 129, 132
institutional development, 2; role of the state
in, 2–3, 17–18, 37–39, 199n. 57. *See also*
industrial relations and institutional
development

Japan, industrial relations in, 166
Jenkins, Clive, 128
Jenson, Jane, 20, 33, 197n. 2, 199n. 54
Jessop, Bob, 34, 199n. 47
Johnson, Alan, 178
Joint Industrial Councils (JICs), 71, 72,
73, 75
Jones, Jack, 114, 118, 123

Kahn-Freund, Otto, 7, 10, 86, 102; on British
industrial relations, 8–9
Katznelson, Ira, 31
Kelly, John, 30, 83, 99, 123, 163, 169
Keynesianism, 98, 144
Klarman, Michael, 62, 63
Kondratieff cycles, 30, 31

labor flexibility, 138–40, 174. *See also* hyperflexibility
labor force: composition of, 138; feminization
of, 137, 138
labor law, 110–13, 177
labor market, 50, 62; and competition, 54–55;
deregulation of, 145
labor movements, 4; decline of, 3–4, 17; and
the state, 108–9. *See also* Thatcherism;
trade unionism; trade unions
labor unions. *See* trade unions
Labour Party, 174, 176, 210n. 143; economic
policy of, 176. *See also* Labour Party industrial relations policy
Labour Party industrial relations policy, 3,
14–15, 113–19, 137. *See also* "New Labour"/New Labour Party
Law, Legislation and Liberty (Hayek), 148

Lehmbruch, Gerhard, 39
liberal-pluralist reformism, 5, 6, 7
Lowe, Rodney, 75
Low Pay Commission (LPC), 179, 180

Maastricht Treaty, 144
MacGregor, Ian, 154
macroeconomic policy, 43, 93, 125
"managerial renaissance," 142–43
Manpower Service Commission, 157
Mansfield, Roger, 140
Marx, Karl, 38
Marxism, 8, 11, 23; structuralist, 33
McCarthy, William, 102
McKay, Sonia, 164
Metcalf, David, 142–43, 148–49
Midland Agreement, 78
Milner, Simon, 56, 74, 79, 89
Ministry of Labour, 72, 73, 81; core principles
   of, 76; leading personnel of, 76; versus the
   Treasury, 75–79
Mond-Turner talks, 74, 75
Monks, John, 175
Morris, William, 51, 175
multinational corporations, 137–38
Munitions Act (1915), 70

National and Local Government Officers' As-
   sociation (NALGO), 91, 98
National Arbitration Tribunal, 91
National Economic Development Council
   (NEDC), 98, 157
National Health Service (NHS), 155–56
National Industrial Conference (NIC), 74, 75
National Industrial Relations Court (NIRC),
   112, 113
National Insurance Act (1966), 111
National Union of Banking Employees
   (NUBE), 97, 127, 128, 129
National Union of Mineworkers (NUM),
   154; membership of, 154
"new collectivism," 165
"New Labour"/New Labour Party, 3, 119, 134,
   144, 160, 174–80, 181; core elements of,
   175; and the European Social Chapter,
   181–82. See also industrial relations, decol-
   lectivization of
newly emerging industries, 51–52, 87, 94
New Unionism, 60
New Zealand, and compulsory arbitration, 82
"Note of Reservation" (Shonfield), 105–6

Order in Council 1305, 91–92
Order in Council 1306, 92
Order in Council 1376, 91–92, 95, 127,
   128, 129
Organization of Economic Cooperation and
   Development (OECD), 111, 163

"Part of the Union" (The Strawbs), 1, 4,
   195n. 1
path dependence, and the structuring of class
   relations, 43–45
pay review bodies (PRBs), 156
Phelps Brown, E. H., 56, 66, 121–22, 130
Pierson, Paul, 44
pluralism, 8–12
Polanyi, Karl, 38
policy discourse, 39–40
"policy paradigms," 197n. 3
political economy: capitalist, 27, 28, 94; Marxist, 23; and the Regulationist tradition, 22
"political time," 20
Pontusson, Jonah, 24
post-Fordism, 133, 144, 175; and construction
   of a British post-Fordism, 134–41
Price, Richard, 52–53
private sector, the, 122, 153, 161, 162
privatization, 155, 179–80
procedure agreements, 57
productivity agreements, 138
productivity bargaining, 95
public sector, the, 43, 122, 135, 153, 156,
   160, 213–14n. 67; and the dues checkoff
   system, 123; and industrial relations reform, 153–56; as a "model employer," 90;
   restructuring of, 145–46, 155, 158
Purcell, John, 109, 159

Quinn v. Leathem (1901), 61

Redundancy Payments Act (1965), 111
regimes of accumulation, 33–35
regulation. See state regulation
Regulation Theory, 19, 22, 23, 31–36, 45
Ridley Plan (1978), 156
Road Haulage Wages Act (1938), 78
Rogers, Joel, 39
Rookes v. Barnard (1963), 100, 101, 114,
   124, 126
Royal Commission on Labour (1894), 40, 48,
   64–66, 79, 80, 200n. 1; committees of, 64
Royal Commission on Trade Disputes and
   Trade Combinations (1906), 62, 82

Royal Commission on Trade Unions and Employers' Associations. *See* Donovan Commission
Royal Mail, 156
Ryan, Paul, 168

Scanlon, Hugh, 114
Scargill, Arthur, 4, 154
Second World War, 90–92
segmentalism, 34
Sellers, Peter, 4
service sector, the, 96–97
Shonfield, Andrew, 105–6
shop stewards, 83, 90, 96, 125; and collective bargaining, 104–5; popular image of, 100; shift in role of, 122–23
Silver, Beverly J., 29
"single union agreement" (SUA), 166
Sisson, Keith, 96, 109
sliding scales, 56
Smith, Justin Davis, 93
Social Contract, 119, 170, 174
Social Democracy, 25, 135
social policy, 43
staple industries, 50–52, 81, 87, 94
state regulation, 14, 55, 110, 177–78, 218n. 24; forms of, 41–43; regulatory institutions, 35–36; revising, 31–36. *See also* collective regulation; Regulation Theory
statutory minimum wage, 92, 152, 170, 179, 180–81, 190, 218n. 24
Storey, John, 165
Stratford v. Lindley (1965), 62
Streeck, Wolfgang, 168
strikes, 54, 103, 111–13, 154, 156, 183; anti-strike strategies, 156; coal strikes (1984–85), 146, 154–55; and industrial conflict, 99–100, 163–64; —comparison of Swedish and British, 58–59; —source of, 66–67; and labor laws, 59–61, 112–13; level of from the 1950s to the 1970s, 99; media representations of, 100; policing of, 146; public sector, 135; and strike waves, 29–30, 61. *See also* "Winter of Discontent"
Summers, Clyde, 129
Swenson, Peter, 34, 38–39, 199n. 60, 200n. 61

Taff Vale Railway Company v. Amalgamated Society of Railway Servants (1901), 61, 62, 157
Tebbit, Norman, 147
Temperton v. Russell (1893), 61

Terms and Conditions of Employment Act (1959), 91–92, 95, 116, 127, 129
Terry, Michael, 125
Thatcher, Margaret, 88, 119, 124
Thatcherism, 2, 5–7, 44, 65, 89, 126, 129, 175, 177
Tillett, Ben, 63
TINA-LEA ("this is not a legally enforceable agreement"), 113
Tolliday, Steven, 14
"Tory reformism," 5–6, 11
Trade Boards Act (1909), 68–69
Trade Boards Act (1918), 72; amendment to, 76
Trade Disputes Act (1906), 62, 63, 65, 68, 75, 77, 81, 101, 112, 114, 141
Trade Disputes and Trade Unions Act (1927), 77, 92
Trades Union Congress (TUC), 59, 63, 108, 109, 110, 112, 118, 157, 171, 172–73, 179, 185, 189; Bridlington Agreement of, 151; lack of representation on the Whitley Committee, 71; and New Unionism initiative, 173; and the "Organising Academy," 173; Partnership Institute of, 177
Trade Union Act (1871), 46, 59
Trade Union Act (1984), 148
Trade Union (Amalgamation) Act (1917), 70–71, 83
Trade Union Amalgamation Act (1964), 208n. 91
Trade Union and Labour Relations Act (TULRA, 1974), 114, 117, 124
trade unionism, 6, 61–62, 64, 120, 168, 195n. 3, 216n. 149; Conservative hostility toward, 146–47, 172; and "managerial unionism," 163; media hostility toward, 143–44; "professional," 163; weakening of, 159–62, 168–69. *See also* New Unionism; Thatcherism
Trade Union Liaison Committee, 178
Trade Union Reform and Employment Rights Act (1993), 148, 152
trade unions, 3, 9–10, 43, 47, 55, 84, 97, 104–5, 107, 114, 131–34, 140, 157–58, 208–9n. 100; and access to government, 157, 178; centralization of union structures, 83; decentralization of, 123, 124; decline in membership, 154, 160–62, 168, 214–15n. 88; effect of decollectivization on, 168; external support for, 151–52; failure of, 141; growth in union membership, 83; ideology and strategy of, 170–73; and industrial action,

149–50, 158, 164; and internal governance, 150–51, 163; and recognition legislation, 209–10n. 125, 211n. 152; and recruitment of members, 84; shift to "participative unionism," 123; twentieth-century peak in membership, 122; and unfair dismissal procedures, 183, 218n. 24; and works committees, 90. *See also* collective bargaining; Employment Relations Act; shop stewards; voluntarism
Transport and General Workers Union (TGWU), 114, 116, 118, 123, 175
Treasury, the, 81; versus the Ministry of Labour, 75–79
Treaty of Rome, 171
Triple Alliance, 68

Union of Shop, Distributive and Allied Workers (USDAW), 127
United States: industrial relations in, 3, 133, 187–88; and technology, 50, 51

Varieties of Capitalism (Hall and Soskice), 28
"Varieties of Capitalism (VoC)" approach, 25, 26–29, 33, 34, 38, 136; and labor, 28
voluntarism, 10, 13, 71, 84, 106–7, 127, 129, 130, 159; abandonment of by trade unions, 170–71, 187

Waddington, Jeremy, 30
wages: minimum, 47, 92; restraint policies, 98, 125; wage competition, 52; wage councils, 116–17. *See also* pay review bodies; statutory minimum wage
Wages Councils Act (1945), 92
Wagner Act, 84, 128, 199n. 60
Wedderburn, Lord, 86, 115, 148
Whitley Committee (1917), 40, 48, 69–74, 80, 90, 141, 153; composition of, 71, 75; and the industry bargaining system, 109–10, 122
Wilson, Harold, 108, 112
"Winter of Discontent" (1978–79), 4, 88, 119, 124, 133, 143–44, 170, 174
Woodcock, George, 102
Workplace Employment Relations Survey (1998), 140, 161, 164, 166–67, 169, 215n. 94
Workplace Industrial Relations Surveys (1980, 1984, 1990), 131, 140, 143, 161, 164, 166, 169, 209n. 119, 215n. 94
World War I. *See* First World War
World War II. *See* Second World War
Wright, Erik Olin, 10–11, 39

Zeitlin, Jonathan, 12, 14, 24, 44, 58, 81